Violence in the U.S.

Volume 1

1956-67

Violence in the U.S.

Volume 1

1956-67

Edited by Thomas F. Parker

FACTS ON FILE, INC.   NEW YORK, N.Y.

Violence
in the U.S.

Volume 1

1956-67

Library of Congress Catalog Card Number 74-81146
ISBN 0-87196-229-2

9 8 7 6 5 4 3 2 1
PRINTED IN
THE UNITED STATES OF AMERICA

CONTENTS

i

INTRODUCTION

THE 1960s AND EARLY 1970s WERE MARKED by serious civil turmoil in the U.S. Anti-Negro bombings, murder and beatings were endemic in the South. Elsewhere in the U.S. major cities were scarred by rioting that left scores dead and injured. A President, his brother and a black Nobel Peace Prize-winner were killed by assassins. Multiple murders took place in the North, South and West. Massive antiwar protests brought clashes between demonstrators and police while troops ringed the U.S. Capitol.

The turmoil of these years, however, had its counterpart in the vigilante violence, urban rioting, assassinations and student disorders of the dark side of U.S. history. Among others, the studies of the National Commission on the Causes & Prevention of Violence outlined many of the violent episodes of the American past.

Anti-Negro violence took place in 1712 during the first slave uprising and continued sporadically into the 1870s, when the Ku Klux Klan forced freedmen to accept the renewed rule of Southern whites. Between 1882 and 1903 1,985 Negroes were lynched in the U.S. Lynchings and night-rider attacks on Negroes continued intermittently into the 1940s and 1950s. The American Protective movement of 1887 used violent tactics against newly arrived Irish and Italian Catholics just as the Know Nothing movement of the 1850s had violently opposed earlier immigrants. In 1885-6 the Bald Knobbers of Missouri mounted vigilante raids to punish theft, drinking, gambling and prostitution. In 1888 the White Cap movement used floggings to intimidate Negroes and Mexicans in Texas.

Urban riots have been a part of the American scene since the brawling days of the Liberty Boys in colonial ports in the 1760s. U.S. cities have been wracked by labor riots, election riots, anti-abolitionist riots, anti-Negro riots and anti-Catholic riots. From the 1830s to the 1850s 35 major riots were recorded in the Northeast. Baltimore had 12 riots, Philadelphia 11, New York 8, Boston and Cincinnati 4 each. Riot control difficulties during this time led to the organization of modern police forces to replace the obsolete watch-and-ward system inherited from colonial times. In 1877 the riots that accompanied a great railroad strike burned entire sections of Pittsburgh, led to street battles in Baltimore and

1

resulted in the creation of the National Guard to quell civil disorders resulting from violent labor-management conflicts.

Major urban riots initiated by whites after the turn of the century inflicted many Negro casualties. There were anti-Negro riots in New York in 1900; in Springfield, O. in 1904, and in Greensburg, Ind. and Atlanta in 1906. National Guardsmen quelled a 3-day riot in which 6 people died in Springfield, Ill. in 1908. Rioting erupted in 1917 in Chester, Pa. and Philadelphia. Chicago was subjected to a week of rioting that killed 22 persons and injured hundreds in 1919. Rioting in 1919 also took place in Washington, D.C.; Omaha, Neb.; Charleston and Longview, Tex. and Knoxville, Tenn. A race riot was reported in Tulsa, Okla. in 1921. Negro rioting erupted in Harlem (New York) in 1935 and 1943. Federal troops were required to quell looting and bloodshed in the massive Detroit riot of 1943. 25 Negroes and 9 whites died in the conflict.

Political assassination and multiple murder have appeared before in American history. In addition to assassinations of minor political figures and endemic murder in New Mexico political life, 3 Presidents lost their lives to assassins after the Civil War—Lincoln in 1865, Garfield in 1881 and McKinley in 1901. Multiple murders were recorded as early as 1798-9, when Micajah and Wiley Harpe killed 20 to 38 persons on the Kentucky and Tennessee frontiers. The Bender family of Kansas killed 12 travelers in 1871-3. H. H. Holmes murdered 27 persons near Chicago in 1890-4.

Violence on college campuses has also been part of the American tradition since a 1766 student rebellion at Harvard. In 1807 more than half of the Princeton student body was suspended for rioting. There was further turmoil at Princeton in 1814 and a student rampage that included arson and window-smashing in 1817. Disorders occurred at Yale in 1828 and 1830. Numerous episodes of campus violence were recorded in the 1830s and 1840s. In 1841 Yale students battled New Haven firemen in the streets, destroying fire-fighting equipment. In 1842 Harvard students clashed with town rowdies. During the 1840s turmoil at the University of Virginia a professor was shot to death. Armed constables were called in to restore order. Students at Yale battled townsmen and firemen in 1854 and 1858. Student activism was evident in 1934-5 when thousands of students participated in a nationwide antiwar strike.

Antiwar protests of the 1960s had their counterparts in the antidraft riots of the 1860s. Riots broke out in Newark, N.J. and in Buffalo and Troy, N.Y. Bitter fighting erupted in Cincinnati in 1862. Anti-draft rioters went on a 3-day rampage in New York City in July, 1863, burning a city block that contained the offices of the provost-marshal in charge of conscription. Federal troops were called in to quell the outburst.

Many other forms of violence have been recorded in America in addition to the types of conflict represented by present-day turmoil. Criminal violence has existed since the organized gangs of colonial days and has contributed a roster of American folk heroes: Jesse James, the Daltons, Billy the Kid, Pretty Boy Floyd, John Dillinger, Machinegun Kelly and others. The Revolutionary, Civil and Indian wars were accompanied by murderous guerilla actions. Labor violence and feuding broke out after the Civil War. Labor-management conflicts erupted in the Haymarket Riot of 1886, the 1892 Homestead and Coeur d'Alene strikes, the violence that drenched Colorado from 1884 to 1910, the coal-mine strikes and the Ludlow massacre of 1913-4.

Bloody family feuds are enshrined in Southern and Western history. The Hatfield-McCoy feud of 1873, the Martin-Tolliver feud in 1884 and the 1902 Hargis-Cockrell conflict took place in the Kentucky-West Virginia border areas. Texas feuds included the Sutton-Taylor conflict of 1869-99 and the Horrell-Higgins feud of 1876-7. The Lincoln County War scarred New Mexico in 1878. A deadly conflict between the cattle-raising Graham family and the sheep-raising Tewksbury clan led to the bloody Pleasant Valley War in Arizona, 1886-92.

This volume records the major outbreaks of violence that began in the U.S. just prior to the 1960s. It covers the upwelling of Southern violence in opposition to the Negro drive for civil rights, the destructive rioting that flamed in urban ghettos, the political assassinations and multiple murders, the disorders that shook the nation's college campuses, the massive antiwar protests and the terrorist bombings. Much of the material included here appeared earlier in FACTS ON FILE publications. As in all FACTS ON FILE books, a sincere effort was made to present this material without bias.

THE SOUTH & RACIAL VIOLENCE (1956-62)

Violent Background to Southern Disturbances

The early years of the 1960s brought a wave of bombings, assassinations, terror and race rioting to the South. Violence had long been part of life in Southern states. Despite the fact that the Southern white elite, aided by the Southern white poor, had been accused of using beatings, mutilation and murder to attain and hold supremacy in the South and to prevent the social, economic and political advancement of black Americans since 1867, such extensive disturbances had not been seen in recent years.

After a lull during World War II, the Ku Klux Klan, traditional source of violent Negro repression, had reappeared in the South as a welter of splinter groups and competing factions. In 1945 fiery crosses, a traditional Klan weapon of intimidation, burned in Tennessee, Alabama, Florida and as far North as New Jersey. 3 years later a wave of kidnappings, floggings and cross burnings swept the Birmingham, Ala. area. 1950 saw the beginning of a 2-year reign of Klan terror in North and South Carolina. In 1953-5 there was a lull in Southern violence as the Klan sought political support for its policies.

Rights Activism Mounts in Late 1950s

A new phase of the black struggle for equality began in Montgomery, Ala. Dec. 5, 1955, when Mrs. Rosa Parks, a black seamstress, refused to give up her seat to a white passenger on a city bus. She was arrested and fined $10.

The Parks case provoked an unprecedented reaction in the black community. In protest against segregated transportation facilities, Montgomery Negroes waged a 381-day economic boycott that fired the imagination of the nation. A Montgomery minister, the Rev. Dr. Martin Luther King Jr., proponent of non-violent protest, led the Montgomery boycott. King became nationally known as Negro direct action spread throughout the South. Boycotts protesting segregation spread to other Southern cities, including Tallahassee, Fla. and Birmingham, Ala.

The home of Martin Luther King was blasted by a bomb in Montgomery in Jan. 1956. In March and July black homes in mixed neighborhoods in Atlanta were damaged by similar explosions. A

5

bomber dynamited the home of another black minister in Montgomery in August.

The U.S. Supreme Court had paved the way for desegregation
of Southern schools by its ruling in 1954 in the landmark case
of *Brown v. Board of Education of Topeka, Kan.*

Autherine J. Lucy, 26, of Birmingham was admitted to the
University of Alabama in Tuscaloosa Feb. 3, 1956 under a Supreme
Court order as the university's first black student (for post-gradu-
ate study of library science). An estimated 1,000 rioters (said to
represent a minority of students and non-student "outsider" segregationists) assembled Feb. 6 at buildings where Miss Lucy was
in class, threw rocks and eggs at her and her car, and similarly
besieged the home of Dr. Oliver C. Carmichael, 64, University
of Alabama president. The rioters chanted "Hey, hey, ho, ho,
Autherine gotta go!"

The university Board of Trustees Feb. 7 approved Miss Lucy's
indefinite suspension as a student "for your safety and for the
safety of the students and faculty members." Carmichael, who had
supported her admission in obedience of the court order, defended her suspension as the only safe alternative to closing the university. Carmichael assured students and faculty members at a con-
vocation at the university Feb. 16 that the suspension was not an
abdication "in favor of mob rule" but an action to protect her
and the university. The university had fought her admittance by
legal means but had admitted her on court order, he said, because
"society could not long endure if its institutions of higher learning array themselves on the side of lawlessness."

Klan Beatings & Torture

Ku Klux Klan activities intensified in the summer of 1957.
Claude Cruell, a black farmer, was beaten severely by Klansmen
in his own home in Greenville, S. C. July 23, 1957. His white attackers were convicted Jan. 23, 1958 by an all-white jury. Greenville Klan leader Andrew Marshall Rochester, 30, was sentenced
by the jury to 6 years at hard labor and Wade Henry Howard, 24,
to 3 years, both for the attack on Cruell.

Ku Klux Klan beatings of 6 Negroes at Maplesville, Ala.
Aug. 9, 1957 and of 4 at Evergreen, Ala. Aug. 8 led Aug. 16 to an
order by Gov. James E. Folsom to state police to aid local authorities in putting down illegal KKK activity.

Judge Edward Aaron, 34, a feeble-minded Negro house paint-
er, was seized by white men in the black community of Zion City

(outside Birmingham, Ala.) the night of Sept. 2-3, driven to a Klu Klux Klan meeting house, tortured, castrated and then dumped by a roadside. State investigators, who arrested 6 members of an unchartered klavern Sept. 7-8, said 2 of the suspects confessed that the 6 had seized Aaron at random since they intended to emasculate "just any Negro man" as a warning to the Rev. Fred L. Shuttlesworth, 35, a black leader of the Birmingham integration movement. State authorities said that Bart A. Floyd, 31, had been identified as having performed the castration to prove himself worthy of promotion to assistant exalted cyclops of the klavern. He was convicted and sentenced to a maximum 20-year term Nov. 7. The castration had been ordered by Joe P. Pritchett, 31, the klavern's exalted cyclops, who was convicted Sept. 2 and also sentenced to 20 years in prison.

School Disturbances Accompany Integration

In the fall of 1957 a school was dynamited in Nashville, Tenn. as the integration of Southern schools moved ahead. A major federal-state controversery developed in Little Rock when Gov. Orval E. Faubus used the Arkansas National Guard to block the integration of Central High School.

In the Nashville case, 13 black first-graders registered Aug. 27, 1957 in 3 of the city's 15 desegregated but previously all-white elementary schools. A campaign of threatening phone calls to families of the 13 began Aug. 28 under a plan announced by New Jersey-born segregationist Frederick John Kasper. The 13 black 6-year-olds, accompanied by parents, were jeered at and in some cases spat at or made the targets of sticks, stones and pop bottles as they were led through crowds of adult segregationists to integrated schools Sept. 9.

Nashville's new $500,000 Hattie Cotton Elementary School, with a registration of one black and 388 white children, was virtually destroyed by a dynamite blast the night of Sept. 9-10. 7 Ku Klux Klan members were arrested by city police as suspects Sept. 10. 19 other persons, including Kasper, were arrested the same day on other charges resulting from the racial tension. Kasper was convicted Sept. 11 on 4 municipal charges of disorderly conduct, offensive conduct, vagrancy and loitering and was jailed for failure to pay $200 in fines.

In Little Rock, 10 black children registered at Central High School, and 9 actually attempted to enter Sept. 4, 1957 with the start of the fall term. Gov. Faubus, however, ordered the Arkansas

National Guard to put the school "off limits" to Negroes. Guard troops were stationed outside Central High School barring entry to blacks from Sept. 2 to Sept. 20, when Faubus was forced to withdraw them in compliance with a federal court order.

A riotous crowd of 800 to 1,000 white supremacists gathered before the school Sept. 23, the first school day after the Guard was withdrawn, in an announced determination to keep black students from entering. A diversion was created shortly before 9 a.m. when 4 black newsmen appeared on the scene and were beaten and chased by members of the mob. While this was happening, 9 black children walked almost unnoticed into the school.

The threat of mob violence, however, resulted in a decision to withdraw the black children from Central High School to prevent mob violence. The decision was made by Little Rock Mayor Woodrow Wilson Mann and Superintendent of Schools Virgil T. Blossom. Both had assailed Faubus' use of the National Guard to keep Negroes out of the school.

In a statement denouncing the mob disorders as "disgraceful occurrences," Pres. Dwight D. Eisenhower warned Sept. 23 that he would "use the full power of the United States, including whatever force may be necessary, to prevent any obstruction of the law and to carry out the orders of the federal court." He said that "the federal law and orders of a United States court, implementing that law, cannot be flouted with impunity by any individual, or any mob of extremists." But he declared that "it will be a sad day for this country—both at home and abroad—if school children can safely attend their classes only under the protection of armed guards."

As a legal preliminary to the use of troops, Eisenhower signed a proclamation commanding "all persons" obstructing court-ordered integration in Little Rock "to cease and desist therefrom and to disperse forthwith."

Mobs gathered before Central High School the morning of Sept. 24 in defiance of the proclamation. At 12:22 p.m. Eisenhower issued an Executive Order directing Defense Secy. Charles E. Wilson to federalize the Arkansas National Guard and authorizing him to use any military forces necessary to prevent obstruction of the Little Rock court order.

An order federalizing the Arkansas Guard was signed by Wilson at 2:25 p.m. Sept. 24. 1,000 members of the 101st Airborne Division, including several Negroes, were flown to Little Rock from Ft. Campbell, Ky. later Sept. 24 to take up posts outside the school. Maj. Gen. Edwin A. Walker, commander of the Arkansas

Military District, was put in command of the regular troops and federalized Guard.

9 black children, protected by the troops, entered the school without major incident Sept. 25. The troops enforced a ban on congregation of groups of segregationists near the high school.

Federal troops remained on call for a year. Little Rock schools closed for the 1958-9 school year, then reopened on a desegregated basis.

Anti-Black & Anti-Semitic Bombings Spread

1958 was marked in the South by a series of bombings that included the dynamiting of Temple Beth El's school in Miami, the dynamiting Mar. 16 of the Jewish Community Center in Nashville, the dynamiting Mar. 17 of an unoccupied house bought by Negroes in a white Atlanta neighborhood, the dynamitings Apr. 27 of the Jewish Center and the James Weldon Johnson Jr. High School for Negroes in Jacksonville and attempted dynamitings of Temple Beth El in Birmingham, Ala. and of synagogues in Charlotte and Gastonia, N.C.

3 Ku Klux Klan members were convicted by a Charlotte jury Mar. 20 of conspiracy to dynamite a Negro school. Lester Francis Caldwell, 32, grand wizard of Klavern 22, was given a 5-to-10-year jail sentence for attempting to bomb the school and a suspended 2-to-5-year sentence on the conspiracy charge. 2-to-5-year terms were imposed on Arthur Brown Jr., 33, and William Oliver Spencer, 28, Klan members convicted of the conspiracy charge but cleared of trying to bomb the school. The Klan members were trapped through the work of Robert Lee Kindley, who had infiltrated the Klan at the request of Charlotte Police Chief Frank N. Littlejohn.

Mayors, police chiefs and other officials of 28 Southern cities gathered in Jacksonville, Fla. in May 1958 for an anti-bombing conference. Plans for joint action to halt the dynamitings were approved by the municipal officials May 3. They agreed to set up a "clearing house" in Jacksonville for information on terroristic acts. The Jacksonville Police Department was to coordinate the work. Rewards totaling $55,700 were offered by cooperating cities or organizations for bomb-case information.

It was reported at the conference that 46 racial bombings had taken place in the South since Jan. 1, 1957. Similar techniques had been used in many of them, particularly in recent attacks on Jewish synagogues and community centers. In these cases: dynamite was used but usually put where risk of property damage or loss of life was not great; phone calls to Jewish leaders or newspapers after the blasts assailed "centers of integration"; in some cases, the caller said he was a member of "the Confederate underground."

The black Baptist Church of Birmingham, Ala. was saved from damage June 29, 1958 when a black miner removed a package of dynamite that had been placed there during darkness. The dynamite exploded in the street, breaking windows in a 4-block radius. The pastor of the church, integrationist leader Fred L. Shuttlesworth, had been beaten by a segregationist mob Sept. 9, 1957 when he attempted unsuccessfully to enter his 2 daughters and 2 other black children in an all-white Birmingham school. The Rev. J. S. Phifer, a black preacher who had driven the car carrying Shuttlesworth and the children, had been arrested for carrying a .25-caliber pistol. Phifer said he had been threatened repeatedly with death, bombing and beating after the incident and feared to be unarmed.

In North Carolina an early-morning explosion July 7, 1958 damaged the home of the Rev. Warren Carr, white chairman of the Durham (N.C.) Human Relations Committee, a local group devoted to bettering interracial relations. 2 formerly all-white rural schools scheduled to be integrated were destroyed by fire in Deep Creek, N.C. Aug. 24-5.

A black home in a former all-white residential section in Birmingham, Ala. was bombed July 17, 1958. Ku Klux Klan member Hubert Eugene Wilcutt was convicted of the bombing Dec. 9. The jury set the sentence at 10 years in jail but recommended probation.

A bomb exploded Oct. 12, 1958 at a Reform Jewish structure in Atlanta. The 3:30 a.m. attack on the building, known as The Temple, was described by police as the work of an expert. The blast tore an 18-foot-square hole around a side entrance of the building, shattered windows, damaged offices, conference rooms and furniture and blew out windows of a nearby apartment house and office building. About 20 minutes after the explosion, the UPI received a phone call from a man identifying himself as "Gen. Gordon of the Confederate underground." He said, "We have just blown up The Temple." He threatened additional incidents and warned, "This is the last empty building I'll blow up in Atlanta."

FBI agents said the Atlanta bombing and phone call almost exactly paralleled recent synagogue dynamitings in Miami, Jacksonville and Birmingham.

Atlanta police officers Oct. 14 arrested 5 men who had been accused in an Oct. 13 statement of having attended a May 5 Atlanta meeting at which the bombing was planned. The informant said he had attended the meeting but had opposed violence and had been excluded from further meetings. According to his statement: a suspect who had done architectural work had drawn a diagram to show where the dynamite was to be placed; the blast was to be set off by a man brought from Birmingham, Ala.; the dynamite was to come from Harlan, Ky. Those arrested, all alleged members of the anti-Semitic National States Rights Party, were Wallace H. Allen, 33, alleged leader of the group, operator of an advertising agency not listed in the phone book; George Michael Bright, 35, a draftsman; Robert A. Bowling, 25, reportedly active in the Christian Anti-Jewish Party; Luther King Corley, 26; Kenneth Chester Griffin, 32, an auditor in the Georgia State Income Tax Division. Bright, Corley, Griffin and 2 others had been arrested July 27 while attempting to picket the *Atlanta Journal & Constitution* with placards of a "National Committee to Free America From Jewish Domination." A raid on Bright's home produced a pencil draft of an unsigned letter threatening Atlanta Jews with "a terrifying experience." A raid on Allen's home turned up a letter from Arlington, Va. saying that "thanks to one man, one 'fat cat' financier" who "put his dollars where his mouth is," "we can now 'do the things we've been planning to do."

Superior Judge Durwood T. Pye declared a mistrial in Atlanta Dec. 10 in the case of George Bright, first of the men tried for the bombing, when the jury deadlocked at 9 to 3 for conviction after 84 hours of deliberation. James DeVore, 33, who had shared Bright's cell, had testified Dec. 5 that Bright had told him "he drew . . . and led the plans for the bombing" and was "lookout" while another defendant placed the explosive.

A list of 46 bombings and attempted bombings of religious institutions, schools and other property in the South since Jan. 1, 1957 was released Oct. 13, 1958 in Atlanta by the Anti-Defamation League of B'nai B'rith.

Black Prisoner Lynched in Mississippi

A young Negro awaiting trial in Poplarville, Miss. on charges of raping a white woman was forcibly removed from the county jail by a white lynch mob Apr. 25, 1959. His body was found near Bogalusa, La. May 4 with 2 fatal bullet wounds. The FBI report on the case named 23 participants, but a U.S. grand jury in

Biloxi, Miss. failed to hand down any indictments.

The black victim, Mack Charles Parker, 23, accused of raping a 23-year-old pregnant white woman before the eyes of her 5-year-old daughter, was kidnapped from the unguarded Pearl River County Jail in Poplarville, Miss. at about 12:30 a.m. Apr. 25 by masked white men. According to witnesses, the kidnappers used 5 cars. At least 8 of them broke into the 3d-floor jail while others waited outside. Locating Parker, they beat him with guns, clubs and a garbage can until his head and face were bloody, dragged him into a car and sped away.

Within hours of the abduction, state and local authorities, under Gov. J. P. Coleman's orders, began a search of nearby swamps and pine forests. Coleman also asked for FBI help, and a special FBI squad was sent to Poplarville the same day. In response to a renewed request from Coleman, Pres. Eisenhower promised Apr. 28 that the FBI would "continue to provide full facilities to help."

Parker's body was retrieved from the Pearl River near Bogalusa, La. May 4.

Anthony Lewis reported in the *N.Y. Times* May 4 that a motive for the Parker lynching may have been the fact that in "a large part" of Mississippi "it is impossible to obtain a constitutionally valid conviction of a Negro." According to Lewis: This "situation, with grave implications for much of the South," existed because judges had ruled that the "systematic exclusion of Negroes from juries in a locality voids any criminal conviction of a Negro constitutionally"; in most of Mississippi few or no Negroes could serve on juries because juries in the state were chosen from voter lists, and election boards registered few or no Negroes; it was "recognized locally" that had Parker been convicted, his conviction probably would have been reversed because no Negroes were registered to vote in the county and no Negroes, therefore, served on the county's juries; the first Supreme Court reversal of a conviction on these grounds took place in 1879, but "strict enforcement of this doctrine in Mississippi" lagged until Jan. 16, 1959, when the U.S. 5th Circuit Court of Appeals granted a *habeas corpus* appeal in the case of Robert Lee Goldsby, a Negro convicted of murder.

A U.S. grand jury in Biloxi, Miss. Jan. 4, 1960 opened an inquiry into the Parker lynching but announced Jan. 14 that it had been unable to indict any alleged lynchers "on the basis of the evidence presented" by the Justice Department. The 23-member jury, including one Negro, had questioned suspected lynchers and several FBI agents.

Sit-Ins Bring Violence & Mass Arrests in 1960

The civil rights movement took a new direction in 1960 when blacks in Southern cities began "sit-in" demonstrations in protest against lunch-counter and department-store segregation. In more than a dozen cities the demonstrations were accompanied by bomb threats and police use of high-pressure fire hoses, dogs, night-sticks and mass arrests. There were clashes between white mobs and demonstrators and black retaliation.

The "sit-in" movement began quietly when black students quietly filled all lunch-counter seats in the Woolworth and Kress variety stores in Greensboro, N.C., starting Feb. 1, 1960 in peaceful "sit-in" protests against the "local custom" of refusing counter service to seated (but not standing) Negroes. The 2 stores were closed Feb. 5 as a result of a false bomb threat and heckling. The "sit-in" movement spread Feb. 8-9 to Charlotte, Durham and Winston-Salem. 8 department and drug store managers closed their lunch counters, and the Greensboro counters remained closed even after North Carolina Agricultural and Technical College and Bennett College students had agreed Feb. 8 to a 2-week cooling-off period. Joseph Charles Jones, graduate ministerial student reportedly leading the Charlotte protest, said the sit-ins were "interrelated" but "not part of a plan and were undertaken independently." He said there was no organization behind the movement.

Police in Portsmouth, Va. used police dogs Feb. 17 to break up a skirmish over a sit-in at a variety store and arrested about 40 students in a crowd of about 300 Negroes and 200 whites.

Students from Alabama State College staged the first "deep South" sit-in Feb. 25 in the lunchroom of the Montgomery County courthouse. Sheriff Mac Sim Butler arrived carrying a club and lined up the 35 demonstrators single file against a wall. Armed deputies patrolled the halls until the passive protesters left.

A group of white men carrying small baseball bats lined a main thoroughfare in Montgomery Feb. 27 and formed groups outside 2 variety stores operating lunch counters. One of the club-carriers struck a black woman on the head and bloodied her as a result of a pushing incident. There were no arrests. Gov. John Patterson warned Feb. 29 that there were "not enough police officers" in the U.S. "to prevent riots and protect everybody" if Negroes "continue to provoke whites."

About 500 state, county and local armed police Mar. 6 halted a march of about 800 Negroes to the Alabama state capitol in Montgomery for a protest meeting after a church rally one block from the old capitol building. Police pushed the marchers back to the church and separated them from a mob of jeering whites. There were a scattered fist fights, but mounted deputies and fire trucks prevented further violence.

Rioting broke out in Chattanooga, Tenn. Feb. 23, 1960 when Negroes and whites, mostly students, fought during a sit-in as the management tried to close an S. H. Kress & Co. store. Police arrested 11 whites and one Negro. 11 Negroes and 9 whites were arrested there Feb. 24 during demonstrations marked by rock and bottle throwing and attacks on cars. Mayor P. R. Olgiati ordered fire hoses used to disperse the mob.

Nashville, Tenn. police arrested about 100 black and white students Feb. 27 after fights had broken out in 2 of 5 stores where Negroes had staged sit-ins. During a 4-hour demonstration, white persons angered by passive resistance to their taunts attacked black demonstrators and a white youth seated beside a black girl at a lunch counter. One white student was fined $50 and 2 Negroes $100 and $10, respectively, Feb. 29.

50 blacks carrying clubs demonstrated Mar. 5 in a Columbia, S.C. drive-in restaurant and pounded on several cars. A white woman was cut by flying glass. A recorder's court in Columbia Mar. 18 found 15 black students from Allen University and Benedict College guilty of the attacks. The 9 admitted leaders were fined $100 each, the others $50.50 each.

Police arrested 388 black students in Orangeburg, S.C. Mar. 15, 1960 on breach-of-peace charges after fire hoses and tear gas were used to disperse about 1,000 Negroes during a mass protest against lunch-counter segregation. Those arrested were released on $10 bail. 15 of the students arrested were sentenced Mar. 19 in magistrate's court to pay $50 each or serve 30 days in jail for disturbing the peace but were freed later on $100 appeal bonds.

Tallahassee, Fla. police arrested 6 white students and 29 Negroes Mar. 12 during a sit-in that had begun in a Woolworth store and that police broke up with tear gas.

The suspension Mar. 30 of 18 students at Southern University in Baton Rouge, La., the U.S.' largest all-black school, touched off a full-scale student rebellion. The suspensions followed student participation in lunch-counter sit-ins Mar. 28-29 and an orderly anti-segregation rally at the state capitol 10 miles from the campus. A majority of the student body of 5,400 boycotted classes Mar. 31 and requested withdrawal forms in protest. The rebellion waned Apr. 1 when the heart-attack death of Prof. J. Warren Lee, 50, was attributed to the students demonstration against school authorities, but class boycotts and withdrawals continued. The Louisiana State Board of Education, an all-white elective body that administered Southern University, had warned Mar. 1 that any student participating in sit-ins faced "stern disciplinary action."

Demonstrations were broken up by police and firemen Mar. 30 in Marshall, an East Texas city with "old South" traditions and a population of about 15,000 Negroes, 15,000 whites. When black students tried Mar. 30, for a 3d time within a week, to be served seated at lunch counters, police officers arrested 20 immediately, took 18 to jail later and then arrested more than 250 as at least 700 singing blacks thronged the courthouse square, reformed the crowd faster than its members could be arrested and surged onto the courthouse steps. Finally, firemen drove 2 trucks into the crowd and forced it to retreat. The police then began freeing those taken into custody, and the firemen dispersed the crowd with high-pressure hoses.

The worst race riots in Mississippi history erupted in Biloxi Apr. 24, 1960 when 40 or 50 Negroes sought to swim in the Gulf of Mexico. The city's entire 26-mile beach was open only to whites. A crowd of whites attacked the blacks with sticks, chains and black-jacks and wounded 4 before being dispersed by police. Later, 2 white men and 8 Negroes suffered gunshot wounds in street clashes, and 7 white airmen from nearby Keesler Air Force Base were attacked by whites. Biloxi police arrested 4 blacks in an auto Apr. 24 on the grounds that one had carried a shotgun. One of those arrested was Dr. Gilbert R. Mason, 31, a leader of the beach demonstrators, who had been in trouble with police before for using the beach. A justice of the peace found him guilty of disturbing the peace and obstructing traffic and fined him $50. Mayor Laz Quave ordered a curfew, and Keesler officials told base personnel to keep out of the city unless they had to visit it on urgent business. Police armed with riot guns patrolled Biloxi Apr. 24-25. Biloxi Negroes began to boycott stores whose policies were considered anti-Negro. (The Mississippi Legislature Apr. 27 enacted an anti-riot law that authorized prison terms of up to 10 years for anybody convicted of inciting riots in which there was death or injury.)

A 9 p.m.-to-6 a.m. curfew on all persons 20 years of age or younger was imposed in Greenville, S.C. July 26 after a series of clashes between whites and Negroes engaged in sit-ins against lunch-counter segregation. The clashes began July 18 after the postponement of a trial of 8 blacks involved in a July 16 "sit-in" at Greenville Public Library. 75 Negroes who had been spectators at the proceeding left the court and demonstrated at several variety stores. New clashes occurred in Greenville during sit-ins July 21-5.

Bombings & Klan Reprisals Plague Rights Movement

Bombings and Ku Klux Klan reprisals accompanied the growth of the civil rights movement in 1960. Dynamite blasts damaged black homes, a Negro was flogged and mutilated, a white minister was beaten and the Klan converged on Jacksonville, Fla. for almost a week of racial violence.

A crude bomb Feb. 9, 1960 tore a 2-foot hole in the home of Carlotta Walls, one of 5 Negroes enrolled in Little Rock (Ark.) Central High School. Police said the blast did "considerable damage." This was the first direct attack on any of the school's 5 black students, except for nonviolent harassment by other students. Little Rock police arrested chauffeur-handyman Maceo Antonio Binns Jr., 31, and student Herbert Odell Monts, 17, both black, on charges of bombing the Walls home Feb. 19. Monts was later convicted by an all-white jury and sentenced to a maximum of 5 years in jail.

On a lonely Houston, Tex. street Mar. 7, 1960, 4 masked white youths kidnaped Felton Turner, 27, an unemployed married Negro, and flogged and mutilated him and hung him upside down. Felton said later that the youths had forced him into a car at gunpoint and driven him to a field, where 3 of them beat him with a tire chain, carved the letters KKK on his chest and stomach and left him loosely trussed up in the branches of a tree, from which he finally freed himself. He said one of his abductors told him: "We were just hired to do a job because of the publicity Texas Southern University Negro students received over sit-ins at a lunch counter at Houston in the past few days." (About 100 TSU students had staged orderly sit-ins Mar. 4 in Houston.)

Police and FBI agents arrested Hubert Sherell Jackson Jr., 16, a self-styled Nazi, in Gadsden, Ala. Mar. 26 on charges of assault with intent to murder after he had thrown a homemade bomb at Beth Israel Synagogue Mar. 25 during ceremonies for a new annex. The high school junior, who used the name Jerry Earl Hunt (since his step-father was named Hunt), confessed boastfully Mar.

26 that he had hurled the bomb and fired a rifle at "a lot of people" who ran from the building. 2 were wounded. The temple was not damaged.

Fiery crosses flamed in Alabama, Florida, Georgia and South Carolina Mar. 26-27, 1960, and nearly 1,000 persons crowded a Monroeville, Ala. coliseum Mar. 26 for a Ku Klux Klan meeting. In Alabama's Calhoun County (where more than 100 crosses were burned Mar. 26), a Klansman said Mar. 27: "We just wanted to show the public we are organized and ready for business." The cross burnings occurred in areas where hundreds of blacks had been jailed for anti-segregation demonstrations. Cities affected included Anniston, Ala.; Clearwater and Jacksonville, Fla.; Marietta and Savannah, Ga.; Charleston, Columbia, Greenville, Greenwood and Orangeburg, S.C.

The Nashville, Tenn. home of Z. Alexander Looby, 62, black city councilman and NAACP lawyer, was destroyed by a dynamite bomb Apr. 19, 1960, but Looby and his wife escaped injury. The bomb damaged several other homes in the black middle-class neighborhood and blew out 147 windows at predominantly-black Meharry Medical College. Several dormitory students were cut by flying glass. Looby had been chief counsel for 153 students arrested in sit-ins. More than 2,000 Negroes (mostly students) marched on Nashville's city hall Apr. 19 in protest against police failure to halt racial violence.

In Little Rock, the FBI arrested 3 white men July 12, 1960 in connection with the attempted bombing of a Philander Smith College dormitory. 2 hours after their arrest, a bomb blew a hole in the wall of a public school warehouse in Little Rock and damaged 2 black homes. The FBI said its agents had caught Emmett E. Miller, 44, and Robert Lloyd Parks, 39, of West Memphis, Ark. lighting a slow fuse on 40 sticks of dynamite under the dormitory staircase July 12. Later July 12 FBI agents arrested Hugh Lynn Adams, 33, of Bassett, Ark. as an accomplice of Miller and Parks. An FBI complaint filed before U.S. Commissioner John E. Coates in Little Rock July 12 indicated that agents had been tipped off to the plot. The complaint said 4 agents had seen Miller and Adams drive from West Memphis, Ark. to Memphis, Tenn. July 8 and get the dynamite, which they later turned over to Parks in West Memphis.

An explosion shattered a 2-family Chattanooga home in a black neighborhood Aug. 21. 2 sleeping children were cut—but not seriously—by flying glass. It was at least the 4th explosion in the city in a month. 2 explosions had been set off Aug. 17 near

the home of a white real estate agent hours after he had adver-
tised homes for sale to Negroes. A black teacher's new house had
been doused with kerosene and destroyed by fire July 15 in a black
Chattanooga district called Jersey Community. A vacant house
owned by the teacher had been burned 4 years previously, and
dynamite had been thrown 2 years previously into a restaurant
operated by his sister and brother-in-law.

Extremists used personal intimidation and other violence as
well as bombings.

The Rev. J. H. Germany, 47, a white minister, was attacked
and beaten Aug. 26 by 6 white men while he worked at his proposed black ministerial college in Union, Miss. The white mob,
about 20 in all, chased 4 black helpers and a constable summoned
during the beating. Germany, a missionary of the Church of God
of Anderson, Ind., said he had recognized several of his attackers
as White Citizens Council members.

Klansmen from Florida and southern Georgia took part in
clashes between blacks and whites in Jacksonville, Fla. after 10
days of sit-ins at 2 downtown stores. Tactics to counteract the
sit-ins were discussed at a meeting of the Jacksonville klavern of
the Florida Knights of the KKK Aug. 23, 1960. A call was sent
out urging other Klan units to converge on Jacksonville on Satur-
day and to bring Klan sympathizers with them. Scores of Klansmen and other whites armed with clubs appeared in downtown
Jacksonville the morning of Aug. 27. Stores selling ax-handles
and baseball bats did a rushing business. Isolated fights started
throughout the town. 50 persons were reported injured. Patrolmen armed with shotguns dispersed a crowd of 3,000. Mayor
Haydon Burns said Aug. 28 that "more than 100 troublemakers
of both races" had been arrested. Black youth gangs roamed the
streets Aug. 27 but were prevailed on by NAACP youth workers
Aug. 30 to declare a truce. Municipal Court Judge John Santora
Aug. 29 imposed short jail terms or fines ($10 to $250) on 26
white and 57 black participants in the disorders. The stiffest sentence—90 days in the road gang—was meted out to Richard Frank
Parker, 25, a white Florida State University student and NAACP
member who had been a sit-in leader.

The first violence in Atlanta since the sit-in campaign began
occurred Dec. 12, 1960 when a bomb exploded before dawn in a
black elementary school. No one was injured. Police did not con-
nect the bombing with the sit-ins. (But many of the 18 explosions
in 4 years in Atlanta were attributed by the police to racial or
religious friction.)

White Mobs Attack Freedom Riders

The U.S. Supreme Court ruled Dec. 5, 1960 that discrimination against blacks in bus-terminal restaurants serving interstate passengers was a violation of the Interstate Commerce Act. In May 1961, groups of "Freedom Riders" began testing conditions at bus-station facilities in the South. After a bus was fire-bombed and bus passengers beaten, the Kennedy Administration sent federal marshals into Alabama to aid local officials in restoring order.

The testing was started by Freedom Riders who left Washington May 4 with New Orleans as their intended destination. Originally, 6 white and 7 black members participated in the tour sponsored by CORE (Congress of Racial Equality), but the number fluctuated. One of the members, Joseph B. Perkins Jr., 27, black field secretary of the Freedom Riders, was arrested in Charlotte, N.C. May 8 for entering a bus-terminal barber shop (he was released May 10). Another, John Lewis, also black, was punched when he tried to enter a rest room at the Greyhound bus terminal in Rock Hill, S.C. May 9. 2 members of the tour—Henry Thomas, 23, black, and James Peck, white—were arrested in Winnsboro, S.C. May 10 after Thomas tried to enter a restaurant (they were held 8 hours).

The Freedom Riders occupied 2 buses by the time the tour reached Alabama. The first members of the group, traveling in a Trailways bus, stopped in Anniston, May 14, 1961 to get sandwiches. According to a member of the group, Dr. Walter Bergman, 61, a former Michigan State University professor, 3 policemen stood nearby while about 10 whites beat and kicked passengers. James Peck was injured and later admitted to a Birmingham hospital.

In Birmingham, according to an eye-witness report by Howard K. Smith of the Columbia Broadcasting System, 30 to 40 white "toughs," who had been waiting all day, "grabbed the passengers into alleys and corridors, pounding them with pipes, with key rings and with fists. . . . Police did not appear until around 10 minutes later, when the hoodlums had got into waiting cars and moved down the street, . . . where I watched some of them discussing their achievements. . . . That took place just under Police Commissioner [Eugene] Connor's window."

Alabama state investigator Ell M. Cowling was on the 2d CORE bus—a Greyhound—when it arrived at Anniston May 14. A crowd of about 200 whites milled about, and several bus

windows were broken. The bus departed with the crowd following by car. Several miles outside Anniston a tire went flat, apparently because it had been cut. This forced the bus to stop, and
Cowling tried to keep the white mob from storming the bus. Then
a fire bomb was thrown into the bus, and the bus was destroyed
by fire while CORE members escaped, some through the windows.
12 were hospitalized briefly for smoke inhalation. 2 patrolmen,
summoned from a nearby house, arrived and dispersed the crowd
by firing shots into the air.

No serious injuries or arrests were reported immediately from
the incidents, but Jesse Oliver Faggard, 20, an alleged member of
one of the white mobs, was arrested in Birmingham May 16 and
charged with participating in the Birmingham incident. Faggard
reportedly signed a statement admitting he had participated at the
request of the Ku Klux Klan.

FBI agents May 22 arrested in Anniston 4 whites, Robert Dale
Couch, 19, Jerry Ronald Eason, 22, Frank B. Johnson, 43, and
Dalford Leonard Roberts, 42, all Anniston residents, on charges of
throwing a fire bomb into the Greyhound bus. When the bus
bombing case came to trial Jan. 16, 1962, U.S. Judge H. Hobart
Grooms in Birmingham sentenced 5 men accused of the bombing
to a year on probation. The men promised to end whatever ties
they might have with the Ku Klux Klan. A 6th defendant, Robert
Couch, was sentenced to one year and one day in jail to be served
at the same time as his current term on a burglary conviction. Of
3 other men indicted on similar charges, charges were dropped
against 2 of them Jan. 16, and another had been acquitted in 1961.

7 black college students from Nashville, Tenn., who had
been arrested following the Freedom Ride incident in Birmingham,
were removed from jail May 19, 1961 and taken by police to the
Tennessee line. Refusing to go back to Tennessee, the 7 students
returned to Birmingham and joined 11 other Negroes and 3 whites
at the Greyhound bus terminal's "white" waiting room to try to
continue the Freedom Ride. After waiting almost 18 hours, they
boarded a bus to Montgomery. When the bus arrived in Montgomery May 20, the Freedom Riders were immediately attacked
by a mob of about 200 whites. Police Commissioner L. P. Sullivan,
sitting in a car on the side of the station away from the fighting,
told a reporter: "We have no intention of standing guard for a
bunch of troublemakers coming into our city. . . ." Police arrived
10 minutes after the fighting erupted, but the crowd, swollen to
about 1,000, continued to beat Freedom Riders and newsmen with
clubs and fists. Alabama Public Safety Director Floyd Mann,

pulling a pistol, forced the mob back from a fallen Negro and rescued a TV newsman. An hour and 15 minutes after the violence had started, 11 mounted sheriff's deputies and 10 more police cars arrived. Then, with the aid of tear gas, the authorities halted the rioting.

On learning of the Montgomery incident, Pres. John F. Kennedy May 20 expressed "deepest concern" and ordered the Attorney General "to take all necessary steps." Atty. Gen. Robert F. Kennedy, the President's brother, then announced that about 350 to 400 U.S. marshals were being dispatched to Montgomery under the direction of Deputy Atty. Gen. Byron R. White. Kennedy said the marshals were being sent "to assist state and local authorities in the protection of persons and property and vehicles in Alabama." The Attorney General May 20 sent Alabama Gov. John Patterson a telegram informing him of the marshals' mission and reviewing negotiations between U.S. and Alabama officials prior to the incident. The wire said: Alabama officials had been told repeatedly of the U.S.' concern over the explosive situation there and of the responsibility of the U.S. to guarantee safe passage in interstate commerce; after Pres. Kennedy and the Attorney General had tried futilely to reach Patterson by phone May 19, John Seigenthaler had been sent to Patterson as the President's representative; Seigenthaler, in Patterson's presence May 19, had informed the Attorney General that Patterson (1) had said Alabama had the "will, the force, the men and the equipment to fully protect everyone in Alabama," (2) had suggested that the U.S. notify the Greyhound Bus Co. of Alabama's guarantee, (3) had considered the offer of U.S. marshals "unnecessary"; "based on this assurance of safe conduct," the students took the trip to Montgomery, but when they arrived, "no police were present, ... an armed mob was"; Seigenthaler "attempted to rescue a young white girl being attacked by the mob, was knocked to the ground and left unconscious in the street."

White groups gathered in Montgomery May 21 in an apparent design to attack Negroes attending a mass meeting in a church. By that evening a mob of about 1,000 whites had formed and was held in uneasy check by U.S. marshals across the street from Montgomery's First Baptist Church, where about 1,500 Negroes held a well-publicized meeting at which the Rev. Ralph D. Abernathy, 34, pastor of the church and president of the Montgomery Improvement Association, introduced the Freedom Riders. A rock was hurled into the church, and several tear-gas bombs thrown at the mob were tossed back at the marshals. Inside the church, the Rev. Dr. Martin Luther King Jr., who had come to Montgomery to advise Negroes, phoned Atty. Gen. Kennedy to express his concern for the Negroes' safety. Kennedy assured King the marshals could handle the situation.

Just prior to King's call, Kennedy, after a report from White that the mob was forming, had called Pres. Kennedy in Middleburg, Va. to apprise him of the situation. He had also called Gov. Patterson to tell him more men were needed. Alabama Public Safety Director Floyd Mann, terming the situation "ugly," asked White to "commit any reserves" of U.S. marshals (they were already committed).

Faced with this situation, Patterson proclaimed martial law in Montgomery May 21 and ordered Adjutant Gen. Henry V. Graham to take whatever steps were necessary to preserve law and order. National Guardsmen arrived on Graham's orders late May 21 and, with drawn bayonets, took up posts around the church. The Negroes inside were told to remain and were given police and National Guard escorts home early May 22.

Martin Luther King met with the Freedom Riders May 23 and announced afterwards that they were determined to continue the Freedom Ride. King said the Rev. James Morris Lawson Jr. would instruct Freedom Riders in Montgomery in the "philosophy and techniques" of nonviolent action. Patterson May 23 called King "a menace to the city" and accused the U.S. marshals of causing the rioting at the church May 21 by bringing King to Montgomery and escorting him to the church.

5 whites were convicted in Montgomery City Court May 26 on charges stemming from May 20 violence against the Freedom Riders.

Gov. Patterson ended martial law in Montgomery May 29 and praised the National Guard for showing "the world that this state can and will continue to maintain law and order without the aid of federal force."

The Freedom Riders meanwhile had boarded 2 buses May 24 for Jackson, Miss. The first bus from Montgomery left at 9:12 a.m. On it were Alabama Adjutant Gen. Henry V. Graham, 11 black and one white Freedom Riders, 17 newsmen and 6 armed National Guardsmen. A squad of city motorcycle police preceded the bus to the city limits, where 16 highway patrol cruisers, carrying 3 National Guardsmen and 2 state troopers each, took over convoy duties. 20 cars with reporters trailed behind, and 3 L-19 reconnaissance planes and 2 helicopters flew overhead. 1,000 National Guardsmen were stationed along U.S. Route 80, the road the bus took.

The trip in Alabama had no major incident. Rest stops were made at isolated spots. At the Mississippi line, Graham and the Alabama Guardsmen were replaced by Lt. Col. Gillespie V. Montgomery (who also was a state senator) and 7 Mississippi National Guardsmen. In Mississippi the bus stopped only once, at Meridian, to change drivers; Montgomery twice refused requests to call a rest stop.

The bus terminal at Jackson was cordoned off by police, who held 3 leashed dogs. About 100 Guardsmen with fixed bayonets were stationed nearby when the bus arrived at 3:55 p.m. The Freedom Riders disembarked and were arrested minutes later as they tried to enter the terminal's "white" rest rooms.

The 2d busload of Freedom Riders—14 black and one white—arrived in Jackson from Montgomery at 6:47 p.m. the same day, and all 15 were arrested 3 minutes later for refusing Police Capt. J. L. Ray's demand they leave the entrance to the terminal's "white" cafeteria. All were held on charges of breaching the peace and refusing to obey an officer.

11 black and white Freedom Riders, including the Rev. William Sloane Coffin Jr., 36, Yale University chaplain, arrived peacefully in Montgomery, Ala. May 24. Their Greyhound bus from Atlanta had been escorted from the Georgia Alabama line by state and city police. 200 National Guardsmen were on duty near the Montgomery station when the bus arrived. Several hundred persons had gathered. The integrationist group did not enter the terminal but got into 2 waiting cars.

Coffin's group had given notice of its intended appearance at the Trailways bus-terminal lunch counter, where 2 groups of Freedom Riders had been served without incident May 24, and had been warned that it faced arrest. Coffin's group was arrested May 25 on charges of breaching the peace when they sought service at the lunch counter. 4 of those arrested were black integration leaders who had joined Coffin's group in Montgomery: the Rev. Ralph D. Abernathy, the Rev. Fred M. Shuttlesworth, the Rev. Wyatt T. Walker, chairman of the Atlanta Southern Christian Leadership Conference, and Atlanta student leader Bernard S. Lee. Coffin, Maguire, Noyce, Swift and Smith were released May 26 after posting bond of $1,000 each.

Gov. Patterson said May 25 that he was not committed "to escort invaders all over Alabama to permit them to flagrantly violate our laws and customs."

The Rev. Solomon Seay, 62, a Negro and executive secretary of the Montgomery Improvement Association, was shot in the wrist in front of his home in Montgomery May 25, the day Coffin's group was arrested. The shot came from passengers in a moving car. 6 white teen-agers, charged with involvement in the shooting, were arrested by Montgomery police May 27 and they were released in the custody of their parents.

Freedom rides continued into the fall with further arrests, more bomb threats and occasional scuffles with segregationists. The movement spread into Arkansas and Florida. An Interstate Commerce Commission ruling ordering the desegregation of all public transportation facilities went into effect Nov. 1, 1961, and the ruling was defied in several Southern cities.

Mob violence broke out in McComb, Miss. after a 3-judge federal court in Jackson, Miss. Nov. 21 ordered McComb authorities to comply with the ICC ruling by removing bus and railroad terminal signs designating separate waiting rooms for black and white intrastate passengers. The violence began Nov. 29 when 5 young blacks from New Orleans went to the terminal and sought service at the ticket window and lunch counter. A white youth struck one of the Negroes. Other whites then joined in beating all the blacks. The Negroes, none severely injured, escaped in a taxi. 5 minutes later police arrived from city hall, a block away. The 5 Negroes stayed overnight at a black hotel and then, escorted by police to the terminal, boarded a New Orleans bus as FBI agents watched.

A 2d CORE-sponsored Freedom Ride to McComb was successful Dec. 1 although it was menaced by a mob of 500 to 700 whites, some of whom struck or threatened 4 out-of-town newsmen. The 6 black riders arrived aboard a bus from Baton Rouge, La. Protected by McComb's 15-man police force, they entered the station but left in a car after a few minutes. The riders later returned to the station. Guarded by police reinforced by 2 sheriffs and 10 deputies from nearby counties, they safely boarded an outgoing bus.

A small group of whites menaced an unheralded 3d Freedom Ride into and out of McComb Dec. 2. 3 Negroes arrived aboard a bus from Jackson, spent a few minutes in the terminal's "white" waiting room, then entered a waiting car driven by CORE Field Secy. Thomas Gaither, a Negro. 4 whites attacked the car but were repulsed by police.

Other Racial Clashes

While attacks on Freedom Riders occupied the headlines

during most of 1961, other violent incidents included a riot at Georgia University, a clash between blacks and whites in Chicago and mass demonstrations quelled with tear gas in Baton Rouge.

The first desegregation in public education in Georgia was started Jan. 10, 1961 when 2 black students, Charlayne Alberta Hunter, 18, and Hamilton E. Holmes, 19, enrolled in Georgia University in Athens. The university, which had more than 7,200 white students, had been ordered to admit the 2 Negroes by U.S. District Judge William A. Bootle in Macon, Ga. Jan. 6. Bootle's ruling barred the university from further discrimination against black applicants.

500 white students demonstrated in Athens Jan. 6 against integration and hanged an effigy of Hamilton Holmes. Police had difficulty with a rowdy parade of more than 1,000 youths in downtown Athens Jan. 9, and Miss Hunter was jeered in an unruly demonstration Jan. 10.

A riot involving about 600 students and some adults took place Jan. 11 following the school's defeat in a basketball game. Rioters threw bricks and firecrackers at the dormitory in which Miss Hunter was staying and surged out of control. A handful of Athens police reportedly watched the beginning of the riot without making any serious attempt to restrain it. Fighting broke out later between the students and police, and 16 persons were arrested. After tear gas had dispersed the rioters, state police arrived. They escorted Miss Hunter from the dormitory, picked up Holmes from the Athens private home in which he had been lodged and drove them to their homes in Atlanta. Miss Hunter and Holmes were suspended Jan. 12 by Joseph A. Williams, dean of students, who said he was acting for "their personal safety." 300 of the university's 600 faculty members met later Jan. 12 and adopted a resolution that condemned the riot and insisted that the 2 black students "be returned to their classes."

Judge Bootle Jan. 13 ordered university officials to reinstate the 2 Negroes. He said their rights were not to be sacrificed to violence.

13 students were expelled or suspended for participating in the riot. 8 of 16 rioters arrested admitted membership in the Ku Klux Klan, it was reported Jan. 14.

In Chicago, police arrested 65 Negroes July 13-15 during an outbreak of racial incidents in which roving gangs of black youths beat 21 whites. Police attributed the attacks to reprisals for the unsolved fatal shooting July 12 of Matthew Tolbert, 17, a Negro.

200 police were on hand when about 200 blacks attempted a

wade-in at Chicago's Rainbow Beach July 16. The demonstrators, watched by angry groups of whites, dispersed; 12 whites were arrested for refusing to obey police. 12 persons had been arrested on the same charge during a black wade-in demonstration at the beach July 9. But 3 Negroes and 3 whites swam together at the beach July 22 without causing any disturbance.

Police officers used tear gas and 2 leashed dogs to quell 5 demonstrations by 1,500 blacks in Baton Rouge, La. Dec. 15, 1961. About 50 of the demonstrators were arrested on disorderly conduct charges. The demonstration had been called to protest the arrest Dec. 14 of 23 Negroes who had picketed downtown stores and had staged CORE-sponsored sit-ins at lunch counters. Many demonstrators were students of Baton Rouge's Southern University.

A CORE-sponsored demonstration was staged by Negroes in New Orleans Dec. 18 to protest alleged brutality by the Baton Rouge police in their use of tear gas and dogs. The Negroes were starting a march to the State Office Building when 292 were arrested on charges of parading without a permit.

A group of Southern University students demonstrated Jan. 16, 1962 to protest the expulsion of 7 students who had participated in the December antisegregation demonstration. (The Louisiana State Education Board had ordered schools under its jurisdiction to expel arrested students.) The expelled students were all members of the Baton Rouge chapter of CORE, which had sponsored the 1961 protest. (The university had suspended an 8th student.) Students picketed the campus and marched through buildings during classes Jan. 31, but a student boycott of classes received little support. University officials barred unauthorized student demonstrations Feb. 1, and attendance was described as near normal Feb. 2

Violence Continues in South, Spreads to North & West

Bombings and killings continued in the South in 1962. Negroes in Albany, Ga. pelted police with rocks and bottles. Night riders fired on black homes. Burning crosses flamed in northern Louisiana; black churches were burned in Georgia. Antisegregation demonstrations also occurred in the North when University of Chicago students demonstrated against segregation in off-campus student housing. 14 Negroes were wounded and a Black Muslim was killed in a shoot-out with police in Los Angeles. 6 blacks and a white were beaten by whites in Cairo, Ill. in an integration attempt.

The bombing involved a house being built in Shreveport, La.

for Dr. C.O. Simpkins, vice president of the Louisiana branch of the National Association for the Advancement of Colored People (NAACP) and a Southern Christian Leadership Conference (SCLC) board member. The house was badly damaged by a bomb blast Feb. 18.

17 Negroes and 2 whites, including Prof. Everett W. McNair of Talladega College, were arrested in Talladega, Ala. Apr. 9 for attempting a sit-in at drugstore lunch counters. Black pickets against the drugstores were dispersed Apr. 25 after whites tore up their placards and a tear-gas bomb was thrown from a passing car. 12 more black pickets and a white youth were arrested Apr. 16.

Lesley Lee Luttes, 16, a white, was shot and killed Apr. 19 in Augusta, Ga. during racial tension arising from a black boycott of 2 supermarkets. The boycott had begun Apr. 16 in a protest against alleged discriminatory hiring practices. Tension developed after a white reportedly had tried to run a picket down with a car. Other incidents of rock and bottle throwing, mostly involving juveniles, were reported as picketing continued Apr. 17-18 and gangs carrying firearms and bats roamed the city. Luttes was killed as he and 2 other white youths were driving through a black section and their car, carrying bricks and an air rifle, was attacked by gunfire from both sides of the street. Another of the youths was seriously wounded and hospitalized. 9 blacks were indicted May 1 for the killing. An agreement to end the picketing and discriminatory hiring practices was reached Apr. 21 by black leaders and the supermarkets' owner.

Shooting incidents by unidentified nightriders in Georgia were reported near Leesburg Aug. 31 and in Dawson Sept. 5. No one was injured in the first incident although 4 rural homes of blacks active in a voter-registration campaign were struck by rifle fire. In the Dawson incident, 3 shotgun blasts were fired into a Negro's home where 7 voter-registration workers, members of the Student Nonviolent Coordinating Committee, were staying. One of the students, John Chatfield, 20, white, was hit by 2 pellets in the arm. 2 others, Prathia Hall, 22, black, and Christopher Allen, 19, a white student from Oxford, England, reported being grazed by buckshot. The integrationists reported that 4 hours prior to the attack 4 of them had been chased out of Sasser by policeman D. E. Short, who, they said, had threatened them and had shot at their car twice.

2 black churches near Sasser, Ga. were destroyed by fires early Sept. 9, 1962. One had been used as the site for weekly voter

registration rallies. A Leesburg church used for voter registration rallies had been razed by fire 3 weeks previously. Pres. Kennedy, denouncing the burning of Georgia churches used in black voter registration drives, pledged Sept. 13 that "we'll do everything we possibly can do to make sure that . . . protection is assured" those seeking to register Negroes. Speaking as his press conference, Mr. Kennedy added that "if it requires extra legislation and extra force, we shall do that." Then a 4th black church was burned near Dawson, Ga. Sept. 17. FBI agents, in Georgia to investigate the previous burnings, announced later Sept. 17 that they had turned over to local authorities 4 white suspects who allegedly had confessed the arson.

While violence continued in the South, student demonstrations, Negro conflict with police and violent white opposition to integrationists appeared in the North during 1962.

Demonstrations against alleged segregation in off-campus student housing were staged by students against the University of Chicago Jan. 23-Feb. 5, 1962. They were sponsored by CORE, which charged that the university operated about 100 segregated apartment houses. The university said that only 12 of its 55 apartment houses were segregated and that it was following a policy to create a "stable inter-racial community" by "stages." The main protest was a continuous student sit-in maintained in shifts in a corridor outside the office of the university president, George Wells Beadle. The sit-in began Jan. 23 and ended Feb. 5 when the students left after being served with an eviction order under threat of suspension. But 41 persons, many of them non-students, were arrested Jan. 24-Feb. 5 after demonstrating at a university-owned real estate office. Charges were dismissed against 13 of those arrested Jan. 24. 10 others were convicted Jan. 31 of trespassing and were fined $10 each (sentences suspended).

In Los Angeles, a member of the Black Muslims was killed and 14 Negroes, including 8 policemen, were wounded in a riot in front of Black Muslim headquarters (Mosque No. 27) on South Broadway Apr. 27, 1962. About 75 policemen had been called out to quell the riot, which began when 2 policemen were attacked as they tried to question a man. One of the officers fired a shot, hitting an attacker. Other Black Muslim members rushed from their headquarters to join the fight, one of them firing a .22-caliber rifle. A county grand jury later indicted 9 of the 16 Black Muslims involved on charges of assaulting and resisting officers. Malcolm X, leader of the black separatist movement in New York, at a press conference, accused Los Angeles Police Chief William

H. Parker of "Gestapo" tactics toward the sect, which, he said, was not anti-white. Parker, testifying before the grand jury, had described the movement as "a hate organization." 90 black ministers issued a statement about the incident in which they denounced the Muslims but called for investigation and elimination of the "image of police brutality" within the Negro community.

6 black youths and Linda Perlstein, 22, white, were beaten by whites Aug. 17, 1962 during an attempt to integrate a skating rink in Cairo, Ill. About 80 Cairo integrationists went Aug. 20 to Springfield, where the group's leaders, including Dr. L. H. Holman, president of the NAACP's Illinois chapter, met with Gov. Otto Kerner to demand protection by National Guard troops or state police and to protest the denial of civil rights in Cairo. The integrationists claimed that since the integration campaign began in Cairo 53 of their members had been arrested while only 4 white youths had been charged with assault. The integration campaign in Cairo had been initiated in June by Student Nonviolent Coordinating Committee leader Mary McCollum, 22, of Nashville, Tenn. and 6 volunteer field workers. The campaign had been successful against a restaurant but was rebuffed at a community swimming pool and the roller rink. The first demonstration at the pool had been held June 29, and 30 integrationists had been arrested July 13-14 in stand-ins there and at the rink. 17 of these, all but one of them Negroes, were convicted July 19 of "mob action" at the rink and were fined $100 each. 4 were found guilty July 20 and fined $50 each for the swimming pool incident. A march was staged through downtown Cairo July 21 by more than 200 blacks and whites in protest against the convictions and fines.

Meredith Registers, Whites Riot at University of Mississippi

The admission of James H. Meredith, a Negro, to the University of Mississippi in the fall of 1962 was accompanied by state defiance of federal authority, rioting on the campus and in nearby Oxford, Miss. and extended harassment of Meredith as he attended classes.

Meredith's registration Oct. 1 was the first desegregation of a public school in Mississippi. But the defiance of federal authority exemplified by the rioting and by Gov. Ross R. Barnett's actions posed what was considered the most serious breach in federal-state relations since the Civil War.

A native Mississippian, born in Kosciusko, Air Force veteran Meredith, 29, was married and the father of a son. His reason for enrolling at the university was that it offered him the best course in his major, political science. He had 3 semesters—a year and a half—to go to complete studies for a degree. After 2 of his applications had been rejected, he had filed a federal suit. An injunction to force Meredith's admission to the school was issued in New Orleans June 25, 1962 by a 2-1 decision of a 3-judge panel of the 5th Circuit Court of Appeals (Judge Dozier De Vane dissenting). The court held that Meredith had been rejected "solely because he was a Negro." U.S. District Judge Ben. F. Cameron in Meridian, Miss. issued 4 stays of this order. 3 of the stays were reversed by the Circuit Court. The 4th, issued Aug. 6, was appealed to the Supreme Court, and Supreme Court Justice Hugo L. Black Sept. 10 nullified Cameron's stays and ordered Meredith's admission to the university. In a statewide TV-radio address Sept. 13 Gov. Barnett (a) invoked the doctrine of interposition of state sovereignty between the federal government and the people of the state, and (b) proclaimed that all public schools and institutions of higher learning would henceforth be operated under state supervision answerable only to state laws.

The legislature Sept. 18 indorsed Barnett's Sept. 13 proclamations and adopted legislation Sept. 19 to block Meredith's entrance to the university.

Just prior to the first attempt Sept. 20 to get Meredith admitted, Barnett had the Board of Trustees of Institutions of Higher Learning appoint him as special registrar for Meredith. He flew to Oxford and rejected Meredith's application at a 20-minute meeting in a campus building. Meredith was accompanied by U.S. Atty. St. John Barrett, Chief U.S. Marshal James J.P. McShane and another U.S. marshal. A crowd of 2,000 students jeered Meredith on the campus.

The first court action against Barnett took place Sept. 25, on application of Meredith's NAACP lawyers, when a 3-judge panel of the 5th Circuit Court (a) enjoined him, as well as other state and local officials, from blocking Meredith's entrance and (b) nullified any state injunctions blocking Meredith's entrance.

Meredith, accompanied Sept. 25 by U.S. Atty. John Doar and McShane, again attempted to register at the trustees' office in Jackson, but Barnett blocked the doorway and again denied him admission to the university. Barnett refused to accept copies of the 5th Circuit Court's restraining orders or of a summons to appear before the court. Meredith then returned to New Orleans. On Justice Department application, a different 3-judge panel of the 5th Circuit Court issued a contempt citation against Barnett the night of Sept. 25. Meredith Sept. 26 attempted a 3d time to enter the university, but he and McShane were halted near the main entrance in Oxford by Lt. Gov. Paul B. Johnson backed by 20 unarmed state troopers and about 15 county sheriffs. Johnson, announcing that he was acting on Barnett's orders, refused to admit Meredith and scuffled several times with McShane as he and the troopers blocked McShane's efforts to push through to the university.

The Justice Department later Sept. 26 obtained a contempt citation against Johnson from the 5th Circuit Court. The court also issued a 2d contempt citation against Barnett, who had evaded attempts to serve him with notice of the court's first action against him. A U.S. marshal trying to deliver the contempt citation to Barnett's office was blocked by state highway police.

A crowd of 2,500 Sept. 27 awaited the scheduled 4th attempt of Meredith to register. 200 police officers equipped with clubs were deployed around the campus by Barnett, who, with Johnson and his top adviser on segregation matters, William J. Simmons, national administrator of the Citizens Council of America, also waited on the campus. But the Justice Department canceled the attempt Sept. 27 and said that the "force accompanying Mr. Meredith [25 U.S. marshals] might not be sufficient to accomplish its mission without major violence and bloodshed for the citizens of Mississippi."

Barnett's defiance of the federal court orders requiring Meredith's registration began to evaporate Sept. 30 when his resistance was shaken by a series of federal steps: Pres. Kennedy, in the mounting tension, federalized the Mississippi National Guard Sept. 30; the force of deputy U.S. marshals was increased, and a staging base had been set up at the Memphis (Tenn.) Naval Air Station by 110 men of the 70th Battalion of Engineers, who arrived in Memphis from Fort Campbell, Ky. Sept. 28.

Barnett, in a statement issued Sept. 30, said: "My heart still says 'never,' but my calm judgment abhors the bloodshed that will follow"; "we are now completely surrounded by armed forces, and . . . we are physically overpowered." He urged Mississippi citizens and officials to try to preserve peace and avoid violence.

A heavy guard of U.S. marshals escorted Meredith when he took up residence on the campus Sept. 30. A few hours later— about 8 p.m.—rioting erupted and continued during a nationally televised plea by Pres. Kennedy at 10:30 p.m. for the students and citizens of Mississippi to comply peacefully with federal law.

The campus had been relatively deserted when Meredith arrived. Many students were away for a Sept. 29 football game in

Jackson. Returning students, joined by some adults, began gathering on campus Sept. 30 before the line of about 300 marshals encircling the administration building, the Lyceum. Tension mounted, heckling increased, and members of the crowd began pelting the marshals with rocks, bottles and bricks. At first, about 100 students took part in the disorder, but the number swelled to 2,500 during the mêlée.

At the height of the riot, 2 charges were made on the line of marshals and were repulsed by tear gas. (According to Edwin O. Guthman, the Justice Department's public information chief, who was in Oxford with the marshals), the marshals did not use tear gas until one of them had been hit on the helmet with an iron pipe.) The 2d charge was led by ex-Maj. Gen. Edwin A. Walker of Texas at the head of a force of about 1,000 students. Students also seized a bulldozer from a nearby construction site and a fire engine and unsuccessfully tried to run the unmanned bulldozer into the line of marshals. The fire engine was run across the campus, which, by this time, was overcast with tear gas and strewn with debris. Then shotgun blasts and rifle fire was begun by hidden snipers, and the marshals retreated inside the Lyceum, on which the snipers continued their fire. Small groups of students roamed the campus and committed acts of vandalism. A favorite target was cars; 5 autos and a mobile TV unit were burned with gasoline fire bombs. Other cars were stoned or overturned and their windows smashed.

The beleaguered marshals were reinforced at about midnight Sept. 30 by the arrival of Mississippi National Guard troops and federal military police. Some MPs were met with flying bricks, stones and molotov cocktails, and rifle fire was heard. They moved in toward the fatigued marshals with fixed bayonets but did not fire. Other MPs arrived by convoy on the campus at about 4:30 a.m. after being detained by an ambush at a railroad trestle, where they had been pelted with heavy objects. After a final assault by 100 hard-core students was turned back at the Lyceum, the troops began rounding up rioters. At about 5:30 a.m. the rioting on the campus had ceased.

Rioting, however, broke out in downtown Oxford at about 9 a.m. Oct. 1 and continued until before noon. Soldiers, blacks and newsmen were beaten and pelted. Cars and homes were damaged. Order finally was restored by troops firing over the heads of the mob. Roadblocks were then set up outside town, and the square was ringed with troops. By Oct. 2, the troops in and around Oxford (population: 6,500) numbered about 13,500 and included the National Guard and Regular Army forces.

The rioting brought death to 2 men—Paul Guihard, 30, a correspondent for Agence France Presse, found dead with a bullet in his back, and Ray Gunter, 23, a jukebox repairman from nearby Abbeville, shot in the head. More than 60 were injured, including 25 U.S. marshals, one seriously from a shotgun blast in the neck. 150 alleged rioters were arrested, including ex-Maj. Gen. Edwin A. Walker, who had commanded federal troops used in the Little Rock, Ark. school desegregation crisis in 1957 and who had resigned from the Army in 1961 following an official reprimand for conducting rightwing political orientation of his troops. Walker, who had appeared downtown in Oxford during the rioting, was arrested Oct. 1. He was charged with assault or opposing federal officers, preventing a federal officer from discharging his duties, inciting or engaging in an insurrection against the U.S., conspiracy to overthrow or oppose by force the execution of U.S. laws. He was arraigned in Oxford Oct. 1, and he was taken to the Federal Bureau of Prisons in Springfield, Mo. that night.

When the Mississippi crisis had arisen, Walker had broadcast a radio appeal from Dallas, Tex. Sept. 28 for segregationists "to move" "to a stand" beside Barnett. Walker urged: "10,000 strong from every state in the union! Rally to the cause of freedom! The battle cry of the Republic: Barnett, yes! Castro, no! Bring your flag, your tent, and your skillet. It's now or never!"

Walker was released from the U.S. Medical Center in Springfield, Mo. Oct. 6 on $50,000 bond after U.S. District Judge Claude F. Clayton Jr. ordered Walker to undergo psychiatric tests.

Atty. Gen. Robert F. Kennedy and Gov. Barnett engaged in a verbal duel Oct. 1 over the responsibility for the violence. Kennedy asserted in a statement that Meredith's entrance to the campus had been "arranged by" Barnett and that Barnett had "assured" the Justice Department that law and order would be maintained by state police. He charged that the state police had been withdrawn from the campus area shortly after the rioting began, were returned after the first violence had subsided and were withdrawn again when further violence erupted. During this latter period, he said, "approximately 150 of the police were observed sitting in their automobiles within 1/2 mile of the rioting and shooting." He praised the marshals' "restraint and judgment" and said their action was "in the finest tradition of the federal service."

Meredith attended 2 classes after his enrollment Oct. 1 with no incidents except jeering by students. Meredith at first was escorted by U.S. Chief Marshal McShane and another marshal, but his guard was increased to 75 marshals before he reached his first class. 4 marshals stood on duty outside his classrooms. He also attended classes peacefully Oct. 2 with an escort of marshals and with his car followed by an Army truck carrying 12 armed soldiers. About 35 to 50 students demonstrated near Meredith's campus residence early Oct. 3 and burned him in effigy. Federal troops dispersed the group. Just after daybreak soldiers removed a 2d effigy hanging from a building nearby. Meredith's attendance continued unmarred by serious incidents Oct. 4-17. A rock was thrown through a window of the campus cafeteria Oct. 8 while he was eating, and he was escorted by marshals back to his troop-guarded dormitory. A crowd of about 400 that gathered during the incident was watched by troops and dispersed by a university dean. During his 2d week of classes Meredith dined in the cafeteria and walked to class unguarded by marshals, conversed with a white student and had coffee with 3 faculty members. Withdrawal of some of the regular troops and federalized National Guard troops deployed on the campus and in and around Oxford was begun Oct. 8.

Late in the month several demonstrations and acts of hooliganism by students were directed against Meredith and troops guarding him. 2 U.S. marshals escorted Meredith from the campus dining room Oct. 24 after about 30 white students had left the room at Meredith's entrance and gathered outside the door, where they blocked Meredith's exit. While Meredith was dining at the cafeteria Oct. 29, about 200 students exploded firecrackers and threw soft drink bottles at soldiers assigned outside. The night of Oct. 30 a bottle was thrown through the window of a car carrying Meredith and 2 marshals, one of whom was injured by the shattering glass. The next night, Oct. 31, a firecracker thrown from a dormitory window hit a military policeman in the face. Troops with fixed bayonets immediately surrounded the dormitory while MPs searched it. The search produced an Army M-1 rifle and pistol, both dismantled, several tear-gas grenades and fireworks. 4 students were expelled Nov. 3 on charges based on the discovery of the weapons in the dormitory. Expulsion had been recommended by the Student Judicial Council.

Shotgun blasts were fired from a speeding car Dec. 23 into Meredith's home in Kosciusko, Miss., but nobody was injured.

VIOLENCE INTENSIFIES (1963)

Violence Hampers Rights Campaigns in South

Racial violence mounted in the South durnig 1963. A voter registration drive in Greenwood, Miss. was met with gunfire and fire bombs. A white integrationist was slain on a road in Alabama. An ambush in Jackson, Miss. resulted in the death of NAACP field secretary Medgar W. Evers. The National Guard was called to control clashes between Negroes and whites in Cambridge, Md. Mass rallies, night marches and violence in Mississippi voter registration drives were accompanied by legal battles to prevent interference with voter registration efforts and to end voting discrimination.

William Higgs, 27, of Jackson, Miss. and attorney William M. Kunstler of New York, had filed in U.S. district court in Washington, D.C. Jan. 2, 1963 a suit requesting that Atty. Gen. Robert F. Kennedy and FBI Director J. Edgar Hoover be ordered to act against alleged interference with black voter registration efforts in Mississippi. The suit was brought on behalf of Higgs and 7 other black Mississippians. The Justice Department sued in Oxford, Miss. Jan. 22 in an effort to end voting discrimination in Sunflower County, Miss. During an unsuccessful black-voter registration drive in 1962, several campaigners had been arrested and shots were fired into the homes of 3 Negroes active in the drive.

A tense situation developed in Greenwood (Leflore County), Miss., where violence and arrests accompanied a major voter registration campaign that got under way Mar. 1, 1963. Dick Gregory, 30, of Chicago, a nationally prominent black comedian, led several marches in Greenwood. During the drive, several hundred Negroes applied for registration in Leflore County. Violence had erupted there as early as Feb. 28, when James Travis, 20, a black registration worker, was wounded (not seriously) by gunfire from an auto carrying 3 white men. 4 major civil rights groups— the National Association for the Advancement of Colored People (NAACP), the Southern Christian Leadership Conference, the Congress of Racial Equality (CORE) and the Student Nonviolent Coordinating Committee (SNCC)—announced the following day that they would coordinate the registration drive.

4 black voter-registration workers were shot in Greenwood Mar. 6, and the Greenwood voter registration headquarters was

35

damaged by fire Mar. 25. Shotgun blasts were fired Mar. 26 into the home of the father of Dewey Roosevelt Green Jr., who had been unsuccessful in an attempt to enroll in the University of Mississippi.

After holding mass rallies at night, Negroes marched during the day from Mar. 27 to Apr. 3 in groups of 35 to 50 to the courthouse in attempts to register. The police, armed and sometimes accompanied by police dogs, attempted to disperse them. A federal suit against vote bias in Leflore County arose out of the arrest of 11 marchers Mar. 27. 8 of those arrested, including Robert P. Moses, 28, an SNCC field secretary and the campaign's leader, and James Foreman, SNCC secretary, were sentenced Mar. 29 to 4 months in prison and fined $200 each for disorderly conduct. The Justice Department sued Mar. 30 for a federal court order barring interference with black voter registrations, but U.S. District Judge Claude F. Clayton Jr. in Aberdeen, Miss. Apr. 1 refused to issue a temporary injunction.

Dick Gregory arrived Apr. 1, addressed mass rallies and led marches to the courthouse Apr. 2-3. A policeman twisted Gregory's left arm in moving him Apr. 2. But the police, who arrested 19 of Gregory's companions, refrained from arresting Gregory although he ignored police orders to disperse and taunted the police, whom he called "dirty dogs" and "a bunch of illiterate whites who couldn't even pass the [vote] test themselves."

Federal and city officials Apr. 4 came to an agreement easing the situation. They agreed on the simultaneous withdrawal of the petition for a temporary injunction and the staying of the sentences of the 8 arrested and sentenced Mar. 27.

Flaming gasoline bombs were thrown Apr. 12 in nearby Clarksdale into the home of Aaron Henry, black president of the NAACP's Mississippi chapter. Henry's overnight guest: Rep. Charles C. Diggs Jr. (D., Mich.), a Negro. No one was injured. 2 whites arrested hours afterwards said they were "just having fun."

William L. Moore, 35, a white integrationist, was found shot to death on a road near Attalla, Ala. Apr. 23, 1963. He had been walking, wearing pro-integration signs, on a personal "Freedom Walk" pilgrimage from Chattanooga, Tenn. to Mississippi to protest segregation. Floyd E. Simpson, 40, white operator of a grocery store in Collbran, DeKalb County, was formally charged in Gadsden Apr. 29 with Moore's slaying.

2 groups of integrationists were arrested by Alabama police May 1 and 3 while attempting to complete the "Freedom Walk"

begun by Moore. The first group, unsponsored, composed of 8 Negroes, were apprehended by Etowah County sheriff deputies near Attalla May 1 and jailed at Gadsden. 3 members of the group had started Apr. 30 from an area near where Moore had been slain and were joined later by 5 others. Another group of walkers, 5 white and 5 black, sponsored by the Congress of Racial Equality (CORE) and the Student Nonviolent Coordinating Committee (SNCC), took up Moore's integration walk May 1 from Chattanooga. City police and Tennessee highway patrolmen accompanied them, and the only incident was the hurling of a handful of gravel from a passing car. The guard shifted to Georgia patrolmen and sheriff's deputies as the group passed into Georgia May 2. When the group stopped for lunch May 3, about 100 whites gathered and one knocked a walker to the ground. Another walker was hit on the head with a rock. Between Rising Fawn and the Alabama line, they were pelted with eggs and followed by about 100 cars carrying whites. As soon as they crossed into Alabama May 3 they were arrested by state patrolmen using electrical prod poles customarily used on cattle. They were jailed at Fort Payne on breach-of-the-peace charges.

A 3d attempt of integrationists to complete Moore's Freedom Walk to Mississippi ended May 19 with the arrest of the participants. Alabama highway patrolmen and Etowah County sheriff's deputies arrested 5 whites and 6 Negroes as they sought to resume the walk at the site of Moore's slaying on U.S. Route 11.

A protest campaign against segregation in Jackson, Miss. led to black-white clashes, a bombing and the use of police dogs. NAACP aide Medgar W. Evers was murdered, and a brief riot followed a march of mourning.

The desegregation drive had barely begun in Jackson, Miss. May 28, 1963 when one of the black demonstrators, Memphis Norman, 21, sitting at a "white-only" F. W. Woolworth lunch counter, was knocked from his stool and kicked in the face by a white man, Benny G. Oliver, 26, a former Jackson policeman. City police, on hand but under orders not to enter private property unless invited, arrested Oliver later. Norman, admitted to the hospital, was charged with disturbing the peace. The charge was dismissed at the city's request May 31. Oliver was sentenced to 30 days in jail and fined $100. The sit-in, begun by Norman and 2 black women, all Tougaloo Southern Christian College students, was joined by Tougaloo Prof. John R. Salter, 29, white, Walter Williams, black, and several white girls. A crowd of about 200 whites gathered and sprinkled the demonstrators with mustard, catsup and sugar from the counter. Salter was struck on the face by a white; Williams was thrown to the floor and beaten; one of the white girls was seized and pushed out of the store by a white youth. All demonstrators continued to sit-in without resisting. None of the blacks were served, and the store, after roping off the section, closed several hours early.

5 other blacks were arrested in Jackson May 28 soon after they started picketing a block away from the store. A bomb explosion that night wrecked the home of one of the integrationist leaders. 6 pickets of both races were arrested in Jackson May 29 in front of the store.

400 black children demonstrated in a Jackson school yard May 30. Police barricaded streets in the area and directed the students back into school. Police dogs brought to the scene were not used. A black mother whose children attended the school and a 17-year-old black girl were arrested. The children began a mass march downtown May 31, and about 600 were arrested by members of the city police force, which was reinforced with sheriff's deputies, and by state highway patrolmen carrying riot guns. The arrested children were loaded into trucks and taken to a temporary jail set up on a fair ground. They were joined June 1 by more than 100 more black children arrested in another march. 300 of them were later released to their parents.

Jackson Mayor Allen Thompson and the City Commission June 1 agreed to 3 of the black demands—to hire Negroes as policemen and school-crossing guards, to desegregate city facilities and to upgrade black employment in city jobs. (Thompson May 28 had denied black leaders' statements, based on a meeting with him that day, that he had agreed to the demands.) The Negroes' key demand for establishment of a biracial committee was rejected June 1.

The protest campaign against segregation in Jackson had been marked by use of black prison trustees to help arrest black demonstrators, by the use of school children in mass parades and by the arrest June 1 of NAACP aide Medgar Evers and NAACP Executive Secy. Roy Wilkins for picketing. Both were freed on bond. The use of the trustees—mostly to carry praying demonstrators to patrol wagons—had begun May 29 with the arrest of 15 pickets.

The Jackson protests continued despite a temporary injunction issued against demonstrations by a county judge June 6 at the city's request. (Black entertainers Lena Horne and Dick Gregory arrived in Jackson June 6 to spur the integration drive.)

Medgar W. Evers, the NAACP's Mississippi field secretary for 9 years, was shot in the back and killed early June 12, 1963 (just after midnight June 11) in front of his home in Jackson. The bullet was fired from ambush. A caliber .30-06 rifle with a telescopic sight was found nearby. Evers had just left his car after appearing at an integration rally at a church.

Gov. Ross Barnett of Mississippi said of the slaying that "apparently it was a dastardly act," and Jackson Mayor Allen Thompson said Jackson citizens were "dreadfully shocked, humiliated and sick at heart" over it.

Jackson Negroes protested June 12 in mass demonstrations that resulted in 158 arrests. 13 of those arrested were ministers walking to city hall in 2s at widely spaced intervals. Several hundred black teen-age demonstrators were halted by a 100-man police force equipped with riot guns and automatic rifles.

About 2,800 persons, including UN Undersecy. Ralph Bunche, attended Evers' funeral services in Jackson June 15 and heard NAACP Executive Secy. Wilkins charge in a eulogy that "the Southern political system put that man behind the rifle" that killed Evers. Pres. and Mrs. Kennedy sent Mrs. Evers a letter of condolence. Evers, who had received 2 Bronze Stars for World War II Army service, was buried in Arlington National Cemetery June 19.

A riot broke out briefly June 15 following a march of mourning for Evers. Officials had granted a parade permit for the march, in which thousands of Negroes and about 50 whites participated. A group of young blacks, breaking from the ranks, stopped at a line of policemen, who were accompanied by police dogs. Several Negroes hurled bottles and rocks, before the police moved forward and began making arrests. U.S. Asst. Atty. Gen. John Doar was credited with keeping the riot from growing worse. Ignoring the rocks and bottles he walked toward the crowd and appealed for calm. Several black leaders aided him. 27 persons, including 2 white integrationists, were arrested.

A 2d march protesting Evers' slaying resulted June 15 in the arrest of 82 persons, including white Prof. John Salter of Tougaloo Southern Christian College, who was beaten by police. 37 black youths were arrested June 16 (Flag Day) as they appeared downtown in 2s and 4s carrying small American flags.

Following a suspension of demonstrations June 17 and several phone calls from Pres. Kennedy and Atty. Gen. Kennedy to Mayor Thompson, Thompson met with 5 black leaders June 18 and announced later that the city would (a) hire 6 black policemen and 8 black school-crossing guards and (b) promote 7 black sanitation workers to truck drivers and a black truck driver to crew leader; all were to serve in black districts.

Black demonstrations in Jackson, which had been under Evers' leadership, were suspended June 20 after a report to black leaders by the Rev. S. L. Whitney on his meeting with Pres. Kennedy June 17. More than 1,000 Negroes and whites had been arrested in the final 4 weeks of Jackson demonstrations.

Byron de la Beckwith, 42, of Greenwood, Miss. was arrested in Greenwood June 22 and charged in Jackson June 23 with murder in Evers' slaying. The charge was made by Hinds County District Atty. William L. Waller. Beckwith, a fertilizer salesman for the Walcott-Steel Chemical Co. in Greenville, Miss., was a member of the Citizens Council of Mississippi. Beckwith's arrest June 22 (June 23 Washington time) by FBI agents was announced in Washington by FBI Director J. Edgar Hoover. The federal charge against Beckwith: violating the 1957 Civil Rights Act by conspiring to prevent Evers from exercising his civil rights. Federal authorities June 24 turned Beckwith over to the Jackson police and deferred the federal case until resolution of the state case. A county grand jury in Jackson, Miss. July 2 indicted Beckwith for the Evers murder and Beckwith pleaded not guilty on his arraignment July 8.

Beckwith's trial began Jan. 31, 1964. The prosecution presented evidence that a rifle with telescopic sight found near the scene of the crime had been owned by Beckwith and had his right index fingerprint on it. Several witnesses testified that they saw Beckwith's car near Evers' home a few days before the crime; 2 witnesses said they saw it parked near where the gun had been found about 45 minutes before the shooting. The defense presented as witnesses 2 police officers and a businessman from Greenwood, Miss., Beckwith's home town, who testified that they saw Beckwith there, 95 miles from the scene of the crime, at about the time of the shooting. Beckwith denied killing Evers and said his rifle had been stolen shortly before the shooting.

Judge Leon F. Hendrick declared a mistrial Feb. 7 after an all-white jury failed to agree on a verdict, and the bailiff reported a 7-5 deadlock for acquittal. A 2d mistrial was declared Apr. 17, 1964 after an all-white jury deadlocked (reportedly 8-4 in favor of acquittal).

Clashes between whites and blacks in Cambridge, Md. led to rioting and to martial law enforced by National Guard troops. A truce between black anti-segregation leaders and city representatives in Cambridge had been imperiled when a black girl, Dinez

White, 15, was held without bail after being arrested May 30, 1963 with 4 others in an individual protest at a recreation center. The incident took place just before the truce was due to expire May 31. Circuit Judge E. McMaster Duer, who had ordered the girl held, released her June 3 on a writ of *habeas corpus*. But negotiations between whites and blacks collapsed June 10 as the Negroes charged that they had been "double-crossed" by Duer's sentencing of Miss White and a 15-year-old black boy demonstrator to indeterminate terms in correction schools. 100 Negroes staged a protest June 10 against the sentencing; 20 were arrested.

A protest march June 11 against the new arrests led to rioting and clashes between whites and Negroes, and 2 white men were injured by shotgun blasts. After several hundred counter-demonstrating whites had been prevented by police and state troopers June 13 from breaking into the black district, the mayor and council and black leaders met in Annapolis June 14 with Gov. J. Millard Tawes, who later June 14 ordered the National Guard to maintain order in Cambridge under a "civilian and military government." 400 to 500 Guardsmen enforced a ban on demonstrations, a 10 p.m. curfew, prohibition of liquor sales and other limited martial law rules in the cannery town.

Negotiations between whites and blacks collapsed again June 16, and a scheduled black march June 18 was canceled only after 2 days of conferences in Washington by Asst. Atty. Gen. Burke Marshall and black leaders.

Much of the controversy centered around black demands for the desegregation of public accommodations. Gov. Tawes had proposed that the City Council adopt an ordinance against such discrimination and that in return the Nergoes promise not to conduct demonstrations for a year. Tawes' plan was rejected by the Cambridge Nonviolent Action Committee, which led the black campaign. The City Council then proposed and finally adopted July 1 a plan even more objectionable to the Negroes—a city charter amendment prohibiting discrimination in public accommodations. Black leaders opposed this plan because, unlike an ordinance, a city charter amendment was subject to referendum by petition of 20% (about 750) of the registered voters. Since white voters in the town of some 12,000 persons outnumbered black voters by about 4 to one, it was assumed that the largely pro-segregation whites would defeat the amendment in a referendum.

The National Guard remained on duty until noon July 8, when Tawes directed the Guard units to leave. Demonstrations resumed the day the Guard departed, and Guard troops were ordered back by Tawes July 11 after the demonstrations led to shootings (no fatalities) and other violence. Brig. Gen. George C. Gelston invoked modified martial law again July 12. Guard troops fired tear gas July 20 to disperse a group of Negroes defying orders to move off the streets. Black leaders who were conferring with Gelston, after being stopped from leading a protest march, intervened to help restore order.

An agreement tentatively settling the racial dispute in Cambridge, was signed July 23, 1963 by black and white leaders representing the city, state and federal governments. The agreement was reached in Atty. Gen. Kennedy's office after 72 hours of intensive federal intervention. Under the agreement the Negro leaders promised to end demonstrations "for an indefinite period."

Bombing & Rioting Mark Birmingham Campaign

A campaign against segregation of lunch counters and public facilities and against hiring bias in Birmingham, Ala. was marked by repeated bombings and outbreaks of rioting. A bomb that killed 4 black girls in a Birmingham church drew international attention. Pres. Kennedy sent federal troops into Alabama, met with black leaders and sent 2 personal representatives to the city to aid in restoring peace.

The desegregation campaign had begun Apr. 2, 1963, and 2 instances of violence were reported during the demonstrations early in the campaign. A Negro slashed with a knife at a police dog during a Palm Sunday demonstration Apr. 7; he was then attacked by the dog; this led to a clash involving other blacks and club-swinging policemen; 26 Negroes were arrested. A crowd of about 2,000 blacks protested the arrest of 26 Negroes during an Easter Sunday demonstration against the arrest of the Rev. Dr. Martin Luther King Jr; members of the crowd hurled rocks at police, who clubbed several of their alleged attackers.

Included among those arrested in the April demonstrations: Al Hibbler, a blind black singer, who was arrested Apr. 9 and immediately released; the Rev. Fred L. Shuttlesworth, president of the Alabama Christian Movement for Human Rights and local director of the campaign, who was arrested Apr. 6, released Apr. 8 and arrested again Apr. 12; the Rev. Dr. Martin Luther King Jr. and the Rev. Dr. Ralph D. Abernathy, who were arrested Apr. 12 with more than 60 others as they led a march of about 1,000 blacks. (King's brother, the Rev. A. D. William King, was arrested Apr. 14.)

Leaders of the drive had applied to both of the city's governments—the newly elected and installed Mayor Albert Boutwell and council and the city's superseded commissioners, who refused to leave office—for permits to stage peaceful protest marches. Both governments refused the request Apr. 30. Their refusals precipitated mass demonstrations.

Thousands of Negroes, many of them children, were arrested in Birmingham May 2-7, 1963 as the drive to desegregate facilities throughout the city intensified.

Initially, hundreds of black children demonstrated May 2 in groups of 10 to 50. More than 700 of them were arrested, and they offered no resistance. Instead, they sang and laughed and some ran to school buses commandeered by police to bring them to jail. The Rev. A. D. King was among those arrested but was later released.

But the situation became worse May 3. The police used high-pressure fire hoses and dogs to repulse groups of marchers, mostly high-school and college students. Most of the marchers did not resist. But rocks and bottles were thrown at the police and firemen from the top of a building, and 2 firemen and a news photographer were injured. 3 students were bitten by the dogs, and a few were injured by the water from the high-pressure hoses. 250 arrests were made May 3.

King said at a mass meeting the night of May 3: "Today was D[emonstration] Day. Tomorrow will be Double-D Day."

Groups of black youths in their teens and younger left 2 black churches early May 4. When the first group neared city hall, they unfurled a banner reading "Love God and Thy Neighbor." They were immediately arrested. Orders were then issued to arrest the other groups, and the churches were closed by the police.

Violence erupted in a park May 3, when an unorganized crowd of about 2,000 black adults became the targets of fire hoses, and the police were pelted with bottles and rocks. As the disturbance mounted, one of King's lieutenants, the Rev. James Bevel of Cleveland, Miss., a field secretary of King's Southern Christian Leadership Conference, borrowed a police bull horn to plead: "If you're not going to demonstrate in a non-violent way, then leave." More than 200 were arrested, including more than 100 juveniles.

The next day, Sunday, several hundred Negroes held a prayer vigil in church, then marched peacefully to nearby Julius Ellsberry park but stopped on the way to pray at a police barricade blocking them from downtown. Only a few arrests, of stragglers, were made.

More mass protests were made May 6 and 7, and the demonstrations built up into riots.

The arrests May 6 totaled about 1,000 and included black comedian Dick Gregory, who attempted to lead 19 teen-agers on a march.

About 3,000 unorganized black adults ran May 7 through the business district. They resisted the police by throwing rocks and bottles but were eventually forced back to the black district by fire hoses spouting water at pressures so high that it took bark off trees. An armored police car was used to herd crowds. An undetermined number of persons were injured, including the Rev. Fred L. Shuttlesworth, one of the black leaders, and 6 policemen hit by rocks thrown by Negroes caught by fire hoses in a park.

Gov. George C. Wallace later May 7 ordered 250 state highway patrolmen to bolster the city force of Birmingham Public Safety Commissioner Eugene (Bull) Connor. 575 more troopers armed with tear gas, submachine guns and sawed-off shotguns moved into the city the night of May 7. About 1,200 law officers were massed in Birmingham by May 8.

As tensions between Negroes and whites increased, a truce was called May 8, only to be jeopardized hours later by the jailing of the Rev. Dr. Martin Luther King Jr. King, released on bail, announced his renewed hope for success in negotiating a settlement. Pres. Kennedy May 8 also expressed hope for a negotiated settlement but called the Birmingham situation "ugly."

An hour after Kennedy spoke, King was in jail. He had been convicted by City Court Judge C. H. Brown of having paraded on Good Friday without a permit. 25 others and one of King's close associates, the Rev. Ralph D. Abernathy, were also convicted and jailed. Brown imposed the maximum penalty on each: 180 days in jail plus $100 fine. Their imprisonment threatened the delicate truce, and several black leaders called for huge demonstrations the next day. But King and Abernathy were released on bond and made conciliatory statements expressing hope for success in the negotiations.

In the Senate May 6, Sens. John Sherman Cooper (R., Ky.) and Wayne Morse (D., Ore.) denounced the treatment of blacks in Birmingham during the demonstrations. Cooper deplored "the use of dogs against human beings . . . just seeking their constitutional rights."

Addressing the opening of the state legislature May 7, Gov. Wallace warned that he was "beginning to tire of agitators, integregationists, and others who seek to destroy law and order in Alabama."

In Birmingham, both black leaders and city officials asserted that the national press had exaggerated the violence of the disturbances. Abernathy said May 8 that "there have been no race riots here."

A limited desegregation plan for Birmingham was worked out by black leaders—the Rev. Dr. Martin Luther King Jr., the Rev. Fred L. Shuttlesworth and the Rev. Ralph D. Abernathy—and the Senior Citizens' Committee, a group of white businessmen set up by the Chamber of Commerce in 1962 to seek some arrangement with black leaders. The latter committee's chief negotiator was lawyer-real estate operator Sidney W. Smyer Sr., who said his group represented employers of about 80% of Birmingham's working force.

But the agreement was attacked May 11 by Commissioner Connor, who appealed by radio for whites to boycott stores honoring the agreement. "That's the best way I know to beat down integration in Birmingham," he said.

A late-night bombing in Birmingham abruptly punctured the truce May 11. The target was the home of the Rev. A. D. King. King, his wife and his 5 children were at home but were not injured, although the front half of their house was demolished. A 2d bombing occurred a few minutes before midnight May 11 at the integrated A.G. Gaston Motel, headquarters for the black campaign. 4 persons were injured (not seriously), and heavy damages were inflicted on the motel and 3 adjoining house trailers. The motel had reported an anonymous warning that afternoon that the Klu Klux Klan was rallying outside the city and that the motel would be bombed.

The bombings triggered a 3-hour riot early May 12 in which about 2,500 Negroes participated and about 50 persons were injured.

Tires on police and fire vehicles were slashed and punctured by blacks gathering at the King home after the bombing late May 11, and police and firemen arriving at the scene of the motel bombing were met with a hail of bottles and rocks. Fires razed 6 nearby neighborhood stores as firemen were driven away by Negroes throwing bottles and rocks. A white taxi driver was pulled from his cab and stabbed, and his cab was burned.

A 28-block area was sealed off eventually by about 250 state troopers and about 100 deputized irregulars under the direction of Col. Albert J. Lingo, state director of public safety. When Lingo had arrived on the scene with an automatic shotgun (his troopers arrived with carbines), he had been urged by Birmingham Chief Police Inspector W. J. Haley and Police Chief Jamie Moore to "please leave." "We don't need any guns down here," Moore said, "you all might get somebody killed." "You're damned right it'll kill somebody," Lingo replied. (The *N.Y. Herald Tribune* reported May 13: After the riot subsided, "the state troopers began clubbing Negroes sitting on their porches." Those clubbed had been watching and "taking no part in the fight." "And so the battle ended with the state policemen, who had played only a very minor rôle in the actual quelling of the riot, rapping old Negro men in rocking chairs.")

In Washington May 12, Pres. Kennedy held an emergency meeting with Atty. Gen. Kennedy, Defense Secy. Robert S. McNamara, Army Secy. Cyrus Vance, Army Chief of Staff Earle G. Wheeler and other officials. The President then went before the press and TV cameras to announce that he had dispatched federal troops to bases near Birmingham and had ordered the "necessary preliminary steps" to federalize the Alabama National Guard. While Kennedy spoke, federal troops, all from outside Alabama, were on the move. By May 13 about 3,000 troops were in the area.

Kennedy's authority to send federal troops into Alabama was questioned by Gov. Wallace May 12. In a telegram to the President, Wallace said there were "sufficient state and local forces" to handle the situation, which he described as being "well in hand." He said that neither he nor the legislature had asked for the troops, and he requested their withdrawal. Earlier May 12 Wallace had issued a statement indicating his belief that the bombings had been perpetrated by "outside subversives" and pledging to stop violence "if it takes 1,000 or 10,000 law enforcement officers, or whatever it takes." Kennedy replied by telegram May 13 that he "would be derelict in my duty" if he did not take steps to "enable this government, if required, to meet its obligations without delay."

With the truce back in effect, the 28-block cordon was lifted by state troopers May 13, but they continued on patrol with carbines. The Rev. King, accompanied by about 100 Negroes, went into 2 pool halls May 13 to urge blacks to avoid violence. King and those with him were stopped by state troopers and told to disperse. Although the Negroes complied, the troopers forcibly cleared the streets of Negroes.

A bomb blast in a black church in Birmingham during Sunday School Sept. 15, 1963 killed 4 black girls. (There had been about 50 bombings of Negro property in Birmingham, all unsolved, since World war II. The Sept. 15 bombing was the 21st bombing of Birmingham Negroes since 1955.) 2 black youths were killed later Sept. 15 in Birmingham, one during protest rioting and the other as he rode a bicycle on the outskirts of town.

In addition to killing the 4 girls, the bomb injured 14 Negroes, blew holes in the walls of the church (the 16th St. Baptist Church), wrecked 2 cars parked outside and badly damaged 3 others. Negroes rushed to the scene after the blast and hurled rocks at passing cars carrying whites and at police. Johnny Robinson, 16, was killed by a shotgun blast fired by a policeman who said he fired low to disperse a rock-throwing group of black youths.

Mayor Albert Boutwell called the bombing "just sickening" as he and Police Chief Jamie Moore appealed Sept. 15 for help from Gov. Wallace in the event of further violence. In response, Wallace sent 500 National Guardsmen and 300 state troopers. He also offered a $5,000 reward for information leading to the arrest and conviction of the bombers.

25 FBI agents were sent to the scene Sept. 15 to investigate the bombing, and Asst. Atty. Gen. Burke Marshall led a team of Justice Department investigators.

Martin Luther King Jr. sent Pres. Kennedy a telegram Sept. 15 urging "immediate steps" by the federal government before "the worst racial holocaust the nation has ever seen" erupted in Birmingham and Alabama. King said he would "plead with my people to remain nonviolent in the face of this terrible provocation." King also sent Wallace a telegram saying "the blood of 4 little children and others critically injured is on your hands" because "your irresponsible and misguided actions created ... the atmosphere that has induced continued violence and now murder." King arrived in Birmingham from Atlanta Sept. 15 and, at a news conference Sept. 16, said the Army "ought to come to Birmingham and take over this city and run it."

Pres. Kennedy in a statement Sept. 16 expressed his "deep sense of outrage and grief" over the bombing and called it "regrettable that public disparagement of law and order has encouraged violence which has fallen on the innocent." Kennedy Sept. 19 appointed ex-Army Secy. Kenneth C. Royall, 69, and ex-West Point football coach Earl H. Blaik, 66, "to represent me personally" in helping Birmingham try to overcome "the fears and suspicions" arising from the racial strife there. The President Sept. 19 also met with 7 black leaders on the situation. In a statement issued after the meeting, the blacks said they had told Kennedy that the city's Negroes were "frustrated, confused and almost on the verge of despair as a result of this reign of terror" in Birmingham. A spokesman for the group, Martin Luther King Jr., said Kennedy had expressed "the kind of federal concern needed" and had "made it clear that the federal government would not stand idly by and allow the lives and property and rights of Negro citizens to be trampled."

A black neighborhood of Birmingham was rocked Sept. 25 by 2 bomb explosions, which damaged 8 homes and 4 autos. The 2d bomb, which went off about 15 minutes after the first, had been loaded with staples, nails, bolts and other metal bits. Most of the damage was from this shrapnel. Police Inspector J. W. Haley said that "this was a booby trap ... made to kill." He indicated a belief that the bomber had expected blacks to rush into the streets after the first explosion and then to be mangled by the shrapnel of the 2d bomb. Most of the residents attracted by the decoy blast had returned to their homes before the 2d explosion.

Incidents in Southern States

Bombings, cross-burnings, rioting and other violence also took place in other parts of the South in 1963. Among incidents reported:

Violence was narrowly averted in a confrontation between Alabama Gov. George C. Wallace and federal officials when 2 black students were enrolled in the University of Alabama in Tuscaloosa June 11, 1963. The Negroes, Vivian Juanita Malone and James Alexander Hood, both 20, took up residence on campus the same day and ate in a school cafeteria, all without violence. Earlier June 11 the 2 Negroes' entry had been blocked by Wallace, who, in fulfillment of a campaign pledge, stood "in the schoolhouse door" to prevent desegregation. But he stepped aside later when requested to do so by a federalized National Guard commander.

Strict security measures had gone into effect in Tuscaloosa and on the campus June 8, when 825 state troopers and deputized law enforcement officers under the command of the state commissioner of public safety, Col. Albert J. Lingo, sealed off access to the university by unauthorized personnel. The school imposed a 10:00 p.m.-to-6:00 a.m. curfew, and 600 Alabama National Guard military police began moving into the city June 9.

The June 11 confrontation took place between Wallace and Deputy Atty. Gen. Nicholas deB. Katzenbach, who carried a Presidential proclamation commanding Wallace "to cease and desist" from "unlawful obstruction" of a federal court order. Wallace, wearing a microphone, stood at the door behind a lectern. Katzenbach asked him to step aside and permit the entry of Miss Malone and Hood, who remained in a car. Wallace refused. Katzenbach told him that "from the outset, governor, all of us have known that the final chapter of this history will be the admission of these students." Katzenbach then accompanied Miss Malone to her dormitory, and John Doar, first assistant in the Justice Department's Civil Rights Division, drove Hood to his dormitory. Both black students were greeted in a friendly fashion by white students, and both then lunched in school cafeterias. Pres. Kennedy, on being informed of Wallace's defiance, signed a previously-prepared executive order putting the Alabama National Guard into federal service. Truckloads of federalized National Guard troops arrived on campus several hours later, led by Brig. Gen. Henry V. Graham, who conferred with Katzenbach and confronted Wallace. Graham told Wallace that it was his "sad duty" to request that the governor step aside. Wallace did so and left. Miss Malone and Hood then entered the auditorium with federal officials and were registered.

2 explosions, 18 hours apart, shattered windows in a black neighborhood Nov. 16 and jolted the University of Alabama campus. A dynamite bomb exploded near the dormitory in which Miss Malone was staying Nov. 19.

In Anniston, Ala., 2 black ministers had been attacked by a group of white men Sept. 15 as they attempted to desegregate the city library. The desegregation was carried out Sept. 16 under police protection as 2 black ministers entered with white city leaders. 4 white men were tried in Anniston Sept. 21 on charges arising from the Sept. 15 attack. Convicted of assault, they were freed on $1,000 appeal bonds each. Also convicted of assault and released on $5,000 appeal bonds were 3 Negroes arrested for attacking a white man shortly after the attack on the ministers.

Black desegregation demonstrations at a segregated Macon, Ga. city park resulted in a bottle and rock battle among 75 youngsters Apr. 1 and another rock-throwing battle involving about 600 whites Apr. 2.

Violence erupted at a demonstration in Savannah, Ga. June 19 when Negroes threw bricks and bottles to protest the arrest of 300 anti-segregation demonstrators. Tear gas was used to disperse the 2d group. Black leader Hosea Williams was arrested July 9, and his arrest led to further demonstrations culminating in a riot broken up by police using tear gas the night of July 10-11. Police began arresting demonstrators on sight July 11, and state troopers were sent in. A night of disorder followed, and the National Guard was alerted by Gov. Carl E. Sanders. But the situation was eased

July 6 when white businessmen named a committee to seek a solution with black leaders. A meeting of the 2 groups produced an agreement providing for a truce in demonstrations and a start by Oct. 1 toward desegregating hotels, motels, bowling alleys and theaters.

In Albany, Ga. more than 140 persons were arrested June 19-21 in antisegregation demonstrations involving clashes between police and black spectators. Among those arrested were 20 of 25 field secretaries of the Student Nonviolent Coordinating Committee, which was aiding the drive begun by the Albany Movement.

Gunfire and an explosion Dec. 8 damaged the home of a black voter-registration worker in Dawson, Ga.

A campaign for total desegregation, begun in Danville, Va. June 1, led to violence when police used fire hoses June 10 to break up a demonstration by about 150 persons. 38 persons were arrested; 47 demonstrators were injured. 200 marched to city hall June 13. Black leaders met with Mayor Julian R. Stinson June 14, but the city council later passed an anti-demonstration ordinance, and 2 police cars were hit by gunfire after police had suppressed another march to city hall. 35 marchers were arrested under the new ordinance June 15. A truce was called June 17 after blacks held their first meeting with the mayor's all-white advisory committee, but the truce was broken June 19 by a demonstration resulting in 29 arrests. Stinson's office had announced earlier June 19 that 10 Negroes had been assigned by the State Pupil Placement Board to 4 previously all-white schools; this was the first school desegregation in the city. 10 leaders of the desegregation drive were indicted by a Corporation Court grand jury June 21 on a charge of "inciting the colored population to acts of violence and war against the white population."

Several Negroes asked for service in Lexington, N.C. June 5 at segregated restaurants, a theater and a bowling alley. The next night a mob of about 2,000 white men gathered and about 500 of them marched to Lexington's black section, where they were met by about 100 Negroes. A riot ensued with rocks and bottles thrown and several shots fired. Fred Link, 24, white, was killed by one of the shots. Mayor C. V. Sink declared a state of emergency June 7 and 200 state troopers were alerted. 10 whites and 7 Negroes were arrested June 7 for alleged involvement in the riot. Superior Court Judge John R. McLaughlin Nov. 13 sentenced 3 black youths who admitted firing a caliber .22 rifle into the crowd of whites during the riot. Roosevelt Smith, 21, and William Chester Johnson, 18, who pleaded guilty to charges of engaging in a riot, were given 6-month jail terms. Joe Poole, 19, who offered no plea to a 2d-degree murder charge, was sentenced to 4-7 years in prison.

After a clash in Fayetteville, N.C. June 14 between Negroes and whites was dispersed by tear gas, the mayor, council and leading citizens tried June 17 to persuade restaurant owners to adopt desegregation policies; but the owners would agree only to a statement offering to desegregate for a 60-day trial period if demonstrations were canceled. The Negroes resumed demonstrations later June 17.

In High Point, N.C., near-riot conditions were reached Sept. 9-11 when black protest marches brought out large antagonistic crowds of whites. Police kept the groups separated but had to use tear gas Sept. 11.

Black anti-segregation sit-ins at Charleston, S.C. lunch counters began June 10 and expanded into mass, NAACP-backed demonstrations spearheaded by the Charleston Movement. A night march July 16 ended in a riot in which 6 policemen and a fireman were injured. The police were reinforced by state highway patrolmen, and National Guard units were alerted. But negotiations between a biracial committee and merchants led July 23 to an agreement by 62 stores to end discriminatory practices. More stores signed the agreement Aug. 1, and picketing against non-complying stores continued. Mass demonstrations had been halted July 25 during negotiations. More than 700 Negroes had been arrested prior to the truce.

In Gillett, Ark. a dynamite blast blew out the front door of a black church June 18.

An explosion June 26 damaged the offices of a black doctor who was president of the Gulfport, Miss. NAACP chapter.

Minor violence followed a series of black demonstrations— marches, restaurant sit-ins, church kneel-ins and picketing—that started in Plaquemine, La. in July and intensified beginning Aug. 19. 330 persons were arrested by Sept. 3. Those arrested included CORE national director James Farmer. Plaquemine had been chosen by CORE as the base of a black voter drive for the area. A major grievance was the charge that a predominantly black area had been gerrymandered out of the city of Plaquemine to deprive Negroes of city services and a vote in city affairs. Farmer, arrested Aug. 19, refused to put up $300 bail until Aug. 29 and spent 10 days in jail. Convicted Sept. 3 on charges of disturbing the peace and obstructing streets and sidewalks, he was sentenced to 30 days in jail and fined $100 on each charge. He was freed on bail pending appeal.

Farmer had been arrested after leading 400 blacks in a demonstration broken up by policemen using tear gas. Negroes continued demonstrations until Aug. 21, when U.S. District Judge E. Gordon West in Baton Rouge issued a temporary injunction banning demonstrations. West's order was voided Aug. 29 by the U.S. 5th Circuit Court of Appeals in New Orleans.

A march on city hall by 500 to 600 Negroes the night of Aug. 31-Sept. 1 was repulsed by police, including state police on horses, who employed tear gas, high-powered hoses and electric cattle prodders. 69 persons were arrested. Farmer charged "police brutality." He said: 15 children had been injured (2 of them hospitalized); the horses had been used "to trample, kick and hospitalize children"; "it was a night of wild terror, . . . and police acted like a legal lynch mob."

Anti-bias demonstrations by black high school students in Plaquemine Oct. 4-10 were broken up by police using tear gas and electric cattle prods. Nearly all the Iberville Negro High School students demonstrated at the school Oct. 4. After the board suspended 35 Oct. 5 for participating, the students began a boycott Oct. 7 and marched on the school board office. Tear gas was used on them then and again Oct. 9 when they tried to assemble in the Freedom Rock Baptist Church after having been chased from the streets during an attempted march on the school. Demonstrations were also broken up by tear gas Oct. 10. The students began the demonstrations after CORE had been barred from racial demonstrations there by Judge West.

An explosion wrecked a classroom and started a fire Aug. 26 in an integrated Catholic school in Buras, La.

4 black St. Augustine, Fla. integration leaders were beaten Sept. 18 when they were seized by Ku Klux Klansmen as they approached the site of a Klan rally. 4 Klansmen were charged with assault and battery in the case, but charges against 3 of them were dismissed Nov. 5, and the 4th was acquitted. Among those beaten was Dr. Robert B. Hayling, 33, local NAACP leader. Hayling's home allegedly had been fired on July 1 from a car carrying 4 white youths. 3 black youths were later arrested and charged with shooting at the car. 4 Negroes were slightly wounded in the incident.

William Kinard, 25, a white, was shot and killed Oct. 25 while riding through a black section of St. Augustine with a loaded shotgun. 2 carloads of whites fired guns Oct. 28 at 2 black homes, a black grocery and 2 black night clubs. A grenade thrown at one of the night clubs failed to explode.

Demonstrators Clash With Police in North

Violent episodes also took place in the North in 1963 and were underscored by warnings sounded by national leaders. Demonstrators clashed with police in Chicago. Black pickets scuffled with police in Philadelphia. White mobs broke windows and firebombed a home bought by a black couple in Folcroft, Pa.

Whitney M. Young Jr., executive director of the National Urban League, released in New York June 9 a league policy statement warning that racial incidents in the South were "mild in comparison with those on the verge of taking flame in the tinderbox of racial unrest in Northern cities."

Pres. Kennedy told the nation in a TV address the evening of June 11 that "the fires of frustration and discord are burning in every city, North and South." The President warned that the crisis "cannot be met by repressive police action. It cannot be left to increased demonstrations in the streets. . . . It is a time to act in the Congress, in your state and local legislative body, and, above all, in all of our daily lives. . . . A great change is at hand and our task, our obligation is to make that revolution, that change peaceful and constructive for all. Those who do nothing are inviting shame as well as violence. Those who act boldly are recognizing right as well as reality."

Mass picketing was begun by Negroes May 24 at a school construction site in Philadelphia, Pa. in protest against alleged discrimination in hiring on city construction projects. Scuffling took place May 27, 29 and 31 between black pickets and police guarding workmen entering the site. 46 persons were injured, including 23 policemen and the Rev. John M. White, black vice president of the Baptist Ministers Conference of Philadelphia & Vicinity. The picketing ended late May 31 after an agreement by contractors, school union and NAACP officials for the immediate hiring of 4 black artisans for the project (black laborers were employed there) and the later hiring of 2 more black artisans.

A black couple moved into a previously all-white housing development in Folcroft, Pa., 5 miles southwest of Philadelphia, despite violence and demonstrations by white mobs Aug. 29-30. The couple, Horace and Sara Baker, who had left their 2-year-old daughter with relatives temporarily, tried to take possession of their home Aug. 29 but were repulsed twice by about 500 jeering demonstrators who smashed windows in their house and car. That night a homemade bomb hurled into the house started a fire, and firemen broke in the front door. Other damage inside and outside the house was reported. The crowd, mostly teenagers, returned Aug. 30 and, despite a force of 50 state policemen, resumed throwing missiles—at the house and at the policemen. When the Bakers returned they were escorted by the police. 2 white clergymen greeted them at the door, but the violence continued. A rear window of the Bakers' car was smashed by teen-age boys wielding belt buckles. 7 persons were arrested during the rioting. Order was restored Aug. 31, and about 100 policemen patrolled the area.

Negroes picketed the New York City construction site of an annex for Harlem Hospital June 12 and 13 in protest against alleged discrimination in the building trades against Negroes and Puerto Ricans. Brief clashes took place both days between police and the demonstrators. There were no arrests. After the first skirmish, Acting Mayor Paul R. Screvane warned that the city, under a never-enforced anti-bias section of its Administration Code, would halt the construction if the unions took no action to end bias. After the 2d skirmish, Screvane called a halt to the work, which the contractor had suspended anyway in fear of violence.

The movement of 4 black families into the mostly white Englewood neighborhood on Chicago's South Side resulted July 29-Aug. 5 in gatherings of protesting white crowds. Bricks and bottles were hurled at the apartment building housing one of the families July 30. The next night 1,000 persons gathered. A force of 200 policemen was sent into the area, and 149 arrests were made. Roman Catholic priests and Protestant ministers mingled with the crowd Aug. 1 in an attempt to restrain violence. About 1,000 whites had demonstrated in the South Side Apr. 17-18 when a black family moved into an all-white section, and 20 arrests were made.

A CORE-sponsored sit-in at Chicago's board of education offices had started July 10 in protest against de facto segregation and temporary mobile classroom units stationed outside predominantly black schools to alleviate overcrowded schools pending construction of new ones. Negroes held that the overflow could be accommodated in predominantly white schools nearby. The sit-in was ended July 18 when police seized 10 of the demonstrators on charges of unlawful assembly and trespass. (3 demonstrators had been arrested in a clash with police July 17.) Pickets taking up the protest clashed with police July 22, when the protest was canceled. Blacks picketing at a construction site of 25 mobile classrooms led to arrests and scuffling with police. 67 Negroes were arrested Aug. 2 and at least 50, including comedian Dick Gregory, Aug. 12 as pickets broke through police lines.

Gregory was jailed and not released until Aug. 23 because he refused to sign a recognizance bond. 3 policemen were hurt in disorders at the site Aug. 13 after 46 pickets had been arrested. Picketing was suspended Aug. 20 pending conferences of the leaders with Mayor Richard Daley. Renewal of the picketing Sept. 6 at the Guggenheim School resulted in 12 arrests after demonstrators wrestled with police. At Beale School on the South Side, where about 200 persons demonstrated Sept. 4, 15 demonstrators were arrested, 13 of them for refusing to end a sit-in in the principal's office.

John F. Kennedy's Assassination

John Fitzgerald Kennedy, 46, 35th President of the U.S., was assassinated in Dallas, Tex. Nov. 22, 1963. He was struck in the head and neck by 2 rifle bullets at 12:30 p.m. CST as he rode in a motorcade, and he was pronounced dead at Parkland Hospital in Dallas at 1 p.m. He was the 4th U.S. President to be killed in office. Vice Pres. Lyndon Baines Johnson, 55, who had been riding 2 cars behind Kennedy, was sworn in as President the same day aboard the Presidential plane at Love Field in Dallas.

Lee Harvey Oswald, 24, a pro-Communist ex-Marine who had once tried to trade his U.S. citizenship for Soviet citizenship, was arrested in Dallas less than 2 hours after the assassination and was arraigned as the President's murderer.

Oswald himself was shot in Dallas' municipal building Nov. 24 as police were about to take him to county jail, and he died at Parkland Hospital. Oswald's assailant, arrested immediately, was Jack Rubenstein (known as Jack Ruby), 52, a Dallas night-club operator said to have been a vehement admirer of Kennedy.

Kennedy had made a speech in Ft. Worth, Tex. the morning of Nov. 22 and then had flown with his wife and with Gov. and Mrs. John B. Connally Jr. of Texas to Dallas' Love Field. Vice Pres. Johnson, as was customary, made the trip in a separate plane. At Love Field, the Kennedys and Connallys entered the special Presidential car, its protective glass bubble-top down, to head a motorcade in Dallas to the Trade Mart, where Kennedy was scheduled to speak. The Presidential limousine was followed by a sedan occupied by Secret Service men.

3 shots were fired as the President's car approached an underpass near the end of its 10-mile journey through Dallas. The first 2 bullets hit the President, who was sitting with Mrs. Kennedy in the rear seat, and he fell face down. The 3d bullet hit Gov.

Connally, who was sharing the "jump" seats with his wife. Connally was injured severely but not fatally. The 2 wives immediately came to the aid of their husbands, and the car was driven to Parkland Hospital.

Kennedy lost consciousness immediately on being hit. He died without regaining consciousness. The cause of death was given as "a gunshot wound in the brain."

Oswald, who was employed in the Texas School Book Depository building, from which the assassination shots were fired, was captured in the Texas Theater in Dallas at 2:15 p.m. Nov. 22 after a 1¾-hour manhunt that started seconds after the President was shot.

Dallas Police Chief Jesse E. Curry, who had been riding in the motorcade ahead of the President's car, said he had realized from the sound of the shots that they came from the depository building and had immediately ordered the building searched. Oswald was in a lunchroom with other workers when the first officer reached the building. By the time other police officers arrived, Oswald had left. Policemen searching the building found near a 6th-floor window an Italian-made Carcano rifle, fitted with a Japanese telescopic sight, that was later proved to be the assassination weapon. An elevator operator told the officers that he had taken Oswald to the building's top floor before the Presidential motorcade arrived. A description of Oswald was immediately broadcast.

Shortly thereafter Patrolman J. D. Tippitt, 38, in a radio patrol car, saw a man answering the broadcast description and got out of his car to question him. According to witnesses, the suspect drew a revolver, killed the policeman with 2 shots and fled. A witness used the police car radio to report the killing, and police spread through the area, where they searched nearby buildings for the killer.

While the search was going on, police headquarters received a call from the cashier of the Texas Theater, 6 blocks from the scene of the patrolman's murder, to report that a man acting suspiciously had entered. Curry and 6 officers sped to the theater and found Oswald in the 3d row from the back. As they approached him, he leaped up and reached for a revolver in his shirt. The police disarmed him after he had pulled the trigger at least once without the revolver firing. The revolver was later proved to be the one used to kill Tippitt.

Oswald met his own death at about 11:20 a.m. CST Nov. 24 in the basement of Dallas' municipal building. He had just been brought down in the elevator to be transferred to the county jail. Suddenly Jack Ruby sprang from a group of newsmen watching Oswald's planned transfer. He punched a revolver into Oswald's left side and fired a single shot.

Oswald cried out and fell to the pavement. A police ambulance rushed him to Parkland Hospital, where he died in surgery at 1:07 without recovering consciousness. At no time did Oswald admit any connection with the President's assassination.

Ruby was seized immediately and was charged with Oswald's murder.

The shooting of Oswald took place before "live" TV cameras and was witnessed by TV viewers throughout the country.

Pres. Johnson Nov. 23 issued a proclamation designating Nov. 25, the day of Kennedy's funeral, "to be a day of national mourning throughout the United States." He asked Americans to assemble Nov. 25 at their places of worship, and he "invite[d] the people of the world who share our grief to join us in this day of mourning and rededication." Increasingly heavily-attended religious and secular services were held throughout the U.S. Nov. 23, 24 and 25 in tribute to Kennedy. TV and radio networks and stations canceled all entertainment programs and commercial announcements Nov. 22-25 to devote their time almost exclusively to the assassination and related events. Thousands of stores, government and business offices, theaters and other establishments were shut down throughout the U.S. beginning at various times Nov. 22 and stretching through Nov. 25 as Americans honored their late President.

The news of Kennedy's assassination was greeted with expressions of shock, desbelief and sorrow in almost every country of the world. Messages of grief and sympathy poured in on Washington from thousands of private citizens and government leaders of most nations.

The funeral took place Nov. 25 with monarchs, presidents, premiers and other high-ranking officials representing 92 countries joining the Kennedy family and other American mourners. Kennedy was buried in the Memorial Area in front of Arlington Mansion (the Custis-Lee House). No other graves were in the immediate vicinity.

Gov. Connally, wounded while riding in the car in which Kennedy was slain, told Nov. 27 the details he remembered of the tragedy. Still hospitalized in Dallas, Connally related his story in an NBC interview. He said: As they were riding "we heard a shot. I turned ..., and the President had slumped. ... As I turned, I was hit. .... Then there was a 3d shot, and the President was hit again. ...."

Connally speculated that "maybe" Kennedy "has been asked to do something in death that he could not do in life, that is to so shock and so stun the nation, the people of the world, of what is happening to us, of the cancerous growth that is being permitted to expand and enlarge upon the world and the society in which we live, that breeds hatred and bigotry and intolerance, indifference and lawlessness, and is an outward manifestation of what occurred here in Dallas, which could have occurred in any other city in America. This is an open manifestation of extremism on both sides that is the genesis of our own self-destruction if we are ever going to be destroyed." Connally agreed that "we should have a memorial" but expressed hope that Americans did not build one "in the sense of absolving themselves . . . for a lack of tolerance, lack of understanding, the passion, the prejudice, the hate and the bigotry which permeates the whole society in which we live and which manifested itself here on Friday. This was only one facet of it. We see it in the bombing of the 5 little children in Birmingham. ...."

Jack Ruby was convicted in Dallas Mar. 14, 1964 of Oswald's murder. The jury directed that Ruby's punishment be death. But Ruby's conviction was reversed by the Texas Court of Criminal Appeals Oct. 5, 1966. While awaiting retrial, Ruby was admitted Dec. 9, 1966 to Parkland Hospital, where doctors discovered that he had extensive cancer. Ruby died in the hospital Jan. 3, 1967 of a blood clot in the lung.

The Warren Commission's final report on the assassination was presented to Pres. Johnson by Chief Justice Warren Sept. 24, 1964. The document, made public Sept. 27, concluded that Oswald had "acted alone" in assassinating Kennedy and that Ruby had acted alone in slaying Oswald. The 7-member commission was unanimous in its denial that either Oswald or Ruby was "part of any conspiracy, domestic or foreign, to assassinate Pres. Kennedy." The 888-page report was written after the commission, assisted by a 27-member staff, had gone over the results of investigations conducted by the FBI and other federal, state and local agencies and had considered the testimony of 552 witnesses. (For the official "Summary and Conclusions" of the Warren Commission Report, see the FACTS ON FILE book *3 Assassinations: The Deaths of John & Robert Kennedy and Martin Luther King.*)

SOUTHERN VIOLENCE & NORTHERN RIOTS (1964)

Fire-bombings, dynamite blasts, beatings, mass demonstrations and night-rider attacks continued in the South during 1964, and 3 civil rights workers and a black educator were murdered there. Violence grew in the summer months as disturbances spread to the North. Riots broke out in New York, Philadelphia, Jersey City and the Chicago suburb of Dixmoor.

Klan & Other Southern Violence

Ku Klux Klan activity intensified in Southern states in the early months of 1964. More than 150 crosses were burned Jan. 18 near black homes, churches and schools in 5 Louisiana parishes. Klansmen clashed with black students Jan. 25 during civil rights demonstrations in Atlanta. Crosses were burned in 7 different places in Vicksburg, Miss. Jan. 31.

A bomb caused extensive damage Feb. 16 to the Jacksonville, Fla. home of Donald Godfrey, 6, who attended the previously all-white Lackawanna elementary school under a court order. FBI agents Mar. 3 arrested William Sterling Rosecrans, an associate of north Florida KKK leaders, and charged him with the bombing. 5 Klansmen—Barton H. Griffin, Jacky Don Harden, Willie Eugene Wilson, Donald Eugene Spegal and Robert Pittman Gentry—were also arrested by the FBI in connection with the bombing. Rosecrans, from Indiana, pleaded guilty Mar. 13 and was sentenced Apr. 17 to 7 years in federal prison. The 5 Klansmen were tried June 30 by a federal jury. Harden and Gentry were acquitted July 5, and a mistrial was declared in the case of the other 3. A 2d jury, all-white, acquitted the 3 Nov. 25 of conspiring to violate the boy's civil rights.

Racial rioting erupted in Jacksonville, Fla. Mar. 23, 1964 and a black housewife, Mrs. Johnnie Mae Chappell, 35, was killed by gunfire from a passing car. Hundreds of young Negroes massed in a park Mar. 23 to initiate a school boycott and demonstration, apparently in defiance of a televised announcement by Mayor Haydon Burns Mar. 21 that the city would not tolerate "illegal" demonstrations. (Negroes had been holding unsuccessful sit-ins at Jacksonville restaurants and hotels for 2 weeks.) Sporadic rioting broke out when police attempted to disperse the group in the park. Rioting continued Mar. 24. The worst incident was at a black high school where students and bystanders hurled stones at police, firemen, school officials and newsmen. More than 265 adults and 200 juveniles were arrested during the 2 days. About a dozen whites were hospitalized after attacks by Negroes. The turmoil subsided after a biracial committee began organizing at Burns' request. The group met Mar. 26 and announced Mar. 28 that it would study ways to "bring about a voluntary desegregation . . . of all establishments serving the public."

Jacksonville police said that 3 white men had admitted Aug. 11 the killing of Mrs. Chappell. They were J. W. Rich, 21, said to have fired a pistol from a car; Wayne M. Chessman, 21, and Elmer Kato, 19. An all-white Circuit Court jury Dec. 2, convicted Rich, who had been charged with first degree murder, of manslaughter.

The Macon County High School in Notasulga, Ala. was destroyed by fire Apr. 18. The school had been ordered to desegregate and was being boycotted by white students.

2 young blacks, Charles E. Moore, 20, and Henry Dee, 19, disappeared suddenly May 2 near Jackson, Miss. Their mutilated corpses were found in the Mississippi River near Tallulah, La. July 12-13 by a search party looking for the bodies of 3 civil rights workers murdered near Philadelphia, Miss. 2 torsos and 2 lower halves of the bodies were found in Mississippi River backwaters. FBI agents and local police officers Nov. 6 arrested James Ford Seale, 29, and Ku Klux Klan member Charles Marcus Edwards, 31, white residents of the Meadville, Miss. area, on charges of killing the 2 Negroes, and the 2 white men were released Nov. 7 in $5,000 bond each. Civil rights leaders said 5 other Negroes had been killed under mysterious circumstances in the area in 1964.

3 black pickets had been hit by pellets in Tuscaloosa, Ala., June 5 during a continuing demonstration against segregation. 2 white men were arrested June 5 on disorderly conduct charges; they were accused of carrying oil of mustard, a skin irritant that had been thrown on demonstrators June 3 and 4. 94 black demonstrators were jailed in Tuscaloosa June 9. The Rev. T. Y. Rogers, leader of the Tuscaloosa campaign, was one of those arrested. The demonstrators reportedly had gone about 100 yards from the First African Baptist Church at the start of an attempted march to the downtown area when the police halted them. (Tuscaloosa had banned parades to the downtown area.) The demonstrators returned to the church, and the police used tear gas and high-pressure water hoses against them. The Negroes threw rocks, bottles and furniture at the police. 33 persons, including one white policeman, were injured. Tuscaloosa police June 11 again surrounded the church,

which was filled with 300 demonstrators, and arrested the leaders.
A Jackson, Miss. Negro was abducted and flogged June 17 by
hooded men. In McComb, Miss., there were explosions the night
of June 20 at the homes of 2 blacks suspected of civil rights activities, at the barbershop owned by another and at the homes of 2
white men who had made remarks opposing KKK violence. The
Sweet Rest Church of Christ Holiness in Branson, Miss. was
rocked by an explosion June 21.

3 Rights Workers Murdered In Mississippi

3 civil rights workers disappeared June 21, 1964 after their
release from jail in Philadelphia, Miss. A massive search by FBI
agents, state and county police and unarmed Navy men located
their bodies in a shallow grave 6 miles from Philadelphia. All 3
had been shot. The FBI arrested 21 white men, including the
sheriff and deputy sheriff of Neshoba County, Miss., for alleged
conspiracy to violate the Civil Rights Code. A U.S. commissioner
dismissed the charges at a preliminary hearing, but a trial resulted
in the conviction of 7 of the 21 on charges of conspiracy to murder.
The 7, including the chief deputy sheriff of Neshoba County and
a Klan imperial wizard, were sentenced to prison. The convictions
were described as the first reported in Mississippi for civil rights
slayings.
    The 3 murdered rights workers were Michael Henry Schwerner,
24, white member of the Congress of Racial Equality (CORE) and
former settlement house worker from Brooklyn, N.Y.; James Earl
Chaney, 21, black plasterer and CORE member from Meridian,
Miss., and Andrew Goodman, 20, white Queens College student
from New York. They were part of a group of 175 rights workers
who had gone to Mississippi during the weekend to aid in a statewide black-voter registration campaign.
    The campaign the 3 rights' workers were engaged in also
focused on education and job-training. It had been organized by
the Council of Federated Organizations, a group sponsored by the
Student Nonviolent Coordinating Committee, CORE, the NAACP,
the Southern Christian Leadership Conference and the National
Council of Churches. The workers had been given intensive orientation for their work in Mississippi during a week-long seminar at
the Western College for Women in Oxford, O. They had been told
by John Doar, deputy chief of the Justice Department's civil rights
division, who conferred with them June 19, that there would be
no federal police force in Mississippi to protect them.

State, county and local police units had been reinforced in Mississippi in anticipation of segregationist reaction to the influx of "agitators." Masked white men June 16 beat 3 blacks attending a church board meeting in the Mount Zion Methodist Church about 12 miles east of Philadelphia; the masked men then burned the church. A Roman Catholic parish hall used by Negroes in Hattiesburg was destroyed by fire the same night.

Schwerner, Chaney and Goodman arrived in Mississippi June 20 and left their base in Meridian June 21 to inspect the site of the Mount Zion church burning. They were arrested at about 5:30 p.m. by Neshoba County deputy sheriff Cecil Price on the outskirts of Philadelphia on a charge of speeding. Chaney paid a $20 fine, and they were released from the county jail in Philadelphia at about 10:30 p.m. They were reported missing June 22, although County Sheriff Lawrence Andrew Rainey, 41, said: "If they're missing, they just hid somewhere, trying to get a lot of publicity out of it, I figure."

A full-scale FBI investigation was ordered June 22 by Atty. Gen. Robert F. Kennedy. Kennedy June 23 postponed his scheduled departure on a European trip to keep abreast of the situation. Pres. Johnson June 22 authorized the use of helicopters from a nearby military base to help in the search. He met June 23 with the parents of the missing whites, who had met earlier with Kennedy. Johnson relayed to the parents the news he had just heard from FBI Director J. Edgar Hoover that the rights workers' abandoned car had been found, empty and burned, in a bog about 15 miles from Philadelphia. Mrs. Rita Schwerner, wife of one of the missing men, was received by the President June 27.

Johnson June 25 authorized the use of 200 unarmed Navy men from the naval air station at Meridian to help in the search. The naval searching team was increased to 400 June 30. 8 naval helicopters also were used.

FBI Director Hoover visited Mississippi July 10 and 11 to investigate the case at the request of Pres. Johnson. Hoover, speaking at a news conference following the opening July 10 of an FBI field headquarters in Jackson, Miss., disclosed that the FBI force in the state had been increased to 153 agents (10 times the normal number) to protect rights workers. He conferred with Mississippi Gov. Paul B. Johnson Jr. July 10 and said later that he believed the 3 civil rights workers were dead.

FBI agents Aug. 4 found 3 bodies in an earth dam recently built 5 miles southwest of Philadelphia, Miss. Pathologists and FBI identification experts examined the bodies in Jackson Aug. 5

and identified them as those of the 3 missing rights workers.

The *Jackson Daily News* reported that the 3 men had been shot to death and the bullets removed, but the FBI declined Aug. 5 to give the cause of death. County Coroner Fulton Jackson, Sheriff L. A. Rainey, Deputy Sheriff Cecil Ray Price and a 6-man coroner's jury visited the dam site Aug. 4 and 5; Jackson said they were not sure what was the cause of death.

Dr. David M. Spain, a New York pathologist, performed a medical examination of Chaney's body Aug. 7. Spain concluded that Chaney had been subjected to an "inhuman beating" before 3 bullets were fired into his body. Mississippi authorities had reported Aug. 5 that none of the 3 had been beaten before being shot. Spain examined Schwerner's body in New York Aug. 10 and reported that he had not been beaten.

A Neshoba County coroner's jury in Philadelphia, Miss. reported Aug. 25 that it had been unable to determine the cause of death of the 3 youths.

Roy K. Moore, chief of the special FBI field office in Jackson, said Aug. 4 that the bodies were found as the result of weeks of systematic searching throughout the countryside by FBI agents. But there were several reports Aug. 5 that an informer had been paid a reward of $25,000 to $30,000 to lead FBI agents to the graves.

Black author Louis Lomax asserted Oct. 25 in *Ramparts,* an independent radical Catholic laymen's magazine published in Menlo Park, Calif., that "eyewitnesses" had identified at least 6 members of a mob that had murdered the rights workers. Lomax wrote that according to the witnesses: A mob had seized the 3 about 3 miles from Philadelphia shortly after their release from jail; Chaney was "tied to a tree and beaten with chains"; Goodman and Schwerner tried to come to Chaney's aid but were subdued; the 3 were loaded into a car and bullets were fired into their chests; they were then taken to the "predetermined" dam burial site.

Homer Bigart reported in the *N.Y. Times* Nov. 29 that moderate leaders in Philadelphia believed that at least 50 Ku Klux Klansmen had carefully plotted to kill Schwerner for at least 6 weeks because he "wore a beard and looked very Jewish." They thought the Klan had "decided to make . . . an example" of Schwerner to discourage an "invasion by Yankee beatniks, Jews and . . . scum." The mob was said to have killed Chaney and Goodman along with Schwerner June 21 when the 3 were trapped outside Philadelphia.

A federal grand jury in Biloxi, Miss. Oct. 2 had indicted 4

law enforcement officials and a former sheriff, all of Philadelphia. They were charged with (a) violating the 1948 Civil Rights Act by conspiring to deprive and depriving Negroes of their rights under the Constitution and (b) violating federal statute by acting against blacks under the guise of law. Specifically, they were accused of unlawfully detaining 7 Negroes and beating them in Oct. 1962 and Jan. 26, 1964. The 5 men, arrested by the FBI Oct. 3, were Sheriff L. A. Rainey, Deputy Sheriff Cecil Price, 26, ex-Sheriff Ethel Glen (Hop) Barnett, 42, and policemen Richard Andrew Willis, 40, and Otha Neal Burkes, 71.

The grand jury investigation had stemmed from the murder of the 3 rights workers, but the indictments made no charges in that case.

FBI agents Dec. 4, 1964 arrested Sheriff Rainey, Deputy Sheriff Price, ex-policeman Burkes and 18 other white men, most of them Ku Klux Klan members, in connection with the murders of Schwerner, Goodman and Chaney.

Among the 21 arrested was the Rev. Edgar Ray Killen, 39, a fundamentalist Baptist minister, and several leaders of the White Knights of the Ku Klux Klan of Mississippi. Rainey, Price and Burkes had been free on bond on their Oct. 3 federal conspiracy indictment charging them with beating Negro prisoners.

The FBI charged that Price and 9 others of the 21 had participated in the actual slaying and that the other 9 (including Rainey, Burkes and Killen) had participated in a conspiracy. The FBI complaint said: "It was part of the plan and purpose of the conspiracy that Cecil Ray Price, deputy sheriff of Neshoba County, acting under the color of his office, did arrest Michael Henry Schwerner, James Earl Chaney and Andrew Goodman without lawful cause and detained them in the Neshoba County jail located in Philadelphia, Miss., and did not release them from custody, and that ... [the 10] did thereupon intercept ... [the 3 rights workers] shortly after they departed from Philadelphia, Miss., by automobile, and did threaten, assault, shoot and kill them."

Those accused of actually participating in the murders were: Price; Jimmy K. Arledge, 27, a Meridian truck driver; Horace Doyle Barnette, 25, a salesman; Travis Maryn Barnette, 36, part owner and operator of B&S Garage in Meridian; James Edward Jordan, 38, a Gulfport, Miss. construction worker; Billy Wayne Posey, 28, a Williamsville, Miss. service station operator; Alton Wayne Roberts, 26, a Meridian salesman; Jimmy Snowden, 31, a Meridian truck driver; Jerry McGrew Sharpe, 21, manager of a Philadelphia pulpwood supply company; Jimmy Lee Townsend, 17, a

Williamsville service station attendant.

Those charged with conspiracy but not with actually participating in the murders: Rainey; Burkes; Killen; Olen Lovell Burrage, 34, owner of a trucking firm and of the farm where the bodies were buried; Herman Tucker, 36, a Philadelphia contractor who built the pond where the bodies were found; Bernard Lee Akin, 50, owner of Akin Mobile Homes in Meridian; James Thomas Harris, 30, a Meridian truck driver; Frank J. Herndon, 46, operator of a Meridian drive-in restaurant; Oliver Richard Warringer Jr., 54, a Meridian drive-in grocery store owner.

U.S. Commissioner Esther Carter in Meridian, Miss. Dec. 12, 1964 dismissed federal charges against 19 of the arrested men. Miss Carter, who acted at a preliminary hearing, ruled that no real evidence had been presented to hold them for federal grand jury action. She did so after dismissing, as incompetent testimony and hearsay evidence, a statement by FBI agent Henry Rask, 39, of Atlanta that the FBI had obtained a signed confession from Horace Doyle Barnette, one of 10 men charged with actually participating in the slaying.

A Justice Department spokesmen said in Washington: "In the experience of the department, the refusal by a U.S. commissioner to accept a law enforcement officer's report of a signed confession in a preliminary hearing is totally without precedent."

U.S. Commissioner Verta Lee Swetman in Biloxi, Miss. Dec. 11, at the request of the Justice Department, dismissed the federal conspiracy charge against a 20th suspect, James Edward Jordan, 38, a construction worker accused of participating in the slaying. The charge against Barnette was dropped by the Justice Department in Shreveport Dec. 14.

A federal grand jury in Jackson, Miss. Jan. 15, 1965 indicted 18 men in connection with the murders of the 3 rights workers. A one-count felony indictment charged the 18 with conspiring to deprive the 3 murdered youths of their civil rights, and a 4-count misdemeanor indictment charged them with violating another federal rights statute by participating in a conspiracy in which law enforcement officials inflicted "summary punishment" on the 3 youths "without due process of law." There was no question of the jury indicting the defendants on murder charges since the crime of murder in this case was under state, not federal, jurisdiction.

The indictment charged that: (a) Price had detained the 3 youths in the Philadelphia jail from shortly after sundown to about 10:30 p.m. June 21; (b) Price then released them so that they could be intercepted by the waiting lynch mob when they tried to drive back to their headquarters in Meridian; (c) Price shortly afterwards halted their car 9 miles south of Philadelphia, put them into a Neshoba County sheriff's car and drove them along a lonely side road to the spot where they were murdered by a 10-man lynch mob, including Price; (d) Posey, 28, a member of the mob, took the bodies to a dam 5 miles southwest of Philadelphia, where a bulldozer was used to cover the bodies with soil.

17 of the men who had been arrested Dec. 4 were among those indicted Jan. 15. In addition, Ptl. Richard Willis, a Philadelphia policeman, was indicted as a participant in the conspiracy. Oliver Richard Warringer Jr., and Otha Neal Burkes, 71, both arrested Dec. 4 and then accused of taking part in the conspiracy, were not indicted Jan. 15.

According to the indictment, the lynch mob was made up of Price, Posey, Barnette, Jordan, Townsend, Sharpe, Roberts, Snowden, Arledge and Travis Maryn Barnette. Those indicted as participating in the conspiracy but not named as members of the lynch mob were Rainey, Willis, Killen, Akin, Burrage, Harris, Herndon and Tucker.

A federal grand jury (including 5 Negroes and 6 women) in Jackson Feb. 27, 1967 returned new conspiracy indictments against 19 men in connection with the murders of the 3 rights workers. Earlier indictments had been dismissed after a July 20, 1966 guideline decision of the U.S. 5th Circuit Court of Appeals invalidated the traditional federal jury selection system of the South for excluding Negroes and women.

The 1967 indictments charged that Rainey, Price, and Willis had acted under color of state law to carry out a "Klan assassination plot." The grand jury also indicted ex-Neshoba County Sheriff Ethel Glen Barnett and Sam Holloway Bowers Jr., 42, a Laurel (Miss.) coin machine distributor described by the FBI as the imperial wizard of the White Knights of the Ku Klux Klan. Neither Barnett nor Bowers had been named in the earlier indictments. The indictments omitted Townsend, one of those previously indicted.

An all-white federal jury of 5 men and 7 women in Meridian, Miss. Oct. 20, 1967 convicted 7 of the defendants of conspiracy in the 3 murders. 8 men were acquitted, and mistrials were declared in the cases of 3 men on whom the jury could not reach a verdict.

Those found guilty were Price, Bowers, Horace Doyle Barnette, Arledge, Posey, Snowden and Roberts. They were convicted of conspiring to deny "life or liberty without due process." They were sentenced Dec. 20 to prison terms ranging from 3 to 10 years. Bowers and Roberts received the maximum terms of 10 years. Price and Posey were sentenced to 6-year terms. 3-year sentences were imposed on Arledge, Snowden and Barnette.

Those who were acquitted were those who had not been accused of participating in the slayings. There were no verdicts reached on Killen, Ethel Glen Barnett and Sharpe.

During the trial Police Sgt. Carlton Wallace Miller, 43, had testified Oct. 11, 1967 that he had joined the local klavern of the White Knights of the Ku Klux Klan in 1964 and had become a paid informer for the FBI. Miller identified 11 of the 18 defendants as either members of the Klan or as having been present at Klan meetings. Miller said that at one meeting, Killen explained the kinds of "pressure" to be used against rights workers: "To begin with, we were to call them up or go see them, threaten them on the job, things of that nature," but the pressure would include "whippings, beatings. ... After the pressure was applied and they didn't respond, then we were to apply physical pressure." Finally, he said, "there was elimination"; "that's a term for murdering them." Miller said Killen had once discussed a plan to "whip" Schwerner but later called it off; "Mr. Killen told us to leave him alone, that another unit was going to take care of him. His elimination had been approved of by the imperial wizard." Miller said that about a week after the 3 rights workers disappeared "Mr. Killen told me they had been shot and were dead and were buried 15 feet in a dam." Miller testified that Killen said he had come to Meridian after receiving word by phone that the rights workers were in custody.

Another former Klan member, Jordan, was the government's key witness. He named 7 defendants as actual participants in the slayings. Jordan had been indicted in the same conspiracy charges but was not a defendant in the trial. Jordan described how Deputy Price had jailed the 3 youths, held them until the mob assembled, then released them only to recapture them after a highway chase. The youths, he said, were driven to the site of the slayings in the deputy's car. Jordan told the court that he was posted as lookout a short distance down the road. "I heard car doors slam, some loud talk that I could not distinguish, and then I heard several shots," he said. Then he walked down the road and found the youths on the ground, apparently dead. The bodies were put in the back of the station wagon, he testified, and were hauled to the dam in Neshoba County, where a bulldozer buried them. Jordan said that Bowers had approved the slayings. He reported that

Bowers had said Schwerner was "a thorn in the side of everyone living, especially the white people, and should be taken care of." The court Oct. 13 heard a statement signed by Horace D. Barnette, a defendant identified as a member of the lynching party. The statement charged Jordan with killing one of the rights workers. Henry Rask, an FBI agent, told the court that he had obtained the 10-page statement from Barnette during a 5-hour 56-minute session Nov. 20, 1964 at a motel near Springhill, La. Rask said that he and James A. Wooten, another FBI agent, had talked with Barnette Nov. 19, 20 and 21 and that Barnette had said the slayings "had been bothering him and he wanted to tell us about it." Rask said: The rights workers had been driven to the shooting site with Jordan. Schwerner was hauled from the back of the car. A mob member "took a pistol in his hand and shot Schwerner." "Schwerner fell to the left so that he was lying alongside the road, and Goodman spun around and fell back toward the bank in back." At that point Jordan stepped forward and said: "Save one for me." Jordan pulled Chaney out onto the road with him. "I remember Chaney backing up, facing the road and standing on the bank on the other side of the ditch, and Jordan stood in the middle of the road and shot him. Jordan then said: 'You didn't leave me anything but a nigger, but at least I killed me a nigger.' "

The defense called on Mrs. Beverly Rawlings to testify Oct. 17 in an effort to discredit Jordan. Mrs. Rawlings said that some time around Sept. 1, 1964 Jordan had indicated to her that he had shot Chaney.

White Mob Attacks Blacks in Florida

A white mob of about 800 attacked part of an integrationist parade of hundreds of Negroes in St. Augustine, Fla. near the city square June 25, 1964 in what was called the city's worst violence in a year. Most of the whites were said to have come from a rally conducted by the Rev. Connie Lynch of California, a white evangelist who had been preaching nightly for action against integrationists. About 30 blacks were hospitalized, and many others suffered minor injuries. 3 whites were hospitalized. The police seized 4 whites among those who had been attacking Negroes with clubs and fists, but the mob forced the police to free the 4. Some of the whites beat several black women and tore off their clothes.

Segregationist leader Holsted Richard (Hoss) Manucy and J. B. Stoner, of Atlanta, a lawyer for the Ku Klux Klan, had held a news conference at the Monson Motor Lodge June 25 shortly before the attacks. Manucy warned: "Violence will continue as long as Negroes continue to invade the public beach which has been used only by whites for hundreds of years. The violence won't stop until all Negroes and white outsiders leave St. Augustine."

State police had watched without acting the morning of June 25 as segregationists forcibly prevented some 50 blacks from swimming at the city beach. But later June 25, under orders to protect integrationists from attack, state troopers clashed with segregationists at the beach and arrested 12 when they tried to stop a "swim-in."

Federal Judge Bryan Simpson held hearings in Jacksonville, Fla. starting June 26 on a motion by civil rights leaders to overturn a ban by Gov. C. Farris Bryant on night-time demonstrations. The governor had acted after Simpson invalidated a similar ban imposed by other officials. St. Augustine Sheriff L. O. Davis testified June 26 that his men had been unable to arrest any of the white assailants June 25 because "everybody was fighting so hard, and besides, we didn't think we could get out ourselves." St. Augustine law enforcement officials denied in testimony June 27 that they had been harassing Northern white youths participating in the rights demonstrations.

Black and white civil rights demonstrators, under the protection of state police, conducted a "wade-in" at the city beach June 29 and marched past the city square. The police held back a white segregationist mob.

The Monson Motor Lodge in St. Augustine, which had integrated in compliance with the rights law, was hit by fire bombs July 24.

Lemuel Penn Slain

Lemuel Augustus Penn, 49, a Negro and assistant superintendent of Washington, D.C. public schools, was killed July 11, 1964 by a shotgun blast fired from a passing car at the car he was driving on Georgia Route 172 about 12 miles northeast of Colbert, Ga. Penn, an Army reserve lieutenant colonel, had been returning to Washington after 2 weeks of reserve training at Ft. Benning, Ga. His 2 passengers, both also returning from reserve duty, Maj. Charles E. Brown and Lt. Col. John D. Howard, were uninjured.

Pres. Johnson telephoned Georgia Gov. Carl E. Sanders July 11 to seek federal-state cooperation in finding Penn's killer. Atty. Gen. Robert F. Kennedy ordered the FBI into the case later that day.

An all-white jury in Madison County, Ga. Sept. 4 acquitted Joseph Howard Sims and Cecil William Myers of Penn's murder. The FBI had arrested Sims, Myers, James Lackey and Herbert Guest, all members of the Ku Klux Klan, Aug. 6. Georgia had filed murder charges against the 4 Aug. 7, and a Madison County grand jury had indicted all except Guest Aug. 25. A statement by Lackey, introduced during the subsequent trial, said that he had driven the car and that Sims and Myers had shot Penn. Lackey, however, later repudiated the statement.

U.S. District Judge William A. Bootle in Macon, Ga. Dec. 29 dismissed federal indictments charging 6 white men, all allegedly active in the Ku Klux Klan, with conspiring to injure and oppress a Negro—Lemuel Penn. Bootle noted that 2 of the 6, Sims and Myers, had been acquitted of murdering Penn. He said the principle must be upheld "that this court not usurp jurisdiction where it has none." The other 4 who had been indicted on the federal charge were James S. Lackey, who faced a state murder charge; Herbert Guest, who had been arrested on a state murder charge but not indicted; Denver Willis Phillips and George Hampton Turner.

The U.S. Supreme Court held Mar. 28, 1966 that federal prosecutions may be instituted against private citizens who interfere with interstate travel. The court affirmed the right to try in federal court under the conspiracy statute the 6 private citizens accused in Penn's murder.

Sims and Myers were sentenced by Judge Bootle in Athens, Ga. July 9 to 10 years' imprisonment for conspiracy to violate the right to interstate travel of Negroes, including Penn. The trial of Sims, Myers and Turner had taken place June 27-July 2; the jury's July 2 verdict had been sealed until the completion of the trial of the 3 other defendants, Lackey, Guest and Phillips. The verdicts in both trials were announced July 8. All defendants other than Sims and Myers were acquitted.

The prosecution in both trials had sought to establish a pattern of conspiracy by the defendants to "injure, intimidate or oppress" Negroes seeking to exercise their rights. The slaying of Penn was presented as only one instance of conspiracy; the prosecution's case included testimony June 29 by 2 black brothers, George and Homer Turner, of a beating they had received in Oct. 1965 from Sims, Myers and 5 other Klansmen.

The major prosecution evidence presented at the 2d trial consisted of confessions by Lackey and Guest. Lackey's statement said that on the day of the murder he had been driving a car also occupied by Sims and Myers, that Sims had told him to follow Penn's car, saying "I'm going to kill me a nigger," and that Sims and Myers had both fired shotgun blasts as he pulled alongside Penn's car. Guest's confession said that Sims, Myers and Lackey had driven away from his garage at about the time of Penn's murder and had returned late that afternoon.

(Sims was sentenced Aug. 13 to 10 years in prison on his July guilty plea to charges of assault with intent to kill in the shooting of his wife, Betty, in May.)

Bombings, Arson & Beatings in Mississippi

The intensity of violence in Mississippi in 1964 was unmatched in other Southern states from June to November.

The homes of 2 McComb, Miss. Negroes active in the civil rights movement were bombed June 22. A Ruleville, Miss. black church was bombed June 25, the same night that a Negro church in Longdale, Miss. was hit by a fire bomb. A Molotov cocktail was hurled June 27 against the front door of the McComb, Miss. *Enterprise Journal*. A note around the bottle was signed: "K.K.K." A black-voter registration worker was wounded by a bullet shot from a passing car as she attended a rally in Moss Point, Miss. July 6.

3 explosions July 7 destroyed a section of the McComb civil rights "Freedom House." The structure occupied by 10 rights workers, was shattered by 3 predawn blasts July 8. 2 of the workers were slightly injured. Rep. Donlon W. Edwards (D., Calif.) said in Washington July 8 that he believed the blasts were an attempt on his life since he and his son, Leonard, 23, a rights worker, had slept in the house July 6. They had left McComb July 7.

Rabbi Arthur J. Lelyveld of Cleveland and 2 other white civil rights workers were beaten with metal weapons by 2 unidentified segregationists in Hattiesburg, Miss. July 10.

2 Natchez, Miss. black churches were leveled by arsonists July 12. The Rev. Snead Baldwin, pastor of 4 congregations in Adams County in the Natchez area, charged July 15 that at least 2 other black churches and one black meeting hall in the area had been destroyed by fires in rural Adams County in the past year.

The owner of a Wesson, Miss. gas station was beaten July 14 by 3 hooded men. He had refused to join the Klan, had hired black help and allowed them to use the cash register.

The Zion Hill Freewill Baptist Church of McComb was burned and 2 men were roughed up by 3 white men July 17. The Madison

County, Miss. Christian Union Baptist Church was destroyed by fire July 19.

A spokesman for the summer rights drive in Mississippi asserted in Jackson July 26 that night riders had used gunfire, dynamite, tear gas and molotov cocktails to harass Negroes and rights workers in 5 Mississippi communities the past few days.

The Mount Moriah Baptist Church near Meridian, Miss. was destroyed by fire July 30. The Pleasant Grove Missionary Baptist Church in Rankin County, 15 miles east of Jackson, Miss., was burned the night of July 30-31. A church meeting hall that had been used for civil rights activities in Gluckstadt, a small community north of Jackson, was burned to the ground Aug. 10.

Dynamite Aug. 15 demolished a Natchez nightclub and bar serving an all-black clientele across the street from a building housing the local Freedom School.

Night riders were reported to have shot and wounded 2 Negroes, burned 6 crosses and clubbed a white civil rights worker in Jackson Aug. 15. Scores of crosses were burned in Mississippi and Louisiana at 10 p.m., presumably by pre-arrangement.

Mrs. Fannie Lou Hamer, 46, vice chairman of the Mississippi Freedom Democratic Party, charged at a meeting of the Mississippi Project Parents Committee in New York Aug. 20 that she had been cursed, kicked and beaten by policemen after returning from a conference to help register black voters in Mississippi. She said policemen had forced 2 other blacks to beat her with blackjacks in a jail cell. She said a federal judge in Mississippi had dismissed her charges against the police. Julius Mendy Samstein, 25, a white field secretary for the Student Nonviolent Coordinating Committee, said at the New York meeting that a "reign of terror" had existed for 5 months in Amite County, in rural southwestern Mississippi. Blacks were dragged from their homes and beaten, he said. "The sheriffs themselves are the people who pull triggers" in some sections of southwestern Mississippi, he declared.

A bomb Aug. 27 shattered the windows and doors in the office of a small weekly Jackson newspaper whose editor had won a Pulitzer Prize for crusading editorials. A dynamite blast in Canton, Miss. Sept. 6 ripped through a white-owned grocery in a black neighborhood. 3 predawn bomb blasts in Summit, Miss. Sept. 7 damaged a home, a store and a shed, all owned by Negroes. A dynamite blast damaged the home of a black minister in McComb Sept. 9.

The number of black churches burned in Mississippi during the summer reached 24 Sept. 17 when 2 churches used in a black-voter registration drive were burned in rural sections of Madison County.

2 small churches in Philadelphia, Miss. were hit by fire Sept. 19.

A black church and the home of Mrs. Aylene Quin, a black rights worker, were bombed in McComb Sept. 20. Police called the bombings a hoax and arrested 24 Negroes under a state "criminal syndicalism" law banning any activity that could lead to political or social change in the state. About 2,000 Negroes had gathered and some threw bricks and bottles at a patrol car. Mrs. Quin, Mrs. Matti Lean Dillon and Mrs. Ora Bryant met with Pres. Johnson Sept. 24 and told him of alleged racial terrorism in McComb. The President ordered the Justice Department to recommend possible federal action. McComb Sheriff R. R. Warren charged Sept. 24 that the latest 4 explosions had been "staged" by blacks to try to induce the federal government to intervene.

Dynamite exploded outside the homes of 2 Negroes, one a former policeman, in McComb Sept. 23 The attack raised to 16 the number of reported house bombings in the McComb area since April. 4 churches had been bombed.

The home of Natchez Mayor John Nosser, a white racial peacemaker, was bombed Sept. 25. This was the 3d explosion in 2 weeks on property he owned. About 15 blocks away, the home of Willie Washington, a black contractor, was bombed Sept. 25 for the 2d time in 3 months.

A bomb went off in Jackson Sept. 27 at the home of I. S. Sanders, black businessman active in the civil rights movement. NAACP field secretary Charles Evers promptly telegraphed Pres. Johnson an appeal for federal intervention to halt "this mounting reign of terror." "I cannot and will not be responsible for the action which the Negroes may take upon themselves," the telegram warned.

2 persons were injured in a dynamite explosion Oct. 4 at the Baptist Academy church in Vicksburg, Miss. The church served as a freedom school operated by COFO. 2 shotgun blasts were fired in Meridian, Miss. Oct. 4 into the bedroom of a black home where white and black rights workers were staying. Nobody was injured.

Fire Oct. 31 destroyed the Antioch Baptist Church, used as a freedom school in Ripley, Miss.

A union official was kidnapped at gunpoint and whipped by masked men Nov. 17 in Laurel, Miss.

Meanwhile Gov. Paul B. Johnson Jr. Sept. 30 had ordered a state investigation of the McComb bombings. He said information indicated some of the bombings "were plants set by COFO [the integrationist Council of Federated Organizations] people" and "some were bombings by white people." Johnson and FBI Dir. J. Edgar Hoover announced the arrests of 3 whites Oct. 1, of one white Oct. 3 and of 7 whites Oct. 5 on charges of illegal use of explosives in connection with the bombings. Arms and ammunition as well as explosives were seized when the arrests were made.

A Pike County grand jury indicted 4 whites Oct. 9 and 5 Oct. 20 as alleged bombers of black homes and churches in the Mc-Comb area. They were charged with conspiracy and illegal use of explosives. 6 of the defendants pleaded guilty on specific counts, but all 9 pleaded no defense to the conspiracy charge at their hearing before Circuit Judge W. H. Watkins in Magnolia, Miss. Oct. 23. Watkins gave 15-year suspended prison sentences to 2 of those who had pleaded guilty, 5-year suspended sentences to 4 who had pleaded guilty and 6-month suspended sentences to 6 defendants. Fines of $500 each were also imposed on the latter 6 defendants. The prosecution and defense attorneys had agreed on the sentences. Watkins put the defendants on probation and warned them not to own or use firearms, live ammunition or dynamite while on probation. He also warned them that they would have to serve their prison terms if there was any more racial violence in McComb—regardless of whether or not they were involved. He said the defendants had been "unduly provoked" by rights workers and merited a 2d chance.

Racial Clashes in 6 Southern States

Clashes between whites and black demonstrators were reported in 6 other Southern states. Fire-bombings, the sound of gunfire and night-rider attacks were frequent. Klan activity was marked by repeated cross-burnings.

In Selma, Ala. 5 Negroes and a white were arrested July 3, 1964 as they tried to enter a restaurant and a theater, several blacks and police officers were injured during a melée at a black rally July 5, and 52 Negroes were arrested July 6 and 7 for demonstrations in support of a voter registration drive.

About 300 whites threw bottles and stones at an integrated movie theater in Tuscaloosa, Ala. July 8. Police dispersed the crowd with tear gas and fire hoses. The outburst occurred after a rumor had spread that actor Jack Palance had escorted a black woman into the theater.

A dynamite bomb wrecked the carport of the Montgomery,

Ala. home of a black family Nov. 29. An explosion was set off Dec. 13 outside a black Montgomery church; 3 men accused of the crime received 6-month sentences but were released on probation after 10 days in jail.

Thomas Booth, 21, a white, was shot in the stomach July 10, 1964 during an attempt to integrate a movie theater in Lake City, Fla.

300 whites and Negroes clashed for 3 hours July 12 after a group of Negroes sought service at the Motor Freight restaurant near Henderson, N.C. 17 persons, including 12 blacks, were jailed on charges of inciting a riot and refusing to obey police officers. 5 Negroes were injured.

A fire bomb was tossed into a recently integrated St. Augustine, Fla. restaurant July 24.

Maurice Lawson, 22, allegedly one of 6 white men who had tried to chase Negroes out of an integrated Atlanta restaurant July 18, was shot and critically wounded during the altercation. Redell Grosby, the white restaurant owner, was charged with shooting him.

A mob at Americus, Ga. beat members of an integrated group emerging from a previously white cafe July 3.

Several white men poured gasoline on a Ferriday, La. shoe shop Dec. 10 and set fire to it, preventing a Negro from leaving. He died in a hospital later.

Northern Protests & Riots

While bombings, murder and arson took place in the South during 1964, conflict was reported in Cleveland, Ohio and Chester, Pa. over school segregation. There were summer riots in July in Harlem and Rochester, N.Y. Racial violence flared in August in Jersey City, Patterson and Elisabeth, N.J. 1,000 blacks clashed with state police in Dixmoor, Ill. Aug. 16. Rioting in Philadelphia Aug. 28-30 injured 348 persons and damaged hundreds of stores. An FBI report in September said that the disturbances were not typical race riots but that racial tensions were a contributing factor.

The racial violence in Cleveland broke out Apr. 7 after a white integrationist, the Rev. Bruce William Klunder, was run over and killed by a bulldozer at a construction site. In reaction to Klunder's death, demonstrations were held at city hall Apr. 8, and Mayor Ralph S. Locher met with United Freedom Movement (UFM) leaders. A memorial service for Klunder was conducted

Apr. 9 by the Rev. Eugene Carson Blake, stated clerk of the United Presbyterian Church in the U.S.A. Blake urged Cleveland to "build the best racially integrated school system" in the nation as a memorial to Klunder.

About 86% of Cleveland's black public school pupils participated Apr. 20 in a boycott of the schools. The protest, against alleged *de facto* segregation, was sponsored by the UFM, which had also called Apr. 13 for a black boycott of downtown stores.

Public schools in Chester, Pa. were closed Apr. 22 following clashes between police and demonstrators protesting alleged *de facto* segregation. The demonstrations, begun in March, had been resumed after a 3-day truce and mediation by the State Human Relations Commission had yielded no results. 219 persons were arrested in the Apr. 22 clashes. State police were called in 3 times to reinforce the city force during the week that followed. The Delaware County, Pa., grand jury June 4-5 indicted 264 persons who had participated in the Chester demonstrations. They were indicted on charges of inciting to riot, riot, obstructing a public highway and conspiracy.

Racial violence broke out in 2 predominately black sections of New York City July 18 and persisted despite strong police anti-riot action, including the firing of thousands of warning shots.

Negroes smashed store windows and hurled debris at police in the city's Harlem section during 4 consecutive nights of turbulence beginning July 18. The police fired thousands of shots in the air in efforts to beat back rioters. The estimated 4-day toll in Harlem: One Negro shot to death; 5 others shot and wounded, none seriously; 81 civilians and 35 policemen injured; 112 stores and business establishments damaged; 185 persons arrested, including at least 10 held for looting.

The Harlem violence was attributed to racial tensions, heightened by an incident in which a black boy was killed by an off-duty white police officer. Police Lt. Thomas Gilligan had shot and killed James Powell, 15, when the boy allegedly threatened him with a knife in New York's Yorkville section July 16. Immediately after the shooting, about 300 teen-agers, mostly Negroes, gathered at the scene and threw bottles and cans at policemen, injuring one of them. 200 Negro teen-agers staged another demonstration in Yorkville July 17 to protest the shooting.

The rioting began after a rally held in Harlem in the evening of July 18 by the Congress of Racial Equality (CORE), at which several black leaders charged New York police with brutality and demanded the dismissal of Gilligan. The rally's final speakers, drawn from the crowd after CORE representatives had turned the platform over to them, denounced the police, city officials and whites in strong language; one of them, the Rev. Nelson C. Dukes, a Harlem minister, declared that it was time for Harlem's blacks to stop talking and to act. At Dukes' urging, the crowd marched to a nearby police station to present its protests and demands for Gilligan's ouster. The police barred the marchers from the precinct house, but the Negroes refused to leave until their demands had been satisfied. The first scuffles ensued when police attempted to set up barricades between demonstrators and the police station. The scuffle became a riot that spread to nearby streets and then throughout much of central Harlem.

For the next several hours blacks on rooftops threw bottles and debris at hundreds of policemen sent to the area to maintain order. Groups of Negroes broke store windows and pillaged goods, and crowds gathered on street corners. The police rushed the crowds with nightsticks and fired volleys of bullets into the air. Jay Jenkins, 41, was shot and killed when he refused to stop throwing bricks at police from a roof-top. Police Commissioner Michael J. Murphy issued general orders to police to try to control the crowds peacefully but to resort to force when necessary.

Acting Mayor Paul R. Screvane and Murphy appealed July 19 for calm in Harlem, and police closed much of Harlem to traffic. But riots on a scale equal to those of the previous night broke out again after a funeral service was held in Harlem that evening for the slain Powell youth.

Jesse Gray, leader of a recent Harlem rent strike, had called earlier July 19 for "100 skilled black revolutionaries who are ready to die" to correct "the police brutality situation in Harlem." Gray had urged guerrilla warfare tactics and was applauded by an audience of about 500, half of whom were said to be black nationalists.

Violence erupted again in Harlem on a reduced scale the night of July 20. Police broke up a march by about 1,000 Negroes. The rioting continued the night of July 21, when a 12-year-old Negro boy reportedly was shot by a policeman.

Meanwhile, in the Brownsville section of Brooklyn, 2 men were shot and acid was thrown in the face of a third during a 5-hour battle between blacks and Puerto Ricans the night of July 19. 12 other men were injured, and police arrested 7 men.

In the predominantly black Bedford-Stuyvesant section of Brooklyn, rioting broke out the nights of July 20, 21 and 22. 3 civilians and 2 policemen were injured, 185 persons were arrested and 112 business establishments were damaged or looted. Each night, the police fired warning shots to disperse crowds of Negroes. 2 of the injured suffered gunshot wounds received July 21, when more than 200 store windows were shattered by rioters. By July 22 policemen were stationed at almost every corner in the area.

Pres. Johnson ordered the FBI July 21 to investigate the Harlem riots for possible violations of federal laws. "It must be made clear, once and for all, that violence and lawlessness cannot, must not and will not be tolerated," he declared.

Mayor Robert F. Wagner flew home from a European vacation July 21 to deal with the crisis. In a message broadcast and televised July 22, Wagner asserted "law and order are the Negro's best friend."

The wave of violence that had begun in Harlem July 18 ended early in the morning of July 23 with widespread rioting and looting in the Bedford-Stuyvesant section. The July 23 rioting, believed to be the worst of the 6 days of unrest in New York, raised the total Bedford-Stuyvesant casualty list to 10 civilians and 12 policemen injured. 276 persons were arrested, and 556 incidents of property damage were reported.

Pres. Johnson, at his July 24 news conference, accused "extremist elements." "I would not hesitate to say that the impression I gain from reading . . . [FBI] reports is that there are extremist elements involved," he asserted.

Police witnesses testified July 27 before N.Y. State Supreme Court Justice Gerald P. Culkin that William Epton, 32, a left-wing Harlem leader, had urged July 18, shortly before the Harlem riots broke out, that Negroes kill "cops" and "judges." The witnesses also testified that Epton, leader of the Harlem Defense Council and chairman of the Progressive Labor Movement in Harlem, had advised that policemen be lured into side streets where they could be subjected to a barrage of bottles and missiles. Detective John Rivera quoted Epton as having told a July 18 Harlem street meeting that "we're going to have to kill cops and judges." "Cops declared war against the people of Harlem" and "we should declare war on them," Epton was reported to have said. Epton and Conrad J. Lynn, 55, a reputed leftist, had been arrested July 25 when they attempted to organize a Harlem protest march in defiance of an injunction. A N.Y. County grand jury Aug. 5 indicted Epton on charges of advocating the overthrow of the state government by force and violence and of calling for the killing of police officers and judges. He was charged with advocating criminal anarchy.

A N.Y. County grand jury refused Sept. 1, 1964 to indict

Police Lt. Gilligan for criminal negligence in the fatal shooting of James Powell. County District Atty. Frank S. Hogan issued a 14-page report on the case Sept. 1. The report said the testimony presented to the grand jury had been contradictory and had failed to substantiate charges that Gilligan had not given adequate warning before firing. Gilligan was said to have been justified in shooting the youth to protect himself. The N.Y. City police department's civilian complaint review board, composed of 3 deputy police commissioners, absolved Gilligan Nov. 6 of wrong-doing in the boy's death.

Racial clashes between Negroes and Puerto Ricans had broken out on the Lower East Side of Manhattan in N.Y. City the nights of Aug. 29 and 30, 1964. The trouble started after a Negro reportedly had shot a Puerto Rican to death Aug. 29. Several hundred persons participated in the disturbances. Molotov cocktails, bottles, stones and bricks were hurled from rooftops at firemen and policemen Aug. 30. The police responded by firing shots into the air.

Violence erupted in Rochester, N.Y. July 24-26 as blacks, whites and police clashed in the streets and angry mobs smashed and looted stores. One white man was killed in the rioting, and about 350 persons, 22 of them policemen, were reported injured. At least 400 persons were arrested. The violence ebbed only after National Guard units and state police had been sent to the city to aid local police in restoring order.

Rochester had a population of 320,000, of whom 40,000 were black. The city's black community had charged police with brutality; whites were said to have become apprehensive at increased Black Muslim activity, and white and black parents had been battling in the courts over racial imbalance in the city's schools.

The rioting started shortly before midnight July 24 in Rochester's black North Side section. The immediate cause was said to have been an incident in which a policeman reportedly tried to arrest a black man who was disturbing a Mother's Improvement Committee street dance. The man reportedly struck the policeman and was attacked by the policeman's dog. Word spread among the dancers that policemen had clubbed and kicked the Negro; they began throwing beer cans and bottles at police, and reinforcements were sent to the area. The crowd quickly grew to 2,000 persons, among them many youths who were reported to have brawled with a band of white youths.

During the next 10 hours, fighting between Negroes, whites and police occurred throughout the North Side. A mob overturned the car of City Police Chief William Lombard, but he escaped unharmed. Police fired volleys of tear-gas grenades at the rioters, and youths picked them up and threw them back. Police dogs were held in readiness but were not used.

200 state troopers were sent to Rochester early July 25 at the request of City Public Safety Commissioner Donald Corbett and the Monroe County sheriff. By dawn July 25 most of the rioting had stopped.

Deputy Police Chief Clarence DePrez reported July 25 that the mobs of looters had bypassed black-owned stores; he called the disturbances "well organized."

City Manager Porter W. Homer July 25 ordered an 8 p.m. curfew for the entire city.

But violence erupted again that evening in Rochester's southwest section, about 1½ miles from the scene of the previous night's riots. Hundreds of Negroes remained on the streets after the curfew went into effect, and state troopers attempted to enforce the order. They were showered with bricks hurled from 2d-story porches and roots. One white man was killed in a melee, and a black man was wounded by shots fired by a white civilian.

The rioting resumed in Rochester's North Side and continued in the southwest section during the day July 26. Black youths pelted police with stones and bottles, and looters broke through the plywood shop fronts that had been put up to replace shattered windows. In the midst of the unrest, a civil defense helicopter circling the southwest area crashed into a house, killing the pilot and 2 occupants of the house. Firemen had to shower a crowd of several hundred with water to clear the street for emergency vehicles.

Gov. Nelson A. Rockefeller mobilized 1,000 National Guardsmen from Rochester, Binghamton and Auburn July 26 and ordered them to immediate emergency duty in Rochester. It was believed to be the first time that New York State National Guard units had been mobilized to deal with any kind of civilian disorder. Rockefeller had warned July 25 that "lawlessness, hoodlumism and extremism" would be met by "every legal means" available to the state and that there was evidence of "organized efforts to incite" the racial unrest. He toured the riot-torn neighborhoods of Rochester July 27 and called them "clear evidence of extremism."

The National Guard units arrived in Rochester late July 26. An estimated 300 Guardsmen rode through the riot-affected sections of the city in open trucks; they displayed steel helmets and bayoneted rifles, but their officers reported that none of the men had been issued ammunition. The Guardsmen made camp in an armory and in 2 city parks. They were under explicit orders not to intervene in any disturbances until summoned by city authorities.

The rioting ebbed soon after the arrival of the Guard units. Earlier July 26, black crowds had thrown rocks, bottles and molotov cocktails at police, and a city fire engine had been the target of rifle fire as it ran through the emergency area. But police were able to disperse the crowds and restore order with warning shots, tear gas, and streams of water from high-pressure hoses.

Victor Turyn, Buffalo FBI agent who worked with the Rochester police, said July 26 that the riots were "spontaneous as the result of the arrest of the youth [at the dance July 24]." "We have no information that Communists or other subversive groups were involved in the riots," he said.

Pres. Johnson pledged Aug. 12 that "we will not permit any part of America to become a jungle, where the weak are the prey of the strong and the many." Speaking before the American Bar Association in New York, the President asserted that "such acts must be stopped and punished—whether they occur in Mississippi or in the State of New York." Law and order could be maintained only if progress was continued toward racial justice, he said. He warned that "those who would hold back progress toward equality, and at the same time promise racial peace, are deluding themselves and the people." Johnson condemned both murders of civil rights workers in the South and black riots in Northern cities. He said: "No person, whatever his grievance, can be allowed to attack the right of every American to be secure in his home, his shop and in his streets." "Fulfillment of rights and prevention of disorder go hand in hand. Resort to violence blocks the path toward racial justice. The denial of rights invites increased disorder and violence."

Racial violence had flared in Jersey City, N.J., late Aug. 2, 1964 after a rumor of police brutality against a Negro who had just been arrested. Widespread looting and clashes between blacks and police were reported in 3 separate outbreaks of violence during the night. Violence was repeated Aug. 3 and 4. At least 56 persons were injured, including 22 policemen and a black youth who was shot and seriously wounded. 36 persons were arrested. 68 stores were damaged and 18 looted. About 50,000 of Jersey City's 300,000 residents were Negroes, and there were repeated charges of police brutality made by Negroes. The city had been declining economically for more than 30 years.

Mayor Thomas J. Whelan Aug. 3 called the riot an "isolated incident" caused by hooligans. But Police Lt. Raymond Blaszak said the rioting had been planned in advance by young agitators.

Rioting broke out in Jersey City again that evening on a more violent scale, and blacks concentrated on attacking policemen and whites instead of looting stores. Youths threw bricks, stones and molotov cocktails at policemen, and policemen fired shots into the air. Teams of civic leaders, black lawyers, clergymen, and representatives of CORE and the NAACP tried to persuade the rioters to disperse. An estimated 450 policemen from Jersey City and surrounding communities tried to quell the rioting.

Scattered violence on a smaller scale took place the evening of Aug. 4. Roving groups of Negroes threw molotov cocktails in the streets and there was some gunfire by policemen. Jersey City was reported comparatively peaceful the evening of Aug. 5.

Racial violence swept through the New Jersey cities of Paterson and Elizabeth the nights of Aug. 11-12 and 12-13, 1964. At least 22 persons were reported arrested and 4 civilians injured in Paterson, and 18 persons were arrested in Elizabeth, 20 miles south of Paterson.

The trouble in Paterson started Aug. 11 when teen-age Negroes, on their way home from a dance sponsored by the City Board of Recreation, threw rocks at police cars sent to the area after a bottle, reportedly thrown from a roof, had smashed a police car's windshield. The incidents were confined to a 10-square-block area in a poor, predominantly black neighborhood.

Paterson Mayor Frank X. Graves Jr. warned during the day Aug. 12 that any further violence would be met with maximum police force. "The basic weapon will still be the nightstick," he said. "We will not use guns unless the lives . . . or the property of the police are threatened. Then we will shoot to kill." He later said threats to police property would not be considered a cause for using guns.

Widespread rioting erupted in a 50-square-block Paterson area the night of Aug. 12. An estimated 100 civilians were involved. Groups of youths threw bottles and rocks at passing cars. Black clergymen and civil rights leaders urged the black youths to go home. Mayor Graves ordered all taverns in the black section closed by midnight. He toured the riot areas and warned the Negroes to "go home" or "you'll be shot." He narrowly missed being struck by a thrown bottle. Graves said later that there was no evidence of outside agitation in Paterson. He denounced the rioters as "just plain, old, lousy law-breakers who're using their color to say they can't be arrested."

Sporadic incidents of racial trouble were first reported in Elizabeth the night of Aug. 11-12. Widespread violence flared the evening of Aug. 12 as an estimated 700 blacks gathered in a 4-square-block section of the city's port area. Negroes threw molotov cocktails into the streets and jostled policemen who tried to restrain them. An emergency force of 200 policemen was on duty in the port area. The policemen fired a dozen shots into the air to disperse the rioters. The Aug. 12 rioting reportedly had started after a policeman, punched when he tried to arrest a demonstrator, retaliated by swinging his nightstick.

Almost 100 whites and Negroes clashed for more than an hour the night of Aug. 28-29, 1964 in a boardwalk amusement area of Keansburg, N.J. 12 white youths were arrested. Police Chief Robert Kronenberger blamed the fighting on "local white punks." The Negroes had arrived at the amusement area from New York in 2 chartered buses earlier Aug. 28. The fighting started when a white youth made a derogatory racial remark to one of the black youths and attacked him. Keansburg's 15 policemen, 20 auxiliary policemen and 4 carloads of state police finally restored order.

Rioting broke out in the integrated Chicago suburb of Dixmoor, Ill. the night of Aug. 16, 1964 after a rumor spread that a white man had attacked a black woman. The white man, a liquor store owner, had accused her of shop-lifting a bottle of gin. About 1,000 Negroes clashed with 225 state troopers and other policemen, who fired shots into the air. 31 blacks were arrested and at least 50 persons, mostly white, were injured. The liquor store was looted, 2 houses set on fire and 50 automobiles (including some police cars) damaged.

Police guards blocked Dixmoor's main streets Aug. 17 to prevent a repetition of the turmoil. Policemen arrested 7 white youths who were exchanging taunts with Negroes, and civil rights workers failed to persuade a black crowd to go home. The liquor store where the riots had begun the previous day was set on fire, and the police were met with gunfire when they tried to disperse the crowd of 100 Negroes. The police used tear gas and dogs to restore order.

Racial rioting erupted the night of Aug. 28 in a 4-square-mile "ghetto" area of North Philadelphia in which 200,000 Negroes lived. The rioting continued on a smaller scale the nights of Aug. 29 and 30. The reported 3-day toll: 248 persons injured (including 66 policemen and 2 firemen), 312 persons arrested and hundreds of stores damaged and looted.

The trouble in Philadelphia started Aug. 28, when a crowd

gathered and menaced 2 policemen—one white and one black—who had pulled a recalcitrant black woman out of a stalled car that had blocked an intersection in the black district. A rumor spread that one of the policemen had killed the woman, and police reinforcements were rushed to the scene as rocks and bottles were thrown. Widespread violence and looting began 90 minutes later. The police tried to repulse the crowds with nightsticks. But, despite their efforts, store windows were smashed, shops were looted, police cars were battered, and the district's streets were littered with debris thrown from windows and roofs.

Philadelphia Mayor James H. J. Tate quarantined the 125 blocks of the black section Aug. 29. He ordered residents "to disperse themselves and peaceably depart to their habitations." 1,500 policemen were sent to the riot area. Some policemen were pelted with stones, but violence the night of Aug. 29 was sporadic and was controlled by the anti-riot forces.

Tate had said at a news conference Aug. 29 that the rioting had "nothing to do with civil rights or any proper or fair grievance" and that he was not aware of any outside influences that could have instigated such rioting. But Terry Chisholm, executive director of the city's Commission on Human Relations, insisted there had been adequate warnings from other riot-torn northern cities that "blood brothers" would start riots in Philadelphia. Police Commissioner Howard R. Leary lauded black leaders, especially Philadelphia NAACP Chapter Pres. Cecil B. Moore, who had toured the black section Aug. 29, appealing to its residents to avoid further violence and remain at home. Moore lauded the police Aug. 30 for having exercised "a remarkable degree of restraint" during the rioting. Rep. Robert N. C. Nix (D., Pa.), a Philadelphia Negro, said of the police: "I think they handled themselves admirably. I have higher respect for them now than I ever had before."

A squad of 100 patrolmen Aug. 31 raided the North Philadelphia headquarters of Shaykh Muhammad Hassan (Abyssinia Hayes), 34, leader of the separatist National Muslim Improvement Association of America, a Philadelphia Black Muslim cult, and found a pistol, 2 bayonets, 2 assembled firebombs and the materials for 10 more. Hassan was arrested on a charge of possessing bombs and explosives.

Hassan and Raymond Hall, 26, also known as Yusseff Abdulla, were arrested Sept. 14 and arraigned Sept. 15 on charges of inciting the Aug. 28-30 Philadelphia riots. They were accused of spreading a rumor that police had beaten a pregnant woman to death and of encouraging looters. Florence Mobley, 23, a typist, was arrested in Philadelphia Sept. 17 on the same charge. An all-white jury Nov. 10 convicted Hassan of complicity in inciting the riot. Hall, also convicted, was sentenced Jan. 8, 1965 to 3 to 9 months in prison. Hassan was sentenced Jan. 11 to 18 months to 3 years in prison and fined $1,000. Florence Mobley had received a suspended sentence Dec. 16, 1964.

FBI Riot Report

The FBI reported to Pres. Johnson Sept. 26, 1964 that the summer riots in Northern cities apparently had been spontaneous and were not " 'race riot[s]' in the accepted meaning of the phrase" although "racial tensions were a contributing factor." The report summarized the results of FBI investigation of riots in New York City, Rochester, N.Y., Jersey City, Elizabeth, Paterson, N.J., Dixmoor, Ill., Philadelphia, Seaside, Ore. and Hampton Beach, N.H.

The FBI report said there was "no systematic planning or organization" behind the riots. They were described as not "riots of Negroes against whites or whites against Negroes" but rather "senseless attack[s] on all constituted authority without purpose or object." The report attributed the riots to youths "variously characterized by responsible people as 'school dropouts,' 'young punks,' 'common hoodlums' and 'drunken kids.' " It said that "rioting by these young people reflects an increasing breakdown across the nation in respect for the law and the rights of other people to be secure in their person and their property."

6 of the 7 major city riots began as "an escalation from a minor incident, normal in character," the FBI reported.

The report said that "the Communist Party U.S.A. does not appear to have officially instigated these riots, though its members were observed taking part" in some.

The report held that "where there is an outside civilian [police] review board, the restraint of the police was so great that effective action against the rioters appeared to be impossible. ... The police were so careful to avoid accusations of improper conduct that they were virtually paralyzed."

The report asserted that "the arrival of large numbers of reporters and television cameras at the riots provided an opportunity for self-seeking individuals to publicize wild charges. ... These circumstances provided additional incitement to the rioters and served to attract others to the scene."

Pres. Johnson Sept. 26 announced these actions to prevent a repetition of the riots:

(a) His orders to the FBI to "make riot training available to all police departments" in the U.S.

(b) His directions that the Army's riot control techniques be made "a larger part of the training of the National Guard of the various states" and "available to local police forces as well."

(c) His instructions that Health-Education-Welfare Secy. Anthony J. Celebrezze study Washington, D.C.'s program to cope with school dropouts and determine "what further steps might be taken by the federal government to assist in meeting this important problem."

(d) His decision to call, at an "appropriate time," a conference of state and city officials to discuss how the federal government could help solve local problems that tended to lead to riots.

FROM SELMA TO WATTS (1965)

Civil Rights Clashes & Urban Riots

Civil rights workers mounted an intensive voter registration drive in Selma, Ala. in 1965 against stiff resistance by police using tear gas, night-sticks and whips. Marchers reached the state capitol at Montgomery only after a federal court order was backed by federal troops. During the campaign, segregationists beat a minister to death and killed a rights worker from Detroit in a highway ambush. Black nationalist leader Malcolm X was slain by gunmen in New York during 1965. An attempted arrest in Los Angeles triggered 6 days of rioting in Watts, a black section. 34 persons died, hundreds were injured and scores of city blocks were destroyed by fires as police and National Guardsmen quelled the outbreak. Racial clashes, arson and bombings took place in many Southern states during the year. Demonstrations against *de facto* segregation in the North were accompanied by violence in Chicago, Cleveland, New York, New Jersey and Massachusetts.

The Southern Regional Council, a nonprofit research organization, reported in Atlanta Jan. 30, 1966 that 17 persons had died in the South during 1965 in race-related violence. (The figure for 1964 was 14, for 1963 13.) 14 of the 1965 slayings were of Negroes and civil rights workers and appeared to have been caused by white Southerners. 7 of the killings occurred in Alabama, 4 in Mississippi, 2 each in Georgia and Louisiana and one each in South Carolina and Arkansas.

Selma Vote Drive Leads to Violence

Civil rights workers met violent opposition from police and segregationists in the Selma, Ala. voter-registration drive. The Rev. Dr. Martin Luther King Jr. was attacked by an assailant while registering in a previously all-white hotel. Sheriff's deputies used clubs and electric cattle prods on blacks lined up to register to vote. State troopers using whips, night-sticks and tear gas turned back rights marchers attempting to reach the state capitol at Montgomery until a federal court order was imposed and National Guardsmen called out. Demonstrations in support of the Selma rights campaign were held throughout the U.S. A federal grand jury investigated charges of police brutality but returned no

87

indictments.

The drive began when 12 Negroes, including the Rev. Dr. Martin Luther King Jr., registered Jan. 18, 1965 at the Hotel Albert in Selma. They were the first blacks accepted by a formerly "white" hotel in Selma. Negroes also were served at 7 "white" Selma restaurants. King was punched and kicked while registering, and his assailant, James George Robinson, 26, of Birmingham, a member of the National States Rights Party, was arrested by City Public Safety Director Wilson Baker. (Robinson was fined $100 and given a 60-day jail sentence in city court Jan. 19.) Baker later Jan. 18 arrested George Lincoln Rockwell, head of the American Nazi Party; Robert Lloyd, 20, an American Nazi Party member, and Jerry Dutton, head of the National States Rights Party, when they appeared at a Selma church rally attended by about 600 blacks.

Dallas County (Ala.) Sheriff James G. Clark Jr. and his deputies arrested 62 blacks in Selma Jan. 19 on charges of unlawful assembly and 5 others on charges of criminal provocation. They were trying to register to vote at the county courthouse and had refused to heed Clark's order to enter the courthouse only through an alley door. Clark was said to have roughed up Mrs. Amelia Boynton, a Selma civil rights leader, whom he arrested when she would not leave the sidewalk in front of the courthouse. King, who was watching from across the street, filed a complaint with the U.S. Justice Department charging Clark with illegal arrests and brutality. Clark's deputies Jan. 20 arrested 156 more Negroes who had tried to enter the courthouse by a front door in defiance of his orders to use a side door.

105 black teachers appeared at the county courthouse Jan. 22 in a voter-registration demonstration, but Clark and 5 deputies forced them away with night-sticks. U.S. District Judge Daniel H. Thomas in Mobile, Ala. Jan. 23 issued an order barring Clark and other officials from intimidating or harassing black voter applicants or "those legally attempting to aid others in registering to vote, or encouraging them." But Thomas limited the registration line to 100.

Annie Lee Cooper, 53, a 226-pound black motel clerk, was subdued by Clark and 3 deputies Jan. 25 when she stepped out of a line of about 200 Negroes waiting to register at the courthouse and punched Clark. The 3 deputies wrestled Miss Cooper to the ground, Clark clubbed her, and she was taken to jail. No blacks were registered. "We have seen another day of violence," Martin Luther King declared after the incident. "We still have . . . a sheriff who is determined to trample over Negroes with iron feet of brutality and oppression."

34 blacks, including chairman John Lewis of the Student Nonviolent Coordinating Committee (SNCC), were arrested Jan. 26 for disobeying orders to leave a voter-registration line of 100 at the courthouse. Policemen, deputy sheriffs, posse men with cattle prods, state troopers, FBI agents and U.S. marshals were in the area to keep order.

Judge Thomas in Mobile ruled Jan. 30 that rights workers could not be arrested for being present in the Dallas County Courthouse to encourage voter-registration applicants as long as the workers were "peaceful and orderly."

King and 263 other Negroes were arrested Feb. 1 while marching to the courthouse to protest discrimination against black voter-registration applicants. They were accused of parading without a permit. In addition, about 500 black school students picketing the courthouse were arrested. 37 were charged with contempt of court, the rest with truancy. King declined to post $200 bail and remained in jail until Feb. 5, when he put up the $200. 120 black adults were arrested Feb. 2 on contempt-of-court charges as they stood in line outside the courthouse, and about 400 black high school students were arrested while marching to the courthouse. More than 300 black schoolchildren were arrested Feb. 3 in front of the courthouse; they were taken in custody after serenading law enforcement officials with civil rights songs. More than 500 Negroes were arrested Feb. 5 when they marched toward the courthouse. Meanwhile, 19 members of the U.S. House of Representatives visited Selma as observers to investigate the situation.

About 50 more black demonstrators were arrested Feb. 8 after the County Board of Registrars had advised a small group of Negroes that they were welcome to sign a sheet to obtain priority numbers but could not register until the next official Alabama registration day, Feb. 15. The group rejected the offer.

Pres. Johnson had declared at his Feb. 4 news conference that "all of us should be concerned with the efforts of our fellow Americans to register to vote in Alabama." He stressed that "the basic problem in Selma is the slow pace of voting registration for Negroes who are qualified to vote." He pledged to use "the tools" of the 1964 Civil Rights Act to enforce the right to vote and said: "I intend to see that that right is secured for all of our citizens."

Alabama Gov. George C. Wallace announced in Montgomery Feb. 20: "I have ordered state troopers to join law enforcement agencies of the counties and cities involved to stop nighttime demonstrations [in Selma and nearby Marion]. Any demonstration evidently conducted for the purpose of creating a breach of the peace will be stopped. . . . No one can contest the right of anyone to register and vote in Alabama if they are qualified under the laws of this state. No one can contest the right of peaceful assembly. However, mass demonstrations in the nighttime led by career and professional agitators with pro-Communist affiliations and associations is not in the interest of any citizen of this state, black or white."

King told 700 Negroes at a Selma meeting Feb. 22: Wallace "said nothing about the problems that brought about the demonstrations. We are going to have a motorcade to Montgomery in the next few days. We hope to have our forces mobilized to have carloads of people from all over the state to march on the capitol. . . . We will be going there to tell Gov. Wallace we aren't going to take it any more." Wallace's ban on nighttime demonstrations was "clearly unconstitutional."

About 100 Negro children and teenagers conducted a twilight march on the courthouse in Selma Feb. 23 but dispersed before nighttime at the urging of Selma Public Safety Director Wilson Baker.

In early March, Alabama law enforcement officers broke up 2 attempts by black and white integrationists to march the 50 miles from Selma to the state capitol in Montgomery to protest the denial of voting rights to Negroes in Selma.

Shortly after the first of the 2 marches got started Mar. 7, the vanguard of about 525 black marchers was attacked by 200 state troopers and sheriff's deputies. The law-enforcement officers, some of them on horses, used tear gas, nightsticks and whips. Some Negroes retaliated by hurling bricks and bottles as they were forced back from the white section of Selma to the black section. Many Negroes were injured. 17, including SNCC Chairman John Lewis, were hospitalized, and 67 others were given emergency treatment for minor injuries and tear-gas effects. The attack by the law-enforcement officers took place in an effort to enforce Gov. Wallace's ban against a protest march from Selma to Montgomery.

Wallace Mar. 8 defended the attacks on Negroes as absolutely necessary to safeguard public safety. He insisted that black lives had been saved by the forcible prevention of the march. Pres. Johnson Mar. 9 issued a statement deploring the "brutality" against Negroes in the Mar. 7 incident and pleading with both demonstrators and state officials to respect the law.

Martin Luther King led 1,500 Negroes and whites from Selma

Mar. 9 in another unsuccessful effort to march to Montgomery. The marchers included many white clergymen and other whites from throughout the U.S. But state troopers, standing shoulder-to-shoulder, formed an impassible barricade and peacefully turned them back on the outskirts of Selma after a march of one mile. LeRoy Collins, head of the Community Relations Service, acting as representative of Pres. Johnson, had worked out an arrangement with King under which the demonstrators would start a token march and then turn back at the first sign of resistance.

3 white Unitarian ministers who had been in the march were beaten by a group of whites on a Selma street corner late Mar. 9. One of the 3, the Rev. James J. Reeb, 38, of Boston, was beaten unconscious with a club, and he died in a Birmingham hospital Mar. 11 of a skull fracture.

Selma police Mar. 10 arrested 4 white men as participants in the assault. Those arrested were William Stanley Hoggle, 36, his brother Namon O'Neal Hoggle, 30, R. B. Kelly, 30, and Elmer L. Cook, 41, all of Selma. They were charged with assault with intent to murder. Following Reeb's death, the 4 men were rearrested Mar. 11 and charged with murder. All but Kelly were indicted by a Dallas County grand jury Apr. 13 on charges of murdering Reeb, and a jury acquitted them Dec. 10, 1965.

About 300 rights workers in Selma sang, prayed and slept in the street the night of Mar. 10 after police had thwarted 3 attempts to march on the courthouse. Almost 1,000 black students from Tuskegee Institute and several white ministers held a peaceful sit-down demonstration in front of the state capitol in Montgomery Mar. 10 in protest against the Mar. 7 actions of the state troopers in Selma.

The U.S. Justice Department Mar. 10 filed suit in Federal Court in Montgomery for an order to prevent Alabama officials from "summarily punishing, by striking, beating, tear-gassing or other means," any person participating in a demonstration for black rights. The suit charged Gov. Wallace, Alabama Public Safety Director Albert J. Lingo and Dallas County Sheriff James G. Clark Jr. with "preventing and discouraging Negroes from exercising their full rights of citizenship." The suit asked that the 3 officials and their agents be: (a) enjoined from intimidating, threatening or coercing anyone for the purpose of interfering with his right to register to vote; (b) prevented from interfering with "lawful, peaceful demonstrations in behalf of the rights of Negroes by attempting forcebly to disperse the demonstrators or seeking to impose unreasonable conditions on the demonstrators";

(c) ordered to provide ordinary police protection for those trying
to exercise the right to vote or demonstrate lawfully in behalf of
Negro rights.

Pres. Johnson Mar. 12 received a wire from Gov. Wallace
asking for a meeting on the Selma situation. The President replied
that he would be "available ... any time," and the 2 met for
more than 3 hours Mar. 13. Afterwards, with Wallace behind
him at a televised news conference Mar. 13, the President said:
"What happened in Selma was an American tragedy." "I told
the governor that the brutality in Selma last Sunday [Mar. 7]
must not be repeated" and that, "whether the governor agrees or
not, that law and order would prevail in Alabama." The "full
power of the federal government" was poised to strike against
"lawlessness." He had asked Wallace to do 3 things—to "publicly
declare his support for universal suffrage in Alabama," to assure
"the right of peaceful assembly" and to call a biracial meeting.
Wallace had expressed concern that the demonstrations were "a
threat" to the peace and security of the people of Alabama. "I
expressed my own concern about the need for remedying those
grievances which led to the demonstrations by the people who
feel their rights have been denied. ...."

Wallace presented his views Mar. 14 on CBS-TV ("Face the
Nation") and at a news conference televised by ABC. He said he
would not permit a rights march from Selma to Montgomery
unless a federal court order to permit the march were upheld on
appeal. He also said he would not receive representatives who
came to see him "at the head of a ... demonstration." He contended that demonstrations would continue regardless of "anything we do in Alabama" and that there had been "more" demonstrations since the 1964 Civil Rights Act was enacted "than we
ever had before." He held up photographs purportedly showing
police in New York, Rochester, N.Y. and Philadelphia, Pa. dispersing demonstrators with clubs and drawn pistols.

Daily demonstrations had started in Selma Mar. 10 after
police had barred a march on the Dallas County Courthouse and
established a line beyond which the blacks were not to pass.
Eventually, a rope was strung Mar. 11 between the police and
demonstrators, who made up a song about "The Berlin Wall" in
Selma. Selma Public Safety Director Baker cut the rope Mar. 12.

An agreement to allow a march as part of a memorial service
for Reeb was arranged Mar. 15 by U.S. District Judge Thomas
in Mobile and representatives of the Federal Community Relations
Service with Baker and Sheriff Clark. More than 2,000 persons,

including many whites, marched from Browns Chapel to the court-house, where Martin Luther King delivered the eulogy. Among those attending: were: United Auto Workers Pres. Walter P. Reuther; Archbishop Iakovos, primate of the Greek Orthodox Church for North & South America; Reps. Edward P. Boland (D., Mass.) and Silvio O. Conte (R., Mass.), representing the Massachusetts Congressional delegation; the Right Rev. William F. Creighton, bishop of the Episcopal Church of Washington; Bishop John D. Bright of the African Methodist Episcopal Church in Philadelphia; Rabbi Eugene Lippman of Washington, representing the Union of American Hebrew Congregations; Methodist bishops Charles F. Golden of Nashville and Richard C. Raines of Indianapolis; about 150 Roman Catholic priests and nuns.

2 attempted marches on the courthouse were stopped by police Mar. 16, but about 600 demonstrators marched to the courthouse Mar. 17 after another agreement worked out with the help of Judge Thomas. Most of the Mar. 17 marchers were white.

Demonstrations in support of the Selma rights campaign had been held in cities throughout the U.S., and the protests gained in intensity after the death of the Rev. Reeb. 14 youths staged a sit-down in the White House in Washington Mar. 11 after entering with tourists and then demanding federal intervention in Selma. Their sit-down, in a main corridor, lasted for 7 hours before they were dragged out by guards and city policemen. Pickets had begun marching outside the White House 3 days previously. Thousands of clergymen from throughout the nation met Mar. 12 for a Washington rally at which the President was denounced for "unbelievable lack of action" in the Selma crisis. A delegation from the rally, sponsored by the Commission on Religion & Race of the National Council of Churches, later was received by Pres. Johnson, who said he had alerted 700 federal troops early Mar. 9 to intervene in Selma.

While demonstrating in Montgomery in a demand to be permitted to stage a Selma-to-Montgomery march, about 600 marchers had been attacked and routed Mar. 16 by mounted state and county policemen wielding ropes, night-sticks and electric prod poles. 8 persons were reported injured. The demonstration had begun as a parade but was stopped by city policemen for lack of a parade permit. The crowd, including about 225 students from northern colleges, remained, however, and 2 separated groups of demonstrators attempted to join forces. The troopers and volunteer possemen from the county sheriff's office then moved in on horses.

A public apology for the attack was made later Mar. 16 by Montgomery County Circuit Solicitor David H. Crozland, who said the attack stemmed from "a mixup and a misunderstanding of orders." The mounted policemen were directed to disperse only a small group of demonstrators considered unruly, Crozland explained. "We are sorry there was a mixup . . ., and we are sorry that anyone got hurt."

A 2d march, of about 1,000 persons who had obtained a parade permit, was held under city police protection later Mar. 16.

A meeting to protest the violence was held that night at a black church. At the meeting, Martin Luther King called for a mass protest march the next day on the county courthouse.

A permit was obtained, and the march was held Mar. 17, with city police protection. The 1,600 demonstrators who participated were led by King, SNCC Executive Secy. James Forman and SNCC Chairman John Lewis. They marched a mile to the courthouse, where the leaders conferred for almost 4 hours with Sheriff Mac Sim Butler and John Doar, head of the Civil Rights Division of the U.S. Justice Department. King emerged from the meeting to tell the 700 persons outside that progress was being made toward an agreement to end police harassment of orderly demonstrations. Then he announced a just-released court decision upholding the demonstrators' right to conduct a 50-mile march from Selma to Montgomery.

U.S. District Judge Frank M. Johnson Jr. in Montgomery Mar. 17 upheld the right of demonstrators to stage an orderly march from Selma to Montgomery. Johnson enjoined Gov. Wallace and other state and county officials from "harassing or threatening" the marchers and ordered them to provide police protection during the march. Pres. Johnson commented later Mar. 17 that "justice has spoken" and expressed satisfaction that the issue "has been determined in the court."

Hearings on the case has been held in Montgomery Mar. 11-16, and King testified Mar. 11 about the march he had led Mar. 9. King said: Thousands of people had come to Selma for demonstrations, and an outlet for "pent-up emotions" had to be provided. "I did it to give them an outlet. Maybe there will be some blood let in the state of Alabama before we get through, but it will be our blood and not the blood of our white brothers." There had been secret negotiations with federal officials in Selma for a limited march, prayer and then dispersal at a certain point.

Judge Johnson reviewed the voter-registration situation in the area. He noted that demonstrations had been peaceful but futile, since few blacks had been registered. He held that Sheriff Clark and his aides, in countering the Selma demonstrations, had exhibited "an almost continuous pattern . . . of harassment, intimidation, coercion, threatening conduct and, sometimes, brutal mistreatment." He asserted that Clark and his men had not been "enforcing any valid law of . . . Alabama or furthering any legitimate policy of the state" and that the attempted Mar. 7 march, which was broken up by mounted police, "involved nothing more than a peaceful effort on the part of Negro citizens to exercise a classic, constitutional right; that is the right to assemble peaceably and to petition one's government for the redress of grievances."

Gov. Wallace, before a joint session of the state Legislature Mar. 18, denounced Judge Johnson for his order upholding the right to undertake the march. Wallace assailed Johnson as a man who "prostitutes our law in favor of . . . mob rule while hypocritically wearing the robes" of a judge. He called the marchers "irresponsible demonstrators . . . many of them Communist-trained." He asked Alabamans, however, for restraint in their reaction to the march. He urged them not "to play into the hands of the enemies of our nation," and he called on them to "obey, even though it be galling," final court orders.

Pres. Johnson summoned reporters to his office later Mar. 18 and read a telegram he had received from Wallace that evening. In the telegram Wallace said it would require 6,171 men, 489 vehicles, 15 buses to furnish adequate security for the march. The state had only 300 troopers and about 150 other officers available, Wallace said, and he "respectfully" requested that the federal government "provide sufficient federal civil authorities" to protect the marchers and citizens in and along the march route. The President then said that federal "civilian personnel approaching the figure" given by Wallace was unavailable but that more than 10,000 Alabama National Guardsmen were at Wallace's disposal. "If he is unable or unwilling to call up the Guard, and to maintain law and order in Alabama," the President said, "I will call the Guard up and give them all the support that may be required."

Pres. Johnson Mar. 20 signed a proclamation noting the danger of "domestic violence" in Alabama and an executive order federalizing the Alabama National Guard and authorizing use of whatever federal troops the Defense Secretary "may deem necessary" in the situation. At a televised news conference the morning of Mar. 20, Johnson announced his action and castigated Wallace. The President said: He had ordered 1,863 federalized Guardsmen to the area, 500 Regular Army military policemen to Maxwell Air Force Base in Montgomery and 509 more MPs to Craig Field near Selma; 100 FBI agents and 75 to 100 U.S. marshals were also being sent to the area; 1,000 regular infantry troops had been alerted at Fort Benning, Ga. Brig. Gen. Henry V. Graham of Birmingham, a National Guard officer, assistant divisional commander of the 31st Division, had been named field commander of all troops in the operation. He was to be aided by Brig. Gen. John M. Wright Jr., assistant commander of the 11th Air Assault Division at Fort Benning. Deputy Atty. Gen. Ramsey Clark had been ordered to Alabama to act as federal coordinator; he was to be assisted by ex-Asst. Atty. Gen. Burke Marshall and his successor as head of the department's Civil Rights Division, John Doar.

The President also said: "It is not a welcome duty for the federal government to ever assume a state government's own responsibility for assuring the protection of citizens in the exercise of their constitutional rights. It has been rare in our history for the governor and the legislature of a sovereign state to decline to exercise their responsibility and to request that duty be assumed by the federal government. . . . I have responded, both to their request, and to what I believe is the sure and the certain duty of the federal government in the protection of constitutional rights of all American citizens."

The 5-day march to Montgomery began from Browns Chapel Methodist Church in Selma Mar. 21. Before leaving the church, Martin Luther King Jr. told the marchers: "You will be the people that will light a new chapter in the history books of our nation. Those of us who are Negroes don't have much. . . . But thank God we have our bodies, our feet and our souls. Walk together, children, . . . and it will lead us to the promised land. And Alabama will be a new Alabama, and America will be a new America."

The 3,200 persons who then began the march were led by King, Dr. Ralph J. Bunche (UN Undersecretary for special political affairs), the Right Rev. Richard Millard (suffragan bishop of the Episcopal Diocese of California), SNCC Chairman John Lewis, Deaconess Phyllis Edwards of the Episcopal Diocese of California, Rabbi Abraham Heschel of the Jewish Theological Seminary in New York, the Rev. Ralph D. Abernathy (King's top aide), the Rev. Frederick D. Reese (a Selma Negro and president of the Dallas County Voters League), and Cager Lee, grandfather of Jimmie Lee Jackson, black youth killed by a state trooper at Marion, Ala. in February.

Among others who started the march were N.Y. City Council Pres. Paul R. Screvane; Mrs. Constance Baker Motley, president of the Borough of Manhattan (N.Y. City), the highest elective office ever held by a black woman (Mrs. Motley, elected to the post Feb. 23, was the first woman to serve as a N.Y. City borough president); Benjamin R. Epstein, national director of the Anti-Defamation League.

The lead car carried Maj. John Cloud of the Alabama state police, who had been in charge of troopers who had routed black marchers with tear gas 2 weeks earlier. Federalized Guardsmen lined the streets leading out of town, and federally manned helicopters flew over the procession. Federal agents, including Doar, who walked near the head of the march, and Maj. Gen. Carl C. Turner, Provost Marshal General of the U.S. Army, reported by radio to the Justice Department and Pentagon in Washington. MPs guarded every crossroad. Army trucks loaded with armed troops were in evidence nearby. Gen. Graham personally directed the security operation along the route.

Equipment, supplies and personnel included: a mobile hospital lent by the AFL-CIO International Ladies Garment Workers Union; a "healthmobile" lent by the National Council of Churches; 13 ambulances, each manned by a physician; hot breakfasts and suppers and cold snacks and lunches prepared at a Negro church in Selma and trucked to the marchers; a tent gang to pitch 2 small and 2 large tents at the nightly campsites; a garbage truck to clear the route and campsites of litter; trucks with portable latrines and washing facilities.

The marchers covered 7.3 miles the first day, then camped on land owned by a Negro. To conform with the federal court order on the march, about 2,750 of the marchers returned to Selma the evening of the first day on the Western Railway of Alabama; the trip was arranged by the Justice Department officials because enough buses could not be found. 150 more marchers returned Mar. 22 to abide by the court-ordered 300-marcher limit where U.S. Highway 80, the march route, had only 2 lanes. Most of the celebrities left the march after the first day.

The marchers walked 16 miles through Lowndes County Mar. 22 and covered 32.3 miles in all by Mar. 23 despite a torrential rain. They stopped for the night Mar. 24 1.7 miles inside Montgomery at the City of St. Jude, a Roman Catholic hospital and school used predominantly by blacks. About 1,500 more marchers joined the procession where Route 80 widened to 4 lanes outside Montgomery.

King left the march Mar. 23 to keep a speaking engagement in Cleveland, then rejoined it with his wife, Coretta, Mar. 24 to lead it into Montgomery. On this last night of the march the marchers were entertained by many show-world celebrities assembled by singer Harry Belafonte at King's request. About 150 participated, on a stage made of coffin crates, under one of the tents.

The march ended in front of the state capitol shortly after noon Mar. 25. The demonstrators numbered about 25,000; their ranks had been swelled for the final 3½ miles from the outskirts of Montgomery. UN Undersecy. Bunche was again in the lead rank with King. Army troops and National Guardsmen lined the final march route and stood guard on roofs.

King addressed the throng at the capitol. He said: Selma had become "a shining moment in the conscience of man. If the worst in American life lurked in the dark streets, the best of American instincts arose passionately from across the nation to overcome it."

The marchers carried a petition to Gov. Wallace. It said: "We have come not only 5 days and 50 miles but we have come from 3 centuries of suffering and hardship. We have come ... to declare that we must have our freedom NOW. We must have the right to vote; we must have equal protection of the law and an end to police brutality."

The governor sent word to the marchers that he would receive a delegation after the rally, but 2 attempts of a delegation to see him were rebuffed. Wallace, however, met with a delegation bearing the petition Mar. 30. This group was led by the Rev. Joseph E. Lowery of Birmingham, who said afterwards they had been "cordially" received and that Wallace had "promised to give careful consideration" to the petition.

Mrs. Liuzzo Slain in Highway Ambush

A white civil rights worker, Mrs. Viola Gregg Liuzzo, 39, of Detroit, a mother of 5 children, was shot to death on U.S. Highway 80 in Alabama Mar. 25, 1965 while she was driving a car to Montgomery after returning civil rights marchers to Selma. (The Selma-to-Montgomery march along Route 80 had ended earlier that day.) Pres. Johnson made a dramatic TV appearance Mar. 26 to deplore "the horrible crime," to announce the arrest of 4 Ku Klux Klansmen in connection with it and to request a Congressional investigation of the Klan, which he described as "a hooded society of bigots."

Mrs. Liuzzo, wife of Anthony J. Liuzzo, 51, a business agent for the International Brotherhood of Teamsters in Detroit, was murdered while on a return trip to Montgomery after having driven some marchers from there back to Selma. Leroy Moton, 19, a black Selma youth helping with the transportation of marchers, was the only other occupant of the car. He reported later that a car had pulled up alongside their car as it sped along a lonely stretch of road and that a volley of shots was fired, killing Mrs. Liuzzo but missing Moton. The death car then ran off the highway out of control and was stopped at a fence. Moton said that another car then approached, that someone walked from it and shined a flashlight into the death car. Moton pretended to be dead. The person with the flashlight then left and drove away. Moton eventually flagged down a truck returning marchers and reported the murder in Selma.

The 4 arrested Klansmen were charged with the federal crime of conspiring to deprive Mrs. Liuzzo of her civil rights (murder was not a federal crime unless committed on federal property). The accused men were Eugene Thomas, 43, and William Orville Eaton, 41, both of Bessemer, Ala.; Gary Thomas Rowe Jr., 31, of Birmingham; Collie LeRoy Wilkins Jr., 21, of Fairfield, Ala. The accused were members of the United Klan of America, Knights of the Ku Klux Klan, Inc., reportedly the largest of several Klan groups.

(The House Un-American Activities Committee voted u-nanimously Mar. 30 to undertake a full investigation of the KKK. Committee Chairman Edwin E. Willis said a preliminary inquiry by the committee had revealed indications of "shocking crimes ... carried out by highly secret action groups within the Klans." The groups, he said, were known as "knock-off squads" or "holy terrors." The preliminary inquiry had been started in February after Rep. Charles L. Weltner had proposed it in a House speech. The early inquiry also covered the Minutemen, the American Nazi Party and the Black Muslims.)

A federal grand jury in Montgomery, Ala. Apr. 6 indicted Wilkins, Thomas and Eaton on charges of conspiring to pursue and assault civil rights workers. Rowe was not indicted. The indictment charged: "It was a part of the plan and purpose of the conspiracy that the defendants would harass, threaten, pursue and assault citizens in the area of Selma and Montgomery, who were participating or had participated in, or who were lending or had lent their support to, the demonstration march [from Selma to Montgomery]."

A Lowndes County (Ala.) grand jury Apr. 22 indicted Wilkins, Thomas and Eaton on charges of first-degree murder in the Liuzzo slaying. They pleaded not guilty at their arraignment Apr. 26 in Haynesville, Ala., the Lowndes County seat. Rowe testified against them before the grand jury and was identified as an undercover FBI informer.

Wilkins was acquitted of Mrs. Liuzzo's murder Oct. 22, 1965 after a mistrial had been declared in an earlier trial in which an all-white jury had voted 10-2 May 7 to convict him of manslaughter. Thomas was acquitted Sept. 27, 1966 by a jury of 8 Negroes and 4 whites. Eaton died of a heart attack Mar. 10, 1966. In Wilkins' first trial, Rowe had testified May 4, 1965 that he had been riding in the car from which the shots that killed Mrs. Liuzzo were fired and that he had seen Wilkins and Eaton shoot pistols at Mrs. Liuzzo after their car had pulled alongside hers.

Wilkins, Thomas and Eaton were convicted in federal court in Montgomery Dec. 3, 1965 on the conspiracy indictment and were sentenced to 10-year prison terms.

Bombings & Killings in Alabama

As national attention focused on the clashes accompanying the Selma voter registration drive, violence was reported elsewhere in Alabama during 1965. State police charged black marchers in Marion, Ala., killing one Negro. A dynamite bomb exploded in Birmingham. A Negro was gunned down near Anniston; a beating-and-torture victim died near Greensboro. A special deputy sheriff killed a white seminarian in Hayneville.

50 state troopers led by Col. Albert Lingo, Alabama public safety director, charged into a crowd of 400 blacks who had been marching on the Perry County jail in Marion the night of Feb. 18. As the Negroes fled, the troopers chased them, following some into a café and others across porches of nearby houses. Jimmy Lee Jackson, 26, reportedly was shot and critically wounded by a trooper in the café after Jackson had come to the assistance of his mother, Mrs. Viola Jackson, who was being clubbed by a trooper. Jackson died in a Selma hospital Fer. 26. At least 10 blacks were injured by troopers' nightsticks, and a trooper reportedly sustained a head injury from a missile thrown from the crowd. White civilians attacked newsmen and smashed their cameras during the clash.

The black marchers were protesting the arrest of James Orange, a member of the Southern Christian Leadership Conference.

Orange had been seized earlier Feb. 18 on a charge of contributing to the delinquency of a minor (who had participated in an Orange-organized demonstration.)

A dynamite bomb exploded in an alley of a black neighborhood in north Birmingham Apr. 1. Weymouth Crowell, 13, a Negro, suffered minor injuries when cut by glass from a bedroom window shattered by the blast. 2 unexploded time bombs were found shortly afterwards outside the homes of Birmingham Mayor Albert Boutwell and City Councilwoman Nina Miglionico, both considered moderates.

Willie Brewster, 38, a Negro, was shot from a passing car July 15 as he was riding home from work in Calhoun County, Ala., near Anniston. He died July 18 in an Anniston hospital. Black companions riding with Brewster at the time of the shooting said the shots had been fired from a car carrying whites. An all-white jury in Anniston, Ala. Dec. 2, 1965 convicted Hubert Damon Strange, 23, of 2d-degree murder in the shooting of Brewster. The jury imposed a 10-year sentence, the minimum for 2d-degree murder, and the State Court of Appeals upheld the verdict Aug. 23, 1966. The prosecution had based its case largely on the testimony of Jimmy Knight, 28, a white Alabaman, who said that 2 hours before the shooting he and Strange had attended a National States Rights Party rally at which the killing of Negroes had been encouraged by the Rev. Connie Lynch. That evening, Knight testified, Strange and 2 other white defendants (Johnny Ira DeFries and Lewis Blevins) had boasted to him of having shot a Negro and had shown him a shotgun and 2 spent shells. DeFries, 23, was acquitted by an all-white jury in Anniston Feb. 17, 1966 of murder charges for Brewster's death.

Perry Small, 87, a Negro, died Aug. 27, 1965, after having been found beaten at his home near Greensboro, Ala. Aug. 22 with his tongue cut off. Hale County authorities said that the attack was in retaliation for Small's outspoken opposition to the local civil rights drive and that 2 black suspects being held had been active in rights work, but a local rights leader said the 2 suspects were not connected with the rights movement.

Jonathan Myrick Daniels, 26, a white seminary student on leave from the Episcopal Theological School in Cambridge, Mass., was slain and a white Roman Catholic priest from Chicago, Richard F. Morrisroe, 26, was seriously wounded by shotgun blasts allegedly fired by a special deputy sheriff in Hayneville, Ala. Aug. 20. The deputy, Tom L. Coleman, 52, a member of one of the county's (Lowndes) most prominent families and an engi-

neer for the Alabama Highway Department, was held on charges
and released on $12,500 bond Aug. 21. Daniels and Morrisroe had
been arrested with 27 other demonstrators in Fort Deposit Aug.
14 after picketing for equal job opportunities. The demonstrators
were jailed in Hayneville and released on recognizance bonds Aug.
20. Shortly afterwards, the 2 men were shot as they approached
a small grocery store with 2 black girls. An all-white jury in
Hayneville Sept. 30, 1965 acquitted Coleman of a first-degree manslaughter charge in Daniels' death.

Malcolm X Slain in New York

Malcolm X (originally Malcolm Little), 39, bearded Negro
founder and leader of a black nationalist movement, was shot to
death in New York Feb. 21, 1965. The assassination took place
shortly after 3 p.m. in the Audubon Ballroom just as Malcolm
started to address a rally of about 400 black followers. He was
apparently hit by 7 bullets. Police said that 3 weapons (a caliber
.38 revolver, a caliber .45 revolver and a sawed-off shotgun) had
been found and as many as 30 shots fired.

Malcolm had just appeared on the stage and had started talking when a fight (believed to have been started by conspirators)
began in the back of the room. Malcolm urged those participating
in the fight to "cool it," and his personal bodyguard, Reuben
Francis, 33, and several plainclothes black policemen (who had
infiltrated the ballroom to keep order) tried to break up the fight.

At that point a Negro later identified as Talmadge Hayer
(alias Thomas Hagan and Hayes), 22, of Paterson, N.J. dashed up
the aisle with a double-barrelled sawed-off shotgun and fired at
Malcolm. As Malcolm fell, his bodyguard, Francis, apparently
shot Hayer in the thigh. Hayer was kicked and beaten by a crowd
of about 150 persons, and his leg was broken. Police finally rescued him from the mob and arrested him. Francis was arrested also
on charges of felonious assault and violation of the Sullivan Law.

2 other blacks, both apparently spectators, were shot, and
many bullets were fired. The injured men were identified as William
Harris, wounded seriously in the abdomen, and William Parker,
wounded in the foot.

It was generally assumed that the assassination was motivated
by the split between the Black Muslims (known officially as the
Nation of Islam) and Malcolm's nationalists (which he had named
the Organization for Afro-American Unity). Malcolm had quit
the Black Muslims in Mar. 1964 and formed his Muslim Mosque,

Inc. (The house in which he had been living in East Elmhurst, Queens [N.Y. City] had been wrecked by a fire set off by firebombs Feb. 13, one week before the assassination; Malcom, his wife and 4 daughters had escaped uninjured. The house had been bought by the Black Muslims for Malcolm's use while Malcolm headed the New York branch of the organization. After he left the group, the Black Muslims began legal action to evict him. Malcolm accused the Black Muslims of setting the fire and said frequently that they planned to murder him. Joseph X, a Black Muslim leader, had charged Feb. 15 that Malcolm had set off the firebombs himself "to get publicity." Malcolm insisted that his home "was bombed by the Black Muslim movement on the orders of Elijah Muhammad," the Black Muslims' leader.)

Police Feb. 22 set up elaborate security precautions to prevent retaliatory murders threatened by Malcolm's followers. Heavy police guards were placed in Chicago around Elijah Muhammad (originally Elijah Poole) and Cassius Clay (who had renamed himself Muhammad Ali), world heavyweight boxing champion who had been converted to the Black Muslim faith by Malcolm but had broken with him to back Elijah Muhammad. Black Muslim headquarters in Harlem (N.Y. City) and San Francisco were burned Feb. 23. Hundreds of extra policemen were sent to Harlem and other sections of N.Y. City to prevent further violence and protect the other Black Muslim headquarters.

Norman 3X (originally Norman Butler), 26, of the Bronx (N.Y. City), a karate expert and member of the Black Muslim élite guard group known as the Fruit of Islam, was arrested in his home Feb. 26 on charges of participating in Malcolm X' assassination. A 3d black suspect, Thomas 15X (Thomas Johnson), 29, of the Bronx, was arrested Mar. 3. (Norman 3X and Thomas 15X had been indicted by a Bronx grand jury Feb. 15 on charges of first-degree assault in the non-fatal shooting Jan. 6 of Benjamin Brown, a N.Y. City corrections officer who had defected from the Black Muslims.)

Hayer, Norman 3X and Thomas 15X were convicted by a jury Mar. 10, 1966 of first-degree murder for Malcolm's assassination. After testifying to his innocence Feb. 23, Hayer had repudiated this testimony Feb. 28 and admitted shooting a pistol at Malcolm "about 4 times." Hayer testified that he and 3 accomplices had been hired to carry out the shooting; he refused to identify his accomplices or the person who had ordered the murder. He insisted that the Black Muslims were not involved and that the other 2 defendants "had nothing to do with this." Hayer,

Norman 3X and Thomas 15X were sentenced to life imprision-
ment Apr. 14,1966.

(59 persons were arrested and 4 hospitalized Aug. 18, 1965 as
a result of a clash between police and Black Muslims at Muhammad's Mosque, a Black Muslim headquarters headed by John
Shabazz, leader of the movement in Los Angeles. The clash took
place when police rushed to the mosque to investigate a report
that men were carrying rifles into the building. As the police surrounded the mosque, a single shot was fired from it. The police
answered with a hail of fire and then entered. They found 2
molotov cocktails, 2 small fires presumably set in an effort to destroy records, no firearms but apparent evidence that some people
had slipped out of the building.)

The Watts Riot

34 persons were killed and a major section of Los Angeles
terrorized Aug. 11-16, 1965 in the U.S.' most destructive episode
of racial violence in decades.

A minor incident in Los Angeles' 95%-black district of Watts
Aug. 11 erupted into 6 days of rioting, looting of stores, arson,
rock-throwing and sniping by an estimated 7,000 to 10,000 blacks.
Weapons used by the rioters included firearms and molotov cock-
tails. The disorders devastated a 150-block area of southwestern
Los Angeles and spread briefly to surrounding areas.

As Gov. Edmund G. (Pat) Brown rushed home from vacation
in Greece, the National Guard was called out by the lieutenant
governor Aug. 13 to help the out-manned municipal police and
county sheriff's deputies in their efforts to restore order. The
authorities finally announced Aug. 15-16 that the violence had
been brought under control. 3,952 people, almost all of them
black, were arrested during the disorders on charges stemming
from the riots. In addition to the 34 deaths, the riot toll included
1,032 people injured (864 treated in hospitals).

28 of those slain were black. Whites among the dead included
a sheriff's deputy and a fireman killed by a falling wall as he fought
a riot-caused fire.

The loss due to looting, fire and other willful destruction
totaled $40 million. 200 buildings were destroyed, more than 600
damaged. Civic, church and civil rights leaders suggested that in
terms of human relations, the riots were responsible for even
greater damage. This damage, which might take years to repair,
was the revival or creation of mutual hate and fear between

blacks and whites.

The apparently unorganized rioting was ascribed by various political, church, civil rights and other observers to a heat wave then prevailing in the area, to charges of police brutality and unfairness to blacks, to resentments, frustrations and hopelessness caused by such conditions as poverty, unemployment and *de facto* school segregation, to the nationwide civil rights movement, to the high percentage of broken families among Negroes, to the presence of a large criminal element in the area and to other sociological, psychological and physical causes. Many observers pointed out that the thousands of rioters represented only a fraction of the nearly 90,000 blacks who lived in Watts and who were the chief sufferers from the disorders. The riots, it was said, were opposed bitterly by a large, frightened majority of Negroes who had as much cause for protest as the rioters had.

The riot-torn district was treated much as a disaster area as the violence subsided. State and municipal officials and volunteer organizations arranged for the distribution of food to residents whose usual food stores had been destroyed or closed. Arrangements were made to restore transportation and other services that had been suspended during the disorders.

The immediate spark that led to the conflagration was an incident in which a white state highway patrolman, Lee Minikus, stopped a car in the Watts district on suspicion that its driver, Marquette Frye, 21, black, was drunk. This took place at 7:45 p.m. Aug. 11. As Minikus was giving Frye a sobriety test, which Frye failed, about 25 blacks gathered at the scene, and Frye's mother, Mrs. Rena Frye, 49, appeared and began scolding her son. Frye then turned angrily on the officer, and Mrs. Frye sprang at Minikus when he tried to force Frye into his patrol car. (Mrs. Frye was convicted Nov. 1, 1965 of interfering with a police officer.) As the Fryes scuffled with Minikus and a 2d white officer, the crowd grew to about 200, and members of the crowd began shouting threats and throwing rocks.

The 2 officers called for help at 8:20 p.m. Other officers arrived with riot guns and forced the crowd to move. But within 2 hours the moving mob had tripled in size. Members of the crowd began stoning cars and buses at random, some began to smash store windows and to loot the stores, and 80 policemen were rushed into the area.

The first night's rioting reached its peak at about 1:30 a.m. Aug. 12 as probably 1,000 or more blacks, most of them teenagers or in their 20s, smashed windows, fought police and stoned cars.

The police reported gaining the upper hand by about 3 a.m., when the mobs began to disperse.

Police Chief William Henry Parker 3d, 63, long a target of charges that he was unfair to Negroes, said Aug. 12 that the rioters were "young hoodlums who have no respect for the law." But he indirectly placed at least some blame on civil rights leaders. "When you keep telling people they are unfairly treated and teach them disrespect for the law," he said, "you must expect this kind of thing sooner or later."

After a nervous day of relative calm, rioting resumed the evening of Aug. 12, when an estimated 7,000 young blacks, including many women, rampaged through Watts. The renewal of rioting, looting and destruction Aug. 12 appeared to be on a more vicious scale than the original outbreak of Aug. 11. Prime targets of looters included gun shops, sporting goods stores and pawnshops, where looters stole firearms and ammunition. Rioters used the weapons to shoot at police, at cars, at whites and even at aircraft. Negro comedian Dick Gregory was shot in the thigh and wounded superficially as he pleaded with rioters Aug. 12 to "get off the streets."

Bands of blacks began late Aug. 12 to engage in gunfights with the police. These groups and others smashed store windows, looted the stores and then set them afire. Blacks of all ages were seen staggering through the streets carrying heavy loads of loot ranging from liquor to home appliances. Many whites unwittingly entering the area in autos were dragged from their cars and beaten, and their autos were smashed and burned. Several cases were reported, however, of individual blacks defying rioters to save whites.

Robert Richardson, a Negro employed as a *Los Angeles Times* advertising salesman, wrote Aug. 13, after watching the rioting for 8 hours: "It's a wonder anyone with white skin got out of there alive. ... Every time a car with whites in it entered the area the word spread like lightning down the street: 'Here comes Whitey—get him!' The older people would stand in the background egging on the teenagers and the people in their 20s. ... One white couple in their 60s ... [was] beaten up and kicked until their faces, hands and clothing were bloody. ... Those not hitting and kicking the couple were standing there shouting 'Kill! Kill!' ... As some areas were blockaded [by police], ... the mobs would move outside looking for more cars with whites. When there were no whites, they started throwing rocks and bottles at Negro cars. ... Everybody got in the looting—children, grownups, old men and women. ... Then everybody started drinking—even little kids 8 and 9 years old. That's when the cry started, 'Let's go where Whitey lives!' That's when I began to see guns. ..."

Oakpark Hospital, where many riot victims were being treated, was attacked by rock-throwing blacks Aug. 13. All the front windows of the hospital were smashed, but police details drove away the attackers. Ambulances sent to aid people injured in the rioting were often attacked. Fire engines sent to fight fires started by rioters were showered with rocks and occasional molotov cocktails, and many firemen were injured.

Most of the stores in Watts were owned by whites, and these largely were the ones destroyed. Many black-owned stores were also looted and burned. But amid the destruction were several untouched stores that apparently had been protected by signs bearing some variation of the announcements "Negro Owned," "Brother" or "Blood."

As about 900 outnumbered Los Angeles police officers and sheriff's deputies fought the rioters Aug. 11, Lt. Gov. Glenn M. Anderson flew to the riot-torn city and, at 5:05 p.m., signed a proclamation ordering California National Guard units "to assist police in restoring law and order in Los Angeles." Serving as acting governor in the absence of vacationing Gov. Brown, Anderson said it had become "clear that local police can no longer control the situation." Los Angeles Mayor Samuel William Yorty and Police Chief Parker, who had appealed for National Guard help at 10:30 a.m., joined other city officials in criticizing Anderson for not moving sooner.

About 2,000 members of the National Guard's 40th Armored Division headed into Los Angeles by truck and began their first anti-riot patrols late Aug. 13. The number of National Guardsmen in the city was increased to about 10,000 Aug. 14 as other members of the 40th Armored reached Los Angeles and Anderson ordered California's other National Guard division, the 49th Infantry, to reinforce the anti-riot forces. Lt. Gen. Roderick Hill, adjutant of the California National Guard, announced Aug. 14 that "we're committing all our National Guard resources in the state."

The National Guard troops, patrolling with police, used machineguns, rifles, bayonets and tear gas to subdue and disarm snipers, confiscate arms and molotov cocktails and end the looting and arson. Guard units set up road-blocks throughout the area, and Guardsmen were assigned to ride fire engines to protect firemen as they fought fires.

(Los Angeles Police Department figures showed 12,364 Guardsmen, 1,430 city policemen, 1,017 county sheriff's deputies and 68 state highway patrolmen on riot duty in Los Angeles by Aug. 16.)

As rioting continued and spread, Anderson Aug. 14, had proclaimed the city a disaster area. By doing so, he put into operation legal machinery permitting the riot fighters to call on police from nearby cities in 4 counties. Anderson Aug. 14 also proclaimed an 8 p.m.-to-dawn curfew.

Leaders of the riot fighters finally reported Aug. 15 that, although some violence continued, they had achieved control of the situation. Some 46 square miles centering on Watts were being patrolled by National Guardsmen and the police.

As disorder was slowly being checked in the Watts district, scattered black outbreaks, all of them quickly subdued, began to be reported from surrounding areas. 110 Negroes were arrested Aug. 14 in the independent municipality of Compton, 5 miles south of Watts, after a mob went on an orgy of smashing windows, looting stores and throwing molotov cocktails. A policeman was killed and a 2d policeman injured in Long Beach, Calif. Aug. 15 as they and other officers fought 50 black youths who had been stoning cars. National Guardsmen were sent to Long Beach, and a 10 p.m.-to-4 a.m. curfew was imposed. Incidents of black rock-throwing, arson, use of molotov cocktails, sniping and other riot-type activity were also reported in San Bernardino, Hollywood, San Diego, Pasadena, Van Nuys and other communities in the vicinity.

Gov. Brown, who had arrived in Los Angeles late Aug. 14, asserted Aug. 16 that the rioting and looting had been "ended" and that the remaining violence was no more than "guerrilla fighting with gangsters." But he continued the curfew for an additional night and announced that the National Guard "will remain here in force until the streets of Los Angeles are safe." Brown suspended the curfew Aug. 17.

At the height of the rioting Pres. Johnson Aug. 14 had "urge[d] every person in a position of leadership to make every effort to restore order in Los Angeles." In a statement issued from his LBJ Ranch in Texas, the President reiterated his deep commitment "to the fulfillment of every American Constitutional right" but held that "rights will not be won through violence." The President announced that he was sending Commerce Undersecy. LeRoy Collins and White House aide Lee C. White to New York to meet Gov. Brown, on the latter's arrival from Greece that afternoon, "to discuss the situation and to inform him of our desire to be of any possible assistance." On the President's orders, an Air Force plane was made available and used by Brown to fly to Los Angeles.

In a statement issued Aug. 15, Johnson again assailed "resort to terror and violence" but asserted that "it is not enough simply to decry disorder" without attacking the cause. He said: "The Los Angeles disorders flow from a violent breach of rooted American principles: The first is that injustices of our society shall be overcome by the peaceful processes of our society. There is no greater wrong in our democracy than violent, willful disregard of law. . . . To resort to terror and violence not only shatters the essential right of every citizen to be secure in his home, his shop and in the streets of his town, it strikes from the hand of the Negro the very weapons with which he is achieving his own emancipation. . . . But it is not enough simply to decry disorder. We must also strike at the unjust conditions from which disorder largely flows. For the 2d great American principle is that all shall have an equal chance to share in the blessings of our society. . . . Aimless violence finds fertile ground among men imprisoned by the shadowed walls of hatred, coming of age in the poverty of slums, facing their future without education or skills and with little hope of rewarding work. These ills, too, we are working to wipe out. We must not only be relentless in condemning violence, but also in taking the necessary steps to prevent violence. We must not let anger drown understanding if domestic peace is ever to rest on its own sure foundation—the faith of all our people that they share, in opportunity and in obligation, the promise of American life."

Gov. Brown met in Los Angeles Aug. 15 with about 50 prominent Negroes, who charged that the Los Angeles police with bias against their race. Brown announced Aug. 16 that he had "decided to appoint a 7-member commission of distinguished Californians to make an objective and dispassionate study of the tragic riots," to "probe both underlying and immediate causes and recommend means to prevent recurrences." Brown Aug. 17 asked Pres. Johnson to assign Commerce Undersecy. Collins as a consultant to the commission, and the White House immediately announced that the President was directing Collins to aid California officials concerned with the riots.

Taking note of what state and city officials had described as a relative lack of anti-Negro discrimination in California, Brown said at a press conference Aug. 16 that California was "paying the penalty for conditions under which Negroes have lived in other parts of the country."

The Rev. Dr. Martin Luther King Jr. said in Miami, Fla. Aug.
15 that he had visited Watts 6 weeks previously, had predicted
trouble and had "proposed a civil rights march just for the purpose
of distilling frustration." "When there is a march, they don't riot,"
he said. "But the white leadership encouraged the Negro leaders
not to march." In San Juan, P.R., where he had gone to address
the world convention of the Disciples of Christ, King Aug. 14 had
indorsed the "use of the full force of the police power to quell the
situation in Los Angeles." But "police power can only bring a
temporary halt," he added, and a full program of aid to Negroes
was needed. King arrived in Los Angeles Aug. 17 to work on the
problem.

NAACP Executive Secy. Roy Wilkins said in New York Aug.
15 that "rioting and looting must be put down with whatever force
is required," that "this is the first necessity toward any resolution
of the problem." He called for "a bi-racial, non-partisan, un-
influenced commission to . . . [study] the causes that led to the
outbreak and to make recommendations to prevent a recurrence."
Wilkins said "the Negro community as well as the white community must assume adult responsibility in facing the revelations of
such a study" and "must be prepared to face up to the critical find-
ings and the recommendations concerning their responsibilities."

Negro writer Louis Lomax said Aug. 14 that "Negro leaders
have been predicting a riot like this for 3 years." "The whites think
they can just bottle people up in an area like Watts and then forget
all about them," he declared. "It didn't work."

A 101-page report on the Watts riot was submitted to Gov.
Brown Dec. 6, 1965 by an 8-member commission headed by former
CIA Director John A. McCone. The document included an analysis
of the immediate and underlying causes of the disturbance. The
commission, appointed by Brown Aug. 19, had taken testimony
from 78 witnesses. Its 29-member staff had interviewed several
hundred witnesses and arrestees and had distributed 10,000 ques-
tionnaires. 26 consultants had aided the professional staff. The
study had been financed by a $150,000 Ford Foundation grant and
a $150,000 state appropriation.

The report, entitled "The Need for Leadership," described the
migration of Southern Negroes to communities such as Los Angeles and the frustrations suffered by the migrants. It cited 3 "ag-
gravating events" of the year preceding the riots: (1) "the angry
exhortations" of civil rights leaders "and the resulting disobedience for law in many parts of our nation," (2) the repeal of

California's Fair Housing Act in Nov. 1964 and (3) the publicity given federal anti-poverty programs that "did not live up to their press notices" in Los Angeles.

The commission found "no reliable evidence of outside leadership or pre-established plans for the rioting," but it asserted that organized gangs had spread the violence once the disturbance had started. The violence was described as "not a race riot in the usual sense" because "what happened was an explosion—a formless, quite senseless, all but hopeless violent protest—engaged in by a few but bringing great distress to all." (2% of Los Angeles' black residents were estimated to have participated in the disorder.) The arrest of Marquette Frye on a drunken-driving charge was seen as the "tinder-igniting incident," but the handling of the arrest by highway patrolmen was not criticized.

The report criticized Lt. Gov. Anderson for delay in providing National Guard support as requested by Police Chief William Parker. It censured the police department for a cumbersome complaint-processing procedure and for the low representation (4%) of Negroes on the police force, but it rejected charges that Parker had exhibited anti-black prejudice.

The document cautioned that implementation of its proposals would not provide a final solution "unless the conscience of the community, the white and the Negro community together, directs a new and, we believe, revolutionary attitude toward the problems of our city." Otherwise, the report warned, the August rioting "may seem by comparison to be only a curtain-raiser for what could blow up one day in the future." In a reference to the situation in other U.S. cities as well as Los Angeles, the commission expressed concern that "the existing breach, if allowed to persist, could in time split our society irretrievably."

Racial Clashes & Arson in Georgia

Segregationists clashed with integrationist demonstrators during 1965 in Crawfordville, Ga. and in Americus, Ga., where a white man was shot and killed. 2 black churches and a house were burned.

In Americus, almost continuous civil rights demonstrations were held following the arrest July 20 of 4 Negro women for refusing to move from a voting line marked "white women only." One of those arrested was Mrs. Mary Kate Bell, an unsuccessful candidate for justice of the peace in the election. The 4 women were jailed, and bail was set at $1,000 each.

At a joint news conference in Atlanta July 26, John Lewis of the Student Nonviolent Coordinating Committee (SNCC) and Hosea L. Williams of the Southern Christian Leadership Conference (SCLC) pledged a "massive united invasion upon segregation" in Americus until (1) the 4 women were freed without bail, (2) the election, which they claimed was illegal because of segregated voting procedures, was voided and rescheduled, (3) demonstrators were protected, (4) at least one black voter registration clerk was appointed and registration periods lengthened, and (5) a biracial committee was set up.

Negroes conducted a "token" march to the county courthouse in Americus July 26 and held vigils at the jail until U.S. District Judge W. A. Bootle July 30 ordered the women released pending the outcome of their suit. Bootle also barred county and city officials from holding segregated elections.

Picketing of white merchants was begun July 28, and 5 black pickets were attacked July 31 by white segregationists. 2 demonstrators, one of them white, were assaulted by white men Aug. 2 while police watched. 23 demonstrators were arrested for trespassing, but 2 whites who attacked the demonstrators were not arrested.

Andrew Aultman Whatley Jr., 21, white, was killed July 28, 3 blocks from a demonstration at the jail, when stones were thrown by a group of whites at a passing car driven by a Negro and shots allegedly were fired from the car. Whatley, a bystander, was wounded fatally. 2 blacks in the car—Charles Lee Hopkins and Eddie James Lamar—were arrested, and they were indicted on first-degree murder charges by a county grand jury Aug. 3. (Hopkins, 23, was convicted Mar. 3, 1966 of murder after he admitted firing a pistol into the white crowd. He received a life sentence. Lamar, who drove the car, pleaded guilty Mar. 4 to voluntary manslaughter and received a 5-year prison sentence.)

Attempts to form a biracial committee were started after a recommendation for such a body had been made by the Americus Merchants Association July 22. White business leaders had offered simultaneously to post the $4,000 total bond for the 4 women arrested in the voting line, but the women had refused the offer because of their stand that they should be released without bail.

The arrest of 6 whites involved in racial incidents was announced by police Aug. 4, and Americus was relatively quiet Aug. 5, with fewer than 10 pickets on post and a "routine protest march" that night by 355 persons. The surprise appointment of 3 black voting clerks was announced Aug. 6 by county officials.

Rights leaders rounded up vote registrants.

A Ku Klux Klan rally took place in Americus Aug. 8, when about 700 persons participated in a silent KKK march and memorial service for the white youth killed July 28. Later, about 300 integrationists marched to the courthouse through a white residential area.

In the Crawfordville case, a 3-judge federal court in Augusta, Ga. Oct. 14 declared the Taliaferro County school system bankrupt and named state Schools Supt. Claude Purcell to take control of the system as receiver. The ruling was handed down in a suit brought by the Southern Christian Leadership Conference (SCLC) and the NAACP Legal Defense & Educational Fund after all 165 white students in the county had transferred to schools in adjoining counties rather than attend school with 72 Negroes who had registered in the county's only white school, in Crawfordville. The school was later closed. The court directed Purcell to reopen the county white school, to allow Negroes to transfer to the other counties or to "come up with some other solution acceptable to the court."

The SCLC had led demonstrations in Crawfordville since Sept. 27, and black children each day had attempted unsuccessfully to board buses used to transport white students to neighboring counties. 200 to 300 of the county's 585 black students had boycotted the black schools and attended a freedom school. Frequent street marches had been held. The Rev. Dr. Martin Luther King Jr. announced after the Oct. 14 court ruling that demonstrations would be halted.

Incidents accompanying the demonstrations had included an attack on a teen-aged demonstrator Oct. 4 by Georgia Ku Klux Klan grand dragon Calvin Craig. Craig twisted the demonstrator's arm and threw him against a car while onlooking crowds shouted "Kill him!" Craig was arrested on an assault charge and released on $100 bond. SCLC photographer Brigido Cabe, 23, was attacked Oct. 12 by Cecil Myers, 26, a member of the Black Knights of the Ku Klux Klan; a fellow Klansman, John Howard Sims, 43, was restrained by state troopers from joining in the assault. Myers was charged with assault and released on $100 bond, and Cabe was arrested on charges of possession of firecrackers. (Myers and Sims had been acquitted in 1964 of the shotgun murder of Negro educator Lemuel Penn.)

Myers, Sims and 5 other Black Knights members were arrested Oct. 17 in Crawfordville on charges of forcing George Turner, a black farmer, off the road in his car and pointing guns at him after attempting to beat him. The 7 were released on bond of $250 each; 7 shotguns, 8 pistols and several clubs were taken from them by the sheriff.

SCLC official Hosea Williams reported that methods used by segregationists to fight the integration drive included beatings, jailings, the dismissal of 2 black teachers and a black principal from black schools, the dismissal of 3 black bus drivers, 2 school cooks and 2 school custodians, the dismissal from various jobs of 22 other Negroes whose children participated in the demonstrations, the evictions of 6 families from their homes and 4 foreclosures on homes and cars.

A Lincolnton, Ga. rights campaign, sponsored by the SCLC, was marked by violence Oct. 22 when about 30 white segregationists, shouting "Kill the niggers," attacked 95 black marchers. Several demonstrators were beaten, and the march was halted. A protest march the following day was called off after 117 demonstrators were turned back by 52 state troopers. Highway Patrol Information Officer William Foster told reporters, "We've got word that the town [population 1,450] is laying in wait for them [the marchers] and with more than their fists." A few minutes later, 7 civil rights workers were injured (one suffered a brain concussion) when their car overturned. SCLC Field Secy. Richard Smith charged that local whites had been "harassing and chasing" the car. Marches were suspended until Oct. 27.

About 50 Lincolnton blacks, most of them pulp mill workers, turned back an Oct. 28 march of 30 young Negroes led by Willie Bolden, 26, the Rev. Charley Brown and Edward Bedford, all of the SCLC. Sylvester Glaze, speaking for the group that confronted the demonstrators, said: "You can't change anything. ... And after you leave here we'll be left alone to catch the devil. ... Our children are too scared to go to school because of all this mess." Bolden led a march of about 65 demonstrators escorted by about 40 state policemen Oct. 29 without interference. Speaking at a rally in front of the courthouse following the march, he accused local black laborers of "selling their souls to feed their families." Daily marches continued without incident through Oct. 31, and more than 20 Negroes lined up at the Lincoln County courthouse Nov. 1 and registered to vote.

Dr. Beverly Holland White, a white Daytona Beach, Fla. physician, was charged Nov. 10 with the burning of an abandoned black church and an abandoned house in Jones County, Ga. and with the burning of another black church in neighboring Twiggs County. The arson had taken place Nov. 8.

Murder & Segregationist Attacks in Bogalusa

A civil rights campaign in Bogalusa, La. led to segregationist attacks on demonstrators and clashes with police during 1965.

O'Neal Moore, 34, a black deputy sheriff of Washington Parish, was killed late June 2 while on car-patrol near Bogalusa by shots fired from a pick-up truck. Creed Rodgers, a black deputy riding in the car, was wounded in the shooting but gave a radio alarm that led an hour later to the arrest in Tylertown, Miss., 40 miles away, of Ernest Ray McElveen, 41, a white resident of Bogalusa, who was charged with murder. The black deputies were the first Negroes to serve in such posts in the parish.

After the shooting, homes of black leaders in Bogalusa were guarded by members of the Deacons of Defense & Justice, a new black organization reportedly being activated in Louisiana, Mississippi and Alabama for armed defense against attacks by whites.

The civil rights campaign in Bogalusa was resumed July 7 and continued despite 2 personal interventions and appeals for a moratorium from Louisiana Gov. John J. McKeithen July 12-13. Both sides in the Bogalusa dispute—Mayor Jesse H. Cutrer Jr. and the city council, and the Bogalusa Civic & Voters League (backed by the Congress of Racial Equality)—appealed to Pres. Johnson July 14 for help in settling the troubled racial situation in the city.

A march to the city hall was held July 7 by about 350 persons, including a few white non-residents, to present desegregation demands to the mayor. 107 state and local police stood guard. Another march was held July 8. As it broke up, a white man, Alton D. Crowe Jr., 25, attacked 2 Negroes—Henry Austin, 21, and Milton Johnson, 26—and was shot and seriously wounded. Austin (who reputedly fired the shots) and Johnson were immediately arrested. Further rights marches were canceled July 9-10 due to increased local racial tension.

U.S. District Court Judge Herbert W. Christenberry July 10 refused an appeal from Bogalusa officials for an order temporarily halting rights demonstrations. Christenberry said that such action was unnecessary since the city already was empowered to prevent or delay demonstrations deemed dangerous. Christenberry, ruling July 10 on a black appeal, enjoined Bogalusa authorities from using violence or threats to prevent Negroes from exercising their civil rights and ordered protection given them from harassment by white townspeople.

Demonstrations were resumed July 11 when more than 600 Negroes and white sympathizers marched in silence behind CORE

National Director James Farmer. Additional state police had been sent to Bogalusa the previous night, and a total of about 400 policemen, some armed with submachine guns, enforced tight security along the parade route. Similar marches were held July 12-14.

A counter-protest march by segregationists was staged in Bogalusa July 11, prior to that day's rights demonstration, and more than 500 whites participated.

Heavy police guard was on hand for the segregationist demonstration. The segregationists were led by J. B. Stoner of Atlanta, Ga. and Connie Lynch of Riverside, Calif. Stoner and Lynch also had staged rallies in the Bogalusa area under sponsorship of the National States Rights Party.

Gov. McKeithen intervened July 12. He conferred in Baton Rouge with A. Z. Young and Robert Hicks, president and vice president, respectively, of the Voters League, and appealed for a 30-day cooling-off period. Young and Hicks, flown to and from the meeting in the governor's private plane, returned to Bogalusa to present his proposal to the League. The McKeithen appeal for a moratorium was opposed at a League meeting held later July 12. Young later phoned McKeithen that his proposal would be rejected unless concessions were made to the black group. McKeithen flew to Bogalusa July 13 and met with the black leaders at the city airport, but he failed to deter their rejection of his plan.

Rights pickets at a Bogalusa shopping center July 16 were attacked 6 times by whites without interference by nearby police. State police witnessed the attacks but remained aloof on the ground that the shopping center was private property outside their jurisdiction. On the 7th attack, they arrested 2 attackers and one demonstrator. City police arrived after the attacks and arrested 7 pickets for trespassing. Shopping center pickets July 17 were soaked with water hoses. No arrests were reported. A rights march July 16 by about 400 integrationists was broken up by city police about midway between its starting point and the Bogalusa city hall, its intended goal. Marchers July 17 were pelted with rocks and fruit by integrationists, and 3 marchers were taken into "protective custody."

Rights demonstrations continued in Bogalusa under more stringent police protection following the filing, by the U.S. Justice Department July 19, of separate criminal and civil contempt actions against Bogalusa Public Safety Commissioner Arnold Spiers and Police Chief Claxton Knight. The suits against Spiers and Knight were filed on the basis of their allegedly "willful disobedience" of Judge Christenberry's July 10 order requiring protection of

Negroes and rights demonstrators. The suits were filed by Asst. Atty. Gen. John Doar, who had been dispatched to Bogalusa by Pres. Johnson as his mediator in the dispute. In addition to the contempt suits, Doar also filed Justice Department suits against: (1) the Original Knights of the Ku Klux Klan, its leader and 20 members and 15 other persons in the Bogalusa area for allegedly following "a violent design to prevent Negro efforts to achieve equal rights"; (2) Washington Parish Deputy Sheriff Walter Vertrees Adams on counts of police brutality against Negroes; (3) 3 restaurants in Bogalusa on grounds of violation of the public accommodations clause of the 1964 Civil Rights Act.

(Acting on the suits filed by Doar, the U.S. 5th Circuit Court of Appeals Dec. 1 issued an injunction ordering the Ku Klux Klan to cease "acts of terror and intimidation" against Negroes in Bogalusa. The defendants were forbidden to interfere with Negroes' rights to use public accommodations, to register and vote and to seek employment. The court found that "the Klan relies on systematic economic coercion, varieties of intimidation and physical violence in attempting to frustrate the national policy expressed in civil rights legislation.")

After the court action was initiated July 19, Knight and Spiers had broadcast over radio and TV a warning that persons attempting to harass rights workers would face arrest "on the spot." (Knight and Spiers were convicted by Judge Christenberry July 30 of civil contempt for violating his July 10 injunction.)

A rights march was staged without incident in Bogalusa later July 19 as police kept crowds from forming. Radio appeals for law and order were continued July 20-21 by police officials and civil leaders. Marches and tests of compliance with the public accommodations provision continued, but without major incident.

Judge Christenberry conducted civil contempt hearings in New Orleans Dec. 28-30 to determine whether Spiers, Knight and Sheriff's Deputies Walter Vertrees Adams and Sidney J. Lyons had violated Christenberry's July 10 injunction. The new charges stemmed from complaints of unprovoked arrests of Negroes and police brutality Oct. 20. Witnesses for the police testified that police had dispersed black marchers with minimum force; Negroes testified, however, that they had been severely beaten and arrested without provocation. Christenberry commented Dec. 29 that the Oct. 20 incident represented "a deliberate scheme to harass these people, confuse them and throw them in jail."

Elsewhere in Lousiana during 1965, police reported the throwing of firebombs into 2 black homes in Ferriday July 27. The home of Robert Lewis Jr., black president of the Ferriday Freedom Movement, was damaged Nov. 21 by what appeared to be a gasoline bomb. Lewis, his wife and 5 children were unhurt. Police arriving on the scene arrested Lewis, who had been standing with a shotgun in front of his house, on a charge of aggravated battery.

2 black churches near Slidell were burned Aug. 3, and a motel and a hotel housing civil rights workers were bombed in Baton Rouge Aug. 12. No injuries were reported.

Violence in Mississippi

Racial violence was reported in various parts of Mississippi during 1965.

Allie W. Shelby, 18, a Flora, Miss. Negro, was shot to death in the Hinds County jail-house in Jackson, Miss. Jan. 22 after he had been arrested, convicted and sentenced to 6 months in jail on charges of making indecent gestures at a white woman in Jackson earlier Jan. 22. Authorities said that Shelby had attacked 2 Jackson policemen as he was being led into the jail. According to the authorities, O. E. Sanderford, a deputy sheriff, then fired one harmless warning shot and finally shot Shelby in the head when he kept resisting. A coroner's jury later Jan. 22 ruled the death justifiable homicide.

A Freedom School and library with 2,000 volumes in Indianola, Miss. was destroyed by fire Mar. 5. Police later Mar. 5 arrested 8 civil rights workers on charges of interfering with an investigation of possible arson suspects. (A Freedom House in Laurel, Miss. had been set afire a few days previously.)

Negroes and white integrationists staged a 2-day 14-mile march from Fannin to Brandon, Miss. May 28-29 to protest vote discrimination, church burnings and the seating in Congress of Mississippi's 5 Representatives. (5 Negro churches had been burned in the area's Rankin County in the past year.) State police, under instructions from Gov. Paul R. Johnson Jr., escorted the marchers.

The march, carried out without incident, was sponsored by the Congress of Racial Equality (CORE) and the Mississippi Freedom Democratic Party, which had challenged the seating of the state's Congressmen on the ground that Mississippi Negroes were denied the vote. The march ended at the county courthouse in Brandon May 29. The marchers were met by city and county officials, who guided the Negroes into the Registrar's Office to begin vote registration.

A temporary restraining order barring Jackson officials from arresting voting-rights demonstrators under the city's parade and handbill ordinances was issued by a 3-judge federal court in New Orleans June 30. More than 800 persons, possibly as many as 1,000, had been arrested under the ordinances during the Mississippi Legislature's current special session in Jackson. The demonstrations, begun June 14, had been staged to protest that the legislature was illegally constituted because of Mississippi's denial of the vote to its black citizens.

70 demonstrators had been arrested in Jackson June 24 on breach-of-peace and resisting-arrest charges after protesting against alleged police brutality. Charges of police brutality against those arrested were made by 3 members of the Commission on Religion & Race of the National Council of Churches and by Dr. David M. French of the Medical Committee on Human Rights. Rights lawyers reported that 60 of those arrested had signed statements charging police brutality. A Jackson medical center reported treating 4 demonstrators with visible injuries.

3 days of peaceful protest marches were begun by rights leaders in Jackson July 1 under the protection afforded by the June 30 court order. The marchers were watched closely by local and federal officers as they followed the procedures specified in the court order: demonstrators were to march 2 abreast and obey all traffic rules and other regulations. The marchers followed a 2-hour route that took them past the state capitol, the governor's mansion and through the downtown section of Jackson. No marchers were arrested during the 3 days of peaceful demonstrations, but police seized a white man July 3 when he attacked the black Rev. Allen Johnson, pastor of the Pratt Memorial Methodist Church, who was leading that day's march.

The Rev. Donald A. Thompson, 59, white minister of the integrated First Unitarian Church in Jackson, Miss., was seriously wounded by 2 shotgun blasts fired from ambush as he was entering his apartment in Jackson Aug. 22. The shooting occurred after Thompson had driven a black member of his church to the Hind County headquarters of the NAACP following a meeting at the church. Thompson was secretary of the integrationist Mississippi Council of Human Relations. Thompson left Mississippi for Boston Nov. 19 after receiving threats on his life.

Headquarters of the integrationist Council of Federated Organizations in Columbia, Miss. was damaged by fire and riddled with bullets in a predawn attack by nightriders July 31.

Civil rights leader George Metcalfe was seriously injured in Natchez, Miss. Aug. 27 when a bomb exploded in his car as he was leaving work. Metcalfe, 55, who suffered a broken arm and leg in the explosion, was president of the NAACP's local branch and chairman of the black-voter registration drive in Adams County. The NAACP's Mississippi field secretary, Charles Evers, went to Natchez after the incident and was credited with averting a retaliatory outbreak from hundreds of incensed Negroes.

544 Negroes were arrested in Natchez, Oct. 1-7 on charges of violating an injunction forbidding demonstrations. The injunction had been issued Sept. 30 by the Chancery Court to halt street protests against segregated public facilities and other alleged discriminatory practices. Marches had begun Sept. 7 with the withdrawal of 650 National Guardsmen. (The Guardsmen had been sent into the city by Gov. Johnson following the Metcalfe bombing.) 265 of those arrested, including Charles Evers, the campaign leader, were sent by bus to the state prison at Parchman, 200 miles from Natchez. After spending up to 5 days in prison, the demonstrators arranged for their release on bond of $200 each.

Demonstrations were suspended in Natchez Oct. 7 to give city officials a chance to consider a revised list of NAACP demands. A boycott of most downtown stores by Negroes continued. Black leaders met with city officials Oct. 13, but disagreement broke out as to what was accomplished. Evers said at a black rally that the city had agreed to hire black policemen, appoint a black school board member, establish a biracial housing commission, integrate the local hospital and instruct city employes to address black adults as "Mr.," "Miss" or "Mrs." Mayor John Nosser Oct. 14 denied that the city had promised to put a Negro on the school board, desegregate the hospital or use courtesy titles in addressing blacks. A march of 600 Negroes through the business district took place Oct. 16 to protest "reneging on agreements"; Evers then said that marches would be suspended but the boycott continued. Nosser Dec. 3 finally announced an agreement under which the boycott would be ended in exchange for concessions by the city. But Evers Dec. 23 announced the resumption of the boycott. Evers charged Natchez police with brutality in quelling a fight Dec. 22 between a white man and one of 7 blacks picketing a store that had refused to hire Negroes. The Negro had been pushed through a store window, and other Negroes resisted police attempts to restore order. 6 Negroes and the white man were arrested.

A bomb exploded early Nov. 29 in a car parked near a black grocery in Vicksburg, Miss., where local black leaders were reported to have been planning an economic boycott of certain white merchants. The explosion caused heavy damage to the store, injured at least 3 persons and demolished the car. Windows in several adjoining homes and stores were shattered and a passing taxi was overturned.

North Carolina Violence

Black voting-rights demonstrations, started in Plymouth, N.C. in early August, were marked by outbursts of violence Aug. 26 and 31, 1965

The first incident involved a reported attack and beating of 27 black and white rights workers in downtown Plymouth after a Ku Klux Klan rally. The 2d incident occurred when a crowd of whites reportedly "closed in" on a small group of Negroes attempting to walk through the crowd after a planned black march had been canceled. One of the Negroes allegedly fired a pistol and wounded a white. Another white was stabbed in the ensuing mêlée. Albien Arrington, 33, a Negro accused of firing the pistol, was later arrested and charged with assault.

100 state highway patrolmen were dispatched to Plymouth by Gov. Dan Moore Aug. 31 on the strength of reports of a movement of Ku Klux Klansmen into the area. 2 white men were arrested by patrolmen Sept. 1 on charges of "going dangerously armed," and 11 more were arrested Sept. 2 at roadblocks set up for weapons checking. The governor met in Raleigh Sept. 2 with Robert Jones, grand dragon of the Ku Klux Klan in North Carolina. Jones said afterwards that he had ordered Klan members to stay out of Plymouth unless they lived there.

The Charlotte, N.C. homes of 4 Negroes active in civil rights were bombed in the early morning of Nov. 22. Damage was extensive, but nobody was hurt. The 4 men were Kelly Alexander, NAACP state president; Fred D. Alexander, his brother and the first Negro since Reconstruction to be elected (in May 1965) to Charlotte's City Council; Julius L. Chambers, 29, a civil rights attorney whose car had been bombed in New Bern, N.C. in January; Dr. Reginald A. Hawkins, a dentist.

Northern Cities Hit by Protests & Racial Strife

Civil rights protests and racial strife increasingly bedeviled Northern cities. Among such developments during 1965:

Chicago—Civil rights demonstrations were started June 10 against the rehiring of Schools Supt. Benjamin C. Willis. Street sit-downs and marches to city hall and the school board June 10 tied up traffic for 4 hours in the business district. In a similar demonstration June 11 225 persons were arrested, including CORE National Director James Farmer, black comedian Dick Gregory and 9 clergymen. 80 persons were arrested June 28 for lying down on a downtown street after a conference between Mayor Richard J. Daley and rights leaders had failed to produce a commitment from Daley to request Willis' resignation. By then the number of persons arrested totaled 656.

The Rev. Dr. Martin Luther King Jr. and his Southern Christian Leadership Conference conducted a civil rights campaign in Chicago July 24-26. The drive culminated in the largest rights demonstration in Chicago's history—a march to city hall July 26 by 10,000 (police estimate) to 20,000 (King's estimate) demonstrators. It was the 42d march to city hall in 47 days in the continuing campaign against alleged school discrimination.

Several hundred Negroes, most of them teen-agers or in their 20s, rioted in the largely-black Lawndale (West Garfield Park) district of Chicago's West Side the nights of Aug. 12-13 and 13-14. Some minor disturbances were reported the night of Aug. 14-15, but the area was considered under effective control by then. About 80 persons were injured and 140 arrested in the incidents. The disorders had broken out after a freak accident in which a black woman was killed by a fire engine from an all-white fire station that had been a target of black demands for integration. Acting on a request of Chicago Police Supt. Orlando W. Wilson, Gov. Otto Kerner ordered 2,000 Illinois National Guard troops Aug. 14 to stand-by alert in Chicago armories, but a force of 500 Chicago policemen subdued the disorders without Guardsmen being used.

The disturbance had begun when a hook-and-ladder truck, answering a false alarm the night of Aug. 12, struck a traffic standard. The standard fell and killed Dessie Mae Williams, 20. A crowd of young blacks gathered, and some members of the crowd began stoning the fire station. The turmoil grew, 7 persons were injured, and the police arrested 18 Negroes.

Negroes gathered near the fire house the evening of Aug. 13 to hear embittered speeches by Lawrence Landry and other leaders of a militant civil rights group called ACT. Rioting followed. Blacks beat whites, fought policemen and attacked cars and stores with rocks, bottles and molotov cocktails. Nearly 1,000 persons were involved. 60 persons, including 18 policemen, were injured and 104 more persons were arrested before the violence was ended early Aug. 14.

Sporadic, minor disturbances the night of Aug. 14-15 brought 18 more arrests.

The home of James Brown, 56, a Negro who had moved Nov. 6 into a white section of South Side Chicago, was pelted with bricks and molotov cocktails Nov. 11.

Cleveland—White and black pupils fought each other at the 3,320-student Collinwood High School in Cleveland, O. Mar. 18 after what were described as a series of minor racial incidents. 2 white boys were hospitalized. Classes were cancelled for the day. When classes resumed Mar. 19, 36 adults and teen-agers were arrested in the school area on charges of disorderly conduct or juvenile delinquency.

Detroit—Eddie Cook, 53, a black sanitation worker, died in Detroit General Hospital Nov. 7 after being hit by a shotgun blast from a car carrying 5 white youths. Police said they had been told that the car had been hit earlier with a bottle thrown by black teen-agers.

Lakewood, N.J.—2 adjacent homes being built for Negroes in a predominantly white section of Lakewood, N.J. were burned Oct. 10 in an apparent case of arson. Members of the Township Council established a fund to help restore the property.

New York—N.Y. City police Feb. 16 arrested 3 black men described as pro-Peking and pro-Castro and a Canadian white woman on charges of plotting to blow up the Statue of Liberty in New York, the Liberty Bell in Philadelphia and the Washington Monument in Washington, D.C.

Those arrested were: Robert Steele Collier, 28, leader of an extremist group known as the Black Liberation Front and alleged leader of the plotters; Walter Augustus Bowe, 32, and Khaleel Sultarn Sayyed, 22, aides of Collier's, and Michelle Duclos, 26, of Montreal, a member of *Rassemblement pour l'Independence,* a wing of the French-Canadian Separatist Party (an organization advocating the secession of Quebec, from Canada). Miss Duclos was said to have driven a car carrying the dynamite from Canada to New York Feb. 15.

The arrest complaint quoted Collier as admitting that he planned the dynamiting "to draw attention to the conditions of my race."

Philadelphia—Black mobs smashed store windows and burned an auto in a series of riot-like disturbances in North Philadelphia, Pa. the night of Aug. 16-17.

Springfield, Mass.—A series of demonstrations against alleged police brutality in Springfield, Mass. led to the burning of 2 white-owned stores by young blacks late Aug. 13 and the arrest of 72 civil rights demonstrators, most of them Negroes, by Aug. 16.

The immediate brutality charge arose from the arrest of 17 black men and a white woman in a disturbance at a Negro bar July 17. After a promised brutality inquiry failed to begin, a CORE-sponsored "camp-out" was started Aug. 7 at City Hall. 25 black and white "camp-out" demonstrators (7 of them from outside Springfield) were arrested Aug. 13, and a few hours later black youths smashed windows and burned the 2 stores a—grocery and a trading stamp center—in the black section of Winchester Square, about 1½ miles from City Hall.

As tensions rose, 250 black and white demonstrators marched late Aug. 14 from Springfield's black section to city hall. At 1:50 a.m. Aug. 15 the police arrested 40 black and 4 white demonstrators who had remained sitting on blankets in the town square across the street from city hall.

NATIONWIDE VIOLENCE (1966)

Violence Across the U.S.

Urban riots blazed in cities throughout the U.S. in 1966. The Watts district of Los Angeles erupted in a 2d riot. In Chicago, Puerto Ricans rioted in June and Negroes in July. Looting, sniping and firebombing swept Cleveland's Hough district. Omaha blacks threw rocks and firecrackers at police before a looting, window-breaking rampage. White youths made a violent invasion of Baltimore's black district. Gangs of white, black and Puerto Rican youths battled in Brooklyn. Negroes rioted in Dayton, Clashes between Cicero, Ill. civil rights activists and white hecklers resulted in the bayoneting of 6 persons by National Guardsmen. Negroes rioted in Atlanta after 2 blacks were shot and killed. Black youths smashed windows and hurled firebombs in San Francisco's Hunter's Point area.

Violence was reported in other cities in the North and West. Individual mass killers ran amok in Chicago and Austin, Tex. Firebombings, dynamite blasts, beatings, riots and murder continued in the South.

2d Watts Outbreak

Violence simmering in the black Watts district of Los Angeles surfaced in an attack on 2 sheriff's deputies Jan. 30. Deputies Raymond Stewart, 25, and Ronald Dowling, 31, were assaulted in Watts by about 20 persons as they intervened in a fight between 2 youths. A crowd of about 100 persons watched the incident but dispersed when police reinforcements arrived. 3 persons were arrested on charges of felony assault on a law enforcement officer.

Full-scale rioting broke out Mar. 15 in a 12-square-block area of Watts about 3 miles from the center of the riot of 1965. Casualties were 2 dead and about 20 injured; 49 persons (26 adults and 23 juveniles) were arrested, and 19 buildings were damaged.

The turmoil started as classes were being released from the Jordan High School. A band of students began to throw stones and bricks at cars, and a white driver was hit and slightly injured. When police arrested a black boy, a mob of about 200 gathered and began throwing things at the police. Sporadic looting and burning of cars and buildings followed, and about 600 persons took part. A Mexican-American truck driver, Lorenz Gomez, 35, was pulled from his truck and shot to death. The other person slain, also by gunfire, was described by police as "a Negro named Crawford."

The rioting was brought under control in about 4 hours, with 200 policemen patrolling the area (the normal force was 24) and roadblocks set up at major streets. Los Angeles Mayor Samuel W. Yorty had instructed Acting Police Chief Harold W. Sullivan to put into effect "a maximum force plan of operations," a troop deployment method worked out after the 1965 riot.

Gov. Edmund G. Brown, who had been in Washington to address the National Press Club, flew to Los Angeles late Mar. 15. On his arrival, Brown said he had been "tipped 3 days ago" that violence might erupt in Watts. In his Washington speech Brown had outlined a pilot program getting under way in California to make "the full range of state services" available "under a single roof." He said the "service-center concept" had been developed in response to "the tragedy of Watts" and "the need to do more to ease tensions around the state which that rioting revealed."

The riot area was calm Mar. 16, but intensive police patrols continued. 3 additional arrests were made Mar. 17. Those arrested were 3 Mexican-American brothers, Joe, Carlos and Robert Garcia, who, police said, had injured 2 black youths Mar. 14 with shotgun blasts. The incident was thought to have created tension that contributed to the Mar. 15 outburst.

Sam Henry Fulton, 18, a Negro, was convicted in Los Angeles July 30 of first-degree murder in the slaying of Lorenz Gomez during the Mar. 15 riot.

The Commerce Department Mar. 8 had released a special census of south Los Angeles; the study, financed by the Office of Economic Opportunity, had been requested by Dr. Andrew F. Brimmer, Assistant Commerce Secretary for Economic Affairs and a member of the McCone Commission, which had conducted a study of the 1965 riot. The study showed that (1) the average annual purchasing power of families in south Los Angeles had declined $400 in the 1960-5 period, when average U.S. family purchasing power rose 14% and non-white purchasing power rose 24%; (2) the male unemployment rate in the area had declined 1% in 1960-5, while the national non-white male unemployment rate had declined 6% (the male unemployment rate in Watts stood at 13.2%).

The Housing & Urban Development Department May 27 announced a grant of funds to California to establish bus service from the eastern border of Watts to an industrial area in western Los Angeles. The new transportation system, based on a recommendation in the McCone Commission report, was designed to enable Watts' black residents to get to an area where jobs were available.

Gov. Brown July 28 had signed legislation making incitement to riot a misdemeanor. The law had been sought by Los Angeles officials.

The McCone Commission Aug. 17 issued a report on progress made in Watts since the 1965 riot. The report stated that there had been "significant progress" on all but a few of the recommendations the commission had made but warned that "tension has continued to be high." It stressed the need to raise the level of Negro education, in Watts and in other parts of the country. The report noted that jobs had been found for 10,000 of Watts' 25,000 unemployed, that bus service to jobs and job-training centers had been expanded and that improvement had been made in law enforcement practices.

A 9-member coroner's jury in Los Angeles May 31 exonerated Ptl. Jerold M. Bova, 23, in the fatal shooting May 7 of Leonard Deadwyler, 25, a Negro. The incident occurred as Bova was apprehending Deadwyler for speeding in Watts. Scattered outbursts of violence, including the tossing of a molotov cocktail outside a police station annex and sniper shots at a police car, occurred in Watts June 1, apparently in reaction to the jury's finding; there were no injuries or arrests in either incident.

The inquest heard 46 witnesses in proceedings that were marked by near-violence. The opening session May 19 was moved from a hall seating 250 persons to one seating 400 when a predominantly black crowd of 1,000 attempted to attend; the session was adjourned after 30 minutes because of the audience's unruliness. Security procedures, including the searching of everyone entering the courthouse, were instituted May 20, and the audience dwindled May 23 when a local TV outlet began to furnish live coverage of the proceedings. Mrs. Barbara Deadwyler, 25, pregnant widow of the victim, testified May 24 that her husband had been speeding to get her to a hospital because she was suffering apparent labor pains; according to her testimony, Ptl. Bova had fired a shot without provocation after her husband had requested a police escort to the hospital. Bova, however, testified May 25 that his service revolver had discharged accidentally when the car had suddenly lurched forward while he was leaning through the right front window, his gun drawn, attempting to gain Deadwyler's attention. Dr. Thomas Noguchi, a medical examiner, testified May 26 that a posthumous blood test showed Deadwyler's blood to have a .35% alcohol content. The standard intoxication threshold was .15%.

Police conduct in Watts was bitterly attacked May 16 by 2 black ministers preaching at Deadwyler's funeral, attended by several hundred Negroes. A rally held May 17 to protest the shooting resulted in violence when members of a crowd of 500, who had marched from the rally to the police station, looted a liquor store, fired shots and attacked 2 *Newsweek* magazine reporters, Karl Fleming, 38, and David Moburg, 22. Fleming was hospitalized with a broken jaw; Moburg suffered a black eye and bruises. Helmeted, shotgun-armed patrolmen dispersed the crowd and arrested 11. 4 additional arrests were made May 24 after rock-throwing blacks injured 2 white motorists driving through Watts.

A Negro-organized Citizens Alert Patrol, whose purpose was "to collect, analyze and channel ... accurate reports growing out of charges of police misbehavior," was inaugurated in Los Angeles' Watts district June 10. The patrol, in which 10 cars equipped with 2-way radios and cameras were to follow police cars each night and observe police investigations, was formed by the Watts Temporary Alliance of Local Organizations as an outgrowth of Deadwyler's death.

Puerto Ricans & Negroes Riot in Chicago

Puerto Ricans rioted in Chicago's Northwest Side in June, and blacks rioted in Chicago's West Side in July. Demonstrations against segregated housing in the Southwest Side brought clashes between whites and police.

An incident involving a policeman and a Puerto Rican youth June 12 set off the 3 days of violence in a Puerto Rican neighborhood on Chicago's Northwest Side. By the time calm was restored June 15, 116 persons had been arrested, most of them on disorderly conduct charges, and at least 16 persons had been injured (8 of them shot).

The rioting was touched off when Patrolman Thomas Munyon shot a Puerto Rican, Cruz Arcelis, 21, in the leg. Munyon said Arcelis had pointed a gun at him; neighborhood witnesses disputed Munyon's story. A crowd of about 1,000 persons—later swelling to 4,000—then set fire to 4 police squad cars and attacked firemen attempting to extinguish the blazes. About 100 helmeted policemen and a number of police dogs were brought in. A *Chicago Tribune* photographer was beaten and his camera smashed by the mob, and a policeman received hospital treatment after being hit by a brick. 49 persons were arrested, but charges against 2 of them were dismissed by Judge George N. Leighton, who said that the 2 policemen making the arrests had used "excessive force." Raymond Howard, one of the patrolmen involved and Patrolman Munyon's squad partner, was transferred from the district June 13 and resigned from the force later in the day.

Violence was resumed the afternoon of June 13 after a squad car hit by a rock swerved onto the sidewalk toward the rock-thrower and barely missed several Puerto Ricans. A crowd of about 500 then gathered; community leaders, identified by red, white and blue ribbons issued by police, attempted to restore order. At a rally that evening attended by 1,200 persons, Puerto Rican leaders called for an end to the rioting. But after the rally a crowd broke windows and stoned cars. 36 persons were arrested, and 7 Puerto Ricans were shot, one of them critically injured with a head wound. Other people, including several policemen and 3 reporters, were injured by rocks and bricks.

Community leaders conferred June 14 with Mayor Richard J. Daley and other city officials. Police Supt. Orlando W. Wilson then announced that the use of police dogs in the riot area would be discontinued, that the police would hold regular meetings with Puerto Rican leaders, that more Latin-American patrolmen would be hired and that other policemen would be encouraged to study Spanish. (The disorder was reported to have been exacerbated by the inability of the police to communicate with the area's Spanish-speaking residents.)

Minor outbreaks of violence June 14 resulted in 31 arrests. Helmeted patrolmen were stationed at close intervals around the riot area, and Police Supt. Wilson ordered 100 neighborhood taverns to remain closed until further notice.

Sentences were meted out in Circuit Court June 17 to about 40 of those arrested during the disturbances. Punishments ranged from $100 fines to 6 months under court supervision.

In the aftermath of the rioting, Puerto Rican community leader Claudio Flores, 42, publisher of the Spanish-language newspaper *El Puertorriqueno,* was sworn in June 22 as a member of the Mayor's Commission on Human Relations.

8 white persons were arrested June 24 in Calumet Park, a Chicago South Side beach along Lake Micigan traditionally used only by whites. Attempts by blacks and Puerto Ricans to use the

park during June had been met by taunts and occasional attacks from whites; a cross had been burned at the beach June 2 while a civil rights group staged a demonstration.

3 nights of rioting swept Chicago's West Side black district July 12-15. The disorders started after police July 12 shut off a fire hydrant that had been opened illegally to give black children relief from the 98° heat. Order was restored with the aid of National Guardsmen July 15, but 2 Negroes were killed, scores of police and civilians wounded or injured and 372 persons arrested. Losses from property damage and looting, primarily suffered by white-owned stores, were reported to be extensive.

The 800-square-block West Side area had an estimated population of 300,000 Negroes. It was the traditional destination in Chicago of blacks newly arrived from the South and appeared to be a greater magnet for disturbances than the more established and somewhat more prosperous South Side black ghetto.

The first arrest, which helped ignite the anger and resentment leading to the rioting, was of a neighborhood resident who had reopened a fire hydrant after police had shut it. On-lookers, some of whom claimed that police had permitted Italian children to play in the water from open fire hydrants in an adjoining Italian section, shouted "Police brutality!" Before long they were stoning police cars, breaking store windows and looting. Police reinforcements were brought in, and 24 others were arrested. 9 persons reportedly were injured, including 2 policemen.

Rioting flared again July 13 after police shut another gushing fire hydrant. A group of at least 100 black youths reacted by throwing rocks, bottles and bricks at a police car. During the night of July 13-14, roving black mobs traded gunfire with police, looted stores, tossed molotov cocktails into buildings and stoned firemen attempting to put out the resulting fires. About 300 policemen restored order early July 14. They arrested about 35 persons. 32 policemen were reported injured (7 required hospitalization). 2 Negroes were hospitalized with gunshot wounds from stray bullets, and about 50 others were otherwise injured.

The night of July 14-15 had 7 hours of rioting in which more than 1,000 police tried to cope with about 5,000 rampaging blacks. 2 Negroes—identified as Rosalynd Howard, 14, and Raymond Williams, 28—were killed in crossfire between police and rioters, and 6 policemen were shot by snipers. 282 area residents were arrested, and about 50 were injured by gunfire or flying objects. A number of firemen were injured as they rushed to fires set with molotov cocktails. 6 neighborhood fire stations were evacuated later July 15 to protect firemen and their equipment. The worst fire set during the night (300 firemen and 60 pieces of equipment fought it) was in a bottling plant and adjoining packing company.

During the night of July 14-15, police raided a basement meeting and arrested 12 blacks, including Frederick Andrews, a leader of the militant ACT group. Plans to charge them with "conspiracy to commit treason" were dropped although the arrest slips bore the treason charge. A gun and pamphlets proposing civil disobedience were seized in the raid.

Daytime looting took place for the first time the afternoon of July 15, and Gov. Otto Kerner called out the National Guard at the request of Chicago Mayor Daley. 4,000 Guardsmen reported to Chicago armories. Armed with rifles, bayonets, pistols, machine-guns and tear-gas grenades, 1,500 of them then entered the riot area in troop trucks and jeeps. Gen. Francis Kane, their commander, said he had ordered his men "to shoot to kill" if they were shot at. Before the Guardsmen entered the area, police had sealed off several streets; they said they were unable to control looting from stores whose windows had been smashed. After the Guardsmen moved in, violence was reduced to isolated outbreaks. 51 persons were arrested the night of July 15-16.

An 80-minute meeting to discuss the rioting was held July 15 by Mayor Daley and the Rev. Dr. Martin Luther King Jr., whose Southern Christian Leadership Conference (SCLC) had been active on the West Side since January. The mayor and King had held an inconclusive meeting July 11 to discuss demands for neighborhood improvement listed by King July 10. At a joint news conference following the July 15 meeting, King and Daley announced agreement by the city to a program to ease tensions. The city agreed to: (1) install spray nozzles on fire hydrants on the West Side; (2) seek federal funds to build swimming pools and other recreational facilities on the West Side (there were 4 public pools in the vicinity of the West Side, but hostile whites reportedly had kept blacks from using all but one); (3) appoint a citizens committee to study relations between the police department and minority groups; (4) assign 2 neighborhood residents as assistants to each precinct captain to work in the area to calm disorders.

Daley charged at the press conference that SCLC staff members working in Chicago had "no other purpose than to bring disorder to the streets" and had been "instructing people in how to conduct violence." King, who had launched the Chicago SCLC drive Jan. 7, retorted that the charge was "absolutely untrue";

he had accused the mayor July 13 of "inviting social disaster" by rejecting his July 10 demands.

King had tried during the riot, without visible success, to stem the disturbances. He had met July 14 with 100 clergymen and nuns; then the group had walked through the West Side, pleading for nonviolence. King's calls for nonviolence won tentative acceptance July 16, after King and other SCLC officials had held a conference through the night with 15 leaders of West Side youth gangs. The Rev. Andrew J. Young, the SCLC's executive director, announced July 16 that the young men had pledged their gangs—the Cobras, Vice Lords and Roman Saints—to "try nonviolence." Young said that gang members had been responsible for most of the rioting and that their leaders were "the only ones who can control them." He outlined a number of grievances presented by the youths, including the "desperate need for jobs" (unemployment in the area was estimated at 25%), the alleged subservience of local politicians to "the Daley machine" and alleged "police intimidation and harassment."

The first of 10 portable swimming pools newly purchased by the city was installed in a West Side playground July 17. Sprinklers had been installed on about 25 fire hydrants in the neighborhood the previous day. The hours during which permanent pools were open were extended, and it was publicly announced that all pools were open to blacks.

Daley July 25 appointed a 23-member citizens committee to recommend "ways and means of improving the relationship of the Police Department with the community." The committee included representatives of the NAACP and the Chicago Urban League but not the SCLC. It was headed by Thomas R. Mulroy, an attorney and ex-head of the Chicago Crime Commission. The last of the National Guardsmen who had been activated during the rioting were released from duty July 25.

Demonstrations against segregated housing in a Southwest Side Chicago neighborhood July 29-31 brought violent reactions from white residents. The demonstrations, part of the SCLC's "open city" campaign, began July 29 with a vigil by 40 demonstrators at the F. M. Halvorsen Realty Co. in the all-white Gage Park district. The participants were removed from the area in police vehicles after an angry crowd of whites gathered at the scene.

About 250 demonstrators, most of them black, marched into the neighborhood July 30 under the leadership of the Rev. James Bevel and the Rev. Jesse L. Jackson, SCLC officials, and Albert

A. Raby, head of the Coordinating Council of Community Organizations (CCCO). They carried signs reading "End Apartheid in Real Estate." Jeering onlookers pelted the marchers with rocks and bottles before being driven away by police. 8 persons were arrested; 6 persons were injured.

About 350 demonstrators led by Bevel staged a car caravan and march into Gage Park July 31 but fled from about 300 white hecklers. 5 of their cars, parked at a nearby park at the request of police, were overturned and burned; 2 cars were pushed into a lagoon, and the windows of 23 others were broken and their tires slashed. 12 whites were arrested, and at least 12 persons were injured by flying objects.

In a statement issued Aug. 1 at SCLC headquarters in Atlanta, Martin Luther King scored the Chicago police for "failure to exercise full responsibility for full protection" of the marchers. King called such police laxity "especially appalling" in view of the fact that "huge masses of police and National Guardsmen were mobilized to put down the violence of a few hundred Negroes on the West Side."

Demonstrators continued protests against alleged housing discrimination in Chicago Aug. 12 and 14. Marchers, numbering in the hundreds, paraded in 3 all-white Chicago neighborhoods— Bogan (Aug. 12 and 14), Gage Park (Aug. 14) and Jefferson Park (Aug. 14). The Aug. 14 marches touched off a clash between police and whites in the Marquette Park area that injured at least 2 policemen and several blacks and led to the arrest of several whites. Demonstrations continued Aug. 16 with the picketing of city offices and real estate agencies.

A group variously estimated at from 500 to 700 persons, half of them whites, marched into the all-white Bogan neighborhood Aug. 12. 1,000 white spectators spat on the marchers, threw stones at them and shouted "Nigger, nigger, nigger" and "Hate, hate, hate." White youths carried signs reading "White Power" and decorated with Nazi swastikas. A force of some 600 policemen protected the marchers as they moved down Pulaski Road and conducted silent vigils in front of 3 real estate offices. Several demonstrators were hit by stones, but there were no serious injuries.

The new marches were preceded by several days of indecision on the part of the rights leaders. The Rev. Jesse Jackson had said at a rally Aug. 8 that marches would be conducted in Bogan and Cicero, a suburb west of Chicago, "by the weekend." As a result, the Illinois state police force was ordered on standby alert Aug. 9, and Cook County Sheriff Richard Ogilvie said the same day that he would seek a court order blocking the march into Cicero if it were not canceled. Mayor Daley appealed to the protestors Aug. 9 to negotiate rather than march, and Archbishop John P. Cody of the Chicago Archdiocese asked the demonstrators Aug. 10 to halt the marches to avert "serious injury to many persons and even the loss of life." Rights leaders agreed Aug. 10 to postpone the marches. King and Albert Raby, coordinator of the CCCO, announced in a telegram to Police Supt. O. W. Wilson Aug. 11, however, that the Bogan march would be held Aug. 12.

The simultaneous marches Aug. 14, 1966 into the Bogan and Gage Park areas of Southwest Chicago and the Jefferson Park neighborhood on the Northwest Side represented the first time that rights leaders had conducted demonstrations in more than one neighborhood in a single day. The Bogan march was led by Jesse Jackson, the Gage Park march by SCLC Executive Secy. Andrew Young and Albert Raby, and the Jefferson Park march by SCLC Program Director James Bevel. As the marchers, estimated at 675 to 1,000 persons, moved into the 3 neighborhoods, white hecklers shouted derisive slogans and threw eggs, tomatoes, bottles and cherry bombs. At least 10 injuries were reported, and police arrested 20 persons.

Rep. Roman C. Pucinski (D., Ill.), whose constituency included Jefferson Park, said Aug. 14 that "I am now convinced that these people [rights leaders] are not looking for any social justice. . . . When they plan 3 simultaneous drives in one day, it is obvious they want to dilute police protection."

After the marches had concluded, at about 7 p.m., police clashed with a crowd of 1,500 to 2,000 whites, most of them teenagers, in the Marquette Park area on the Southwest Side. Most of the whites had attended an American Nazi Party rally at which John Patler, a Nazi Party captain, had urged a "white revolution" and said that "if Negroes can march into white areas, we can march into Negro areas." Attendance at the Nazi rally was estimated at 2,000. After the rally broke up, white youths began throwing rocks, bottles and firecrackers at black motorists. 2 cars containing Negroes were damaged and a 3d burned. The arrival of 30 policemen restored order temporarily, but later 50 reinforcements had to be called in. Police fired shots in the air and used their night-sticks to break up the renewed disorder. At least 2 policemen and several blacks were injured and several whites were arrested.

Rights leaders stepped up demonstrations Aug. 16. Small numbers of pickets paraded in front of the City Hall, the Chicago

Real Estate Board headquarters, a downtown savings and loan building, Cook County Welfare Department offices and Chicago Housing Authority offices. There were no violent incidents.

That evening, however, violence broke out briefly during picketing of 6 real estate firms in the Jefferson Park neighborhood. About 500 jeering whites threw bricks and firecrackers at the pickets. About 500 policemen dispersed the crowd.

Opposition to terms of a Chicago open-housing accord signed Aug. 26 led to plans for protest marches by 2 hostile groups, but only one of the marches actually took place. George Lincoln Rockwell, 46, head of the American Nazi Party, set Sept. 10 for a march to pressure officials to withdraw their promises to Negroes. Robert L. Lucas, head of the Chicago chapter of CORE, called for a Sept. 11 march to draw attention to the need for stronger federal open-housing laws. Both men were arrested Sept. 10 shortly after the start of the anti-Negro march. 4 persons were injured and 3 others were arrested. The CORE march was canceled Sept. 11.

Rockwell was arrested Sept. 10 shortly after he had started a sidewalk march in the Englewood section of Southwest Chicago. He was charged with having solicited funds and having made a speech on Park District property without a permit during a Nazi Party rally Aug. 28 at Marquette Park. Rockwell pleaded guilty Sept. 20 and paid a $400 fine.

After Rockwell's arrest, the march was led by John Patler of Arlington, Va., Rockwell's chief aide, and Christopher Vidnjevich, head of the Chicago branch of the American Nazis. About 150 predominantly teen-age marchers participated. They were escorted by about 400 helmeted policemen. Only about 7 blocks of the 36-block march route had black residents. About 700 Negroes and 1,000 whites lined the streets; but despite minor clashes and some boos and catcalls, the marchers were ignored by most of the black community. 2 black youths were arrested in connection with the throwing of a bottle of acid at the marchers. 2 policemen and a black bystander were taken to St. Bernard Hospital and treated for acid burns.

Racial Turmoil in Cleveland

After a rock-throwing incident in June 1966, racial conflict in Cleveland's Hough area escalated into rioting in July. 4 persons died in widespread shooting, arson and looting. A grand jury report charged a small group of professional radicals and Communists with organizing and exploiting the violence.

The disturbance started when black youths in Cleveland's black neighborhood of Hough began throwing rocks at passing cars June 23 and smashing windows of Gale's Super Valu Market, a white-owned supermarket. There were also reports of black and white youths stoning each other. Several shots were fired by a white motorist at a group of black youths; Steven Griffin, 10, was hospitalized with a groin wound. Several others were taken to hospitals for treatment of cuts. The outbreaks reportedly stemmed from a fight June 22 between white and black youths who had been playing baseball in Gordon Park, between Hough and the white section of Sowinski.

Molotov cocktails were thrown from rooftops into the streets June 24, and an unsuccessful attempt was made to set fire to the supermarket that had been vandalized the previous night. At least 3 persons, 2 of them white, were treated for minor injuries. The supermarket was destroyed by a firebomb June 26.

Shooting, firebombing and looting swept through Hough July 18-23. 4 persons were killed and 50 injured; property damage, much of it stemming from about 250 fires, was widespread. 164 persons were arrested, most of them on looting charges.

The incident setting off the riot took place in a neighborhood bar. One version was that the bar's white management had refused to serve water to Negroes; another was that a woman soliciting funds for a friend's funeral had been ejected. As the disturbance escalated, bands of blacks began roaming the area, looting and throwing firebombs. Firemen who tried to put out fires were driven away by gunfire. During the night's rioting one black woman was killed and 2 black men were wounded in crossfire between snipers and police (300 policemen had been sent into the area). 6 policemen, one fireman and 2 Negroes were injured by flying objects. At least 10 buildings were destroyed by fire. More than 50 blacks were arrested. The dead woman, identified as Mrs. Joyce Arnett, 26, was shot as she leaned out of a 2d-story window to call her children.

Mayor Ralph S. Locher conferred with city officials and black leaders July 19 and then requested that the National Guard be sent to Hough. Gov. James A. Rhodes later July 19 issued a proclamation declaring that "a state of tumult, riot and other emergency" existed in Cleveland and activating 1,600 National Guardsmen for riot duty. An additional 400 Guardsmen were called up July 20 at Locher's request.

Rioting resumed shortly before nightfall July 19 with a sniper attack on police. In the ensuing exchange of fire, a black man, identified as Percy Giles, 36, was killed and 2 other persons were wounded. During 4 hours of violence, almost 40 fires were started with molotov cocktails.

Guardsmen moved into Hough late July 19; beginning July 20 they patrolled the area in 2 1,000-man units on 12-hour shifts. Traffic in the riot area was barred by Guardsmen July 20 to all but residents and persons on business, but scattered looting and firebombing broke out in midafternoon and spread during the night to black sections south and east of Hough.

Members of a black family driving from their apartment in an area east of Hough were shot at by police July 21 after the driver, Henry Towns, 22, refused to get out of the car. Towns' wife, Diana, 16, and her 3-year-old son by another marriage were wounded critically; the couple's 7-month-old son and Mrs. Towns' half-brother, Ernest Williams, 12, were also wounded, but not seriously. Towns was arrested and was charged July 22 with assault with a deadly weapon (the auto). The family, reportedly frightened by a fire in a nearby building, had been driving to a relative's home outside the riot area.

A rash of fires set with molotov cocktails broke out shortly after nightfall July 21, but no full-scale rioting took place. Scattered firebombing continued in the riot area July 22, and a Negro was killed as he walked to a bus stop about 2 miles from Hough. The victim, Sam Winchester, 54, told police before he died that he had been shot by whites in a passing car. Another Negro, Benoris Toney, 29, was attacked by whites July 23 as he drove through a lumber company parking lot between Hough and the Italian neighborhood of Murray Hill; his attackers drove their car alongside his and fired shotgun blasts through the closed window. Toney died of head wounds after 3 hours of surgery. Warren R. Lariche, 28, and Patsy C. Sabetta, 21, said to be members of a white "vigilante" group, were charged July 25 with 2d-degree murder in the shooting of Toney and were freed on $5,000 bail. A 3d suspect, Michael Jacobucci, 17, faced Juvenile Court proceedings. Police said July 25 that the shooting was a reaction to a rumor that 2 "vigilantes" had been shot by Negroes.

Calm continued in the riot area July 24 and 25; the National Guard force began reducing its strength July 26 and was completely disbanded July 31.

Cleveland Police Chief Richard R. Wagner charged July 22 that "someone has been training juveniles in the manufacture and use of firebombs." He cited a privately operated center known as the JFK House, whose initials stood for Jomo (Freedom) Kenyatta, a reference to the president of Kenya. A JFK House spokesman commented that "nobody in this town has to be taught how to make a molotov cocktail."

Public Safety Director John N. McCormick July 20 had traced the riot to "a plan to stir up trouble." He said the plotters were "200 to 300 persons," who included "young offsprings that are very difficult to control, joined by adults who thrive on disorder in the community."

The Cuyahoga County Grand Jury began an investigation of the riots July 26 and returned 8 indictments of Hough residents July 29 on charges ranging from larceny to carrying concealed weapons; the grand jury declined to indict Henry Towns for his part in the July 21 incident.

The county grand jury Aug. 9 issued its report on the Cleveland riots. The grand jury, headed by Louis B. Seltzer, retired editor of *The Cleveland Press*, had heard 7 days of testimony by about 40 witnesses, black and white. The report charged that the rioting had been "organized and exploited" by a small group of "trained and disciplined professionals," who were aided by "misguided people, many of whom are avowed believers in violence and extremism and some of whom also are either members or officers in the Communist Party." It specifically mentioned leaders of the JFK House. The report said: "Irrefutable evidence was shown to the effect that [director of the center Lewis G.] Robinson pledged reciprocal support to and with the Communist Party of Ohio. In addition, Robinson attended many meetings at which imported Communist speakers talked and was arrested at one of these." (Robinson Aug. 10 denied any Communist ties and dismissed the report as "nothing but a lot of garbage.")

The report also singled out the W.E.B. DuBois Club, asserting that its leaders, together with leaders of the Communist Youth Party, had arrived in Cleveland only a few days before the violence erupted. (Keith Allen, 25, a newscaster who had joined the club for a short time to get a feature story, had told the grand jury Aug. 1 that "as early as November of last year the Marxist-oriented group had planned racial strife in the Hough area to further the aims of socialism." Hugh Fowler, executive secretary of the clubs' national organization, rejected Allen's testimony Aug. 6. Fowler admitted that members of the club had been in the riot area but claimed that "the only thing [they] tried to do was to keep people from getting hurt.")

Black leaders in Cleveland denounced the report Aug. 10 as a "camouflage" to cover the white community's responsibility for the riots. Bertram E. Gardner, black director of the Municipal

Community Relations Board, said: "Actually, the living conditions were the things that caused the riots. . . . They [the rioters] didn't need any Communists to tell them they're suffering. . . . I think [the grand jury report] represents generally the average white man's emotional blindness against the real causes. . . ."

2 undercover agents for the Cleveland police force's anti-subversive squad, Jessie Thomas and Fred L. Giardini, both 26, who had infiltrated allegedly subversive organizations, said Aug. 11 that they had "no personal knowledge of direct Communist involvement in the riots." They said, however, that a link existed between the W.E.B. DuBois Club and JFK House.

Atty. Gen. Nicholas deB. Katzenbach testified before a Senate subcommittee Aug. 17 that "there is no indication" that the Hough and Watts riots "were planned, controlled or run by extreme leftwing elements." He discounted claims that the riots had been fomented by "Communists or black nationalists or terrorists." The real causes, he held, were "disease and despair, joblessness and hopelessness, rat-infested housing and long-impacted cynicism." Katzenbach blamed the riots on "generations of indifference by all the American people to the rot and rust and mold which we have allowed to eat into the core of our cities." During his testimony, Katzenbach warned that "some unpredictable event" could touch off rioting in "30 to 40 cities with the same problems, the same frustrations, the same tensions." He revealed that his department's Community Relations Service had assigned mediators to 40 cities with racial problems, but he agreed that some cities reject such aid.

(A black minister's newly-purchased but as yet unoccupied home in the wealthy all-white Westlake suburb of Cleveland was swept by fire Sept. 24. The Rev. John R. Compton, recently appointed executive director of the Cleveland Metropolitan Commission of the Ohio Society of Christian Churches, had bought the $23,250 home with the assistance of Fair Housing, Inc. Westlake Mayor Roman R. Alexander said Sept. 26 that Compton and his wife should have warned local officials they were moving into the neighborhood. "I think it would have been better if we knew this was coming up," he said.)

Academic & Political Comment

Dr. Sidney M. Peck, associate sociology professor at Cleveland's Western Reserve University, described the disturbances July 21 as "nothing more than the making visible of the just demands of a people that are subjected to continual indignities." "Break a few windows and things get done," he said. "It shows that violence pays off in action." He predicted that violence "may be expected to grow" unless needs of the black community were met.

Robert B. Johnson, chairman of Wilberforce University's social sciences division, commented July 21 that, unlike blacks in the South, Hough's Negroes were "destroy[ing] their own neighborhood." He said: "In the South, Negroes feel that the state or city belongs to them, and they wanted their part of it. Here, the Negro does not feel a part of the community, nor does he want any part of it."

Pres. Johnson commented on racial unrest in such cities as Chicago and Cleveland at his July 20 news conference and made general reference to such outbreaks at an Indianapolis speech July 23. The President cautioned July 20 that "while there's a Negro minority of 10% in this country, there is a majority of 90% that are not Negroes." Although most of the majority "have come around to the viewpoint of wanting to see equality and justice given their fellow citizens," he said, "they want to see it done . . . without violence." Asked whether he thought "professional agitators" were behind the riots, Johnson said he "would not want to say that the protests and the demonstrations are inspired by foreign foes," although "people who do not approve of our system" might be a contributing factor. In his July 23 address, Johnson warned that "riots . . . do not bring about lasting reforms" but rather "make reform more difficult by turning away the very people who can and must support reform." "We refuse to condone riots and disorders," he added, "not only to protect the society at large," but also "to serve the real interests of those for whose cause we struggle."

Vice Pres. Hubert H. Humphrey July 20 issued a statement clarifying a July 18 speech that had come under attack from some Republican Congressmen, who had objected to Humphrey's saying that if he were subjected to slum conditions, he might "lead a mighty good revolt" himself. The clarification cited the "opportunity for peaceful protest" afforded by "the American political and social system" and said that "there is no room in this nation for violence, riot and disorder. Such actions only add to the troubles." To "solve the basic problems" leading to riots, the statement concluded, "people who believe in law and order and social justice. must redouble their efforts to provide every American with equal opportunity and a decent place in which to live, work and play."

Ex-Sen. Barry Goldwater called on Pres. Johnson July 27 to visit urban black ghettos to talk with their residents "straight from the shoulder and heart," using his "personal persuasion" to ward off violence. Answering questions following an address at the National Press Club in Washington, Goldwater traced the rioting to "an inclination [of Negroes] to blow off" because they had been "promised the moon in the field of civil rights." He recommended strengthened police forces as more effective than legislation and concluded: "When white and black and brown and every other color decide they're going to live together as Christians, then and only then are we going to see an end to these troubles."

National Guard Called in Omaha

Rioting and looting broke out in Omaha's black Near North Side section July 3-5, 1966. Guardsmen dispersed crowds during the 3d night of vandalism, but renewed vandalism took place July 30-Aug. 2.

The July 3-5 rioting, rock-throwing and looting resulted in the arrest of 122 persons by the time order was restored July 5. Most white-owned stores in the neighborhood's business district had their windows broken, but black-owned stores were spared. All those arrested were released by July 7.

The outburst began early July 3, when youths threw a firecracker and a bottle into a police car answering a report that firecrackers were being exploded at a supermarket parking lot. A crowd of about 200 gathered. Members of the mob smashed windows and looted several stores. A policeman was burned by the firecracker thrown into the squad car, and a TV cameraman was cut by flying glass. Police restored order after 90 minutes of violence; they arrested 8 persons.

Police leaves were canceled July 3 as the threat of renewed disorder grew. 500 National Guardsmen were called into Omaha July 4, and 2 companies of Guardsmen and 40 state highway patrolmen were placed on alert. There was renewed window-breaking and looting by a band of black youths the night of July 3-4; more than 50 were arrested, and one 15-year-old boy was shot in the leg by an off-duty patrolman. A 3d night of vandalism July 4-5 brought 128 Guardsmen into the area to disperse crowds; 47 arrests were made. No incidents were reported July 6, and the Guardsmen were released from duty.

Nebraska Gov. Frank B. Morrison, who was in Los Angeles attending the National Governors Conference, said July 4 that the riot area was "an environment unfit for human habitation."

Omaha Mayor A. V. Sorensen, who had asserted July 4 that the outburst had no racial overtones, said July 5 at a news conference that meetings that day with black leaders had led him to change his assessment. He said of the riot: "It was an expression of discontent. It was a desire to be recognized and have all the nice things first-class citizens in America have."

Gov. Morrison flew to Omaha the night of July 5 and toured the riot-torn neighborhood. He met July 6 with 4 men who had been arrested during the rioting and then said at a news conference that unemployment had been presented as the major underlying cause of the outburst. About 30% of Omaha's Negroes were unemployed.

Mayor Sorensen announced July 6 that he had appointed a commission to study recreation needs of the riot area; the mayor had met July 5 with neighborhood teen-agers, who had told him that the supermarket parking lot was a habitual gathering place because there was nowhere else for local youth to go. The youths had also charged the police with using unnecessary force in dispersing the crowd at the supermarket in the riot's original incident.

3 nights of vandalism occurred July 30-Aug. 2 in the same area. 4 youths were arrested early July 31 after store windows had been broken and 2 stores looted near the supermarket parking lot that had been the focus of the earlier disturbances. Fires were set with molotov cocktails the night of July 31-Aug. 1 in 3 businesses in the black area, and police dispersed a crowd of about 150 after a patrol car was stoned. 24 adults and 7 juveniles were arrested, and one youth discovered looting a store was wounded by a police shotgun. Sporadic firebombing with molotov cocktails continued the night of Aug. 1-2.

Officials indicated Aug. 2 that they had dropped the conciliatory policy adopted after the earlier outbreaks. Gov. Morrison said Aug. 2 that officials were "having no truck with advocates of violence." Mayor Sorensen warned that "we're not going to listen to a lot of grievances that have been chewed over and over again." The mayor added, however, that he had ordered an investigation of a fatal shooting by police July 25 of a young black suspected of burglary; the incident reportedly had created black resentments that had sparked the latest outbreaks.

Baltimore: Prisoners Riot, Whites Invade Black District

About 1,000 inmates of the Maryland Penitentiary in Baltimore rioted July 8, 1966 in protest against alleged guard brutality and poor living conditions. Racial causes were also blamed; perhaps 2/3 of the prison's 1,461 convicts were black. 50 persons were injured in the 2-hour mêlée, during which 4 buildings were burned, windows smashed, a guardhouse demolished and the prison commissary looted. The disorder ended after authorities fired tear gas into the yard and Warden Roger L. Copinger appealed to the convicts.

The disturbance was the 2d within a year at the 163-year-old institution. (The earlier disorder, a one-day sitdown strike in Oct. 1965, had led to the dismissal of Warden Franklin Bough.) The riot followed a clash between a black inmate, John E. Jones, 24, and a black guard July 7. Jones, who suffered minor injuries, was called a victim of guard brutality. 5 additional guards had been required to subdue him. Warden Copinger admitted that a heat wave had made the overcrowded cells almost unbearable and that the prison food was poor. A Baltimore grand jury indicted 36 prisoners July 21 and 26 on charges of arson, burglary and rioting.

A black district in East Baltimore was invaded July 28 by white teen-age gangs. The attack followed a National States Rights Party rally at which Charles Conley (Connie) Lynch, 53, a minister from San Bernardino, Calif., had attacked Baltimore Mayor Theodore R. McKeldin as a "superpompous jackassie nigger-lover" and had told the audience of about 1,000 whites: "To hell with the niggers, and those who don't like it, they can get the hell out of here." As hundreds of white youths then moved from the rally into the black neighborhood, most Negroes fled into their homes, but some retaliated by throwing bricks and bottles. 10 persons were arrested, most of them white; a few people were injured, none seriously.

About 20 white youths invaded the black district again late July 29 and engaged in a brief street battle with young Negroes. 2 persons were injured, and one person was arrested. Several Baltimore clergymen rode through the city in patrol cars during the night, urging white and black residents to remain calm.

Earlier July 29 Circuit Court Judge William O'Donnell, acting at the request of city officials, had issued an injunction forbidding the National States Rights Party to hold public meetings in the city for 10 days (the party had planned to hold a rally that night). A grand jury July 29 indicted Lynch and 4 other party leaders on charges of riot and conspiracy to riot.

Maj. Gen. George M. Gelston, the city's acting police commissioner, said July 30 that the clashes had been "caused by the segregationists and not by the Negroes." Earle R. Poorbaugh, Mayor McKeldin's press secretary, said the National States Rights Party had come to Baltimore "because they figured the white people here would have gotten tired of the CORE program." The Congress of Racial Equality had been conducting an anti-segregation drive in the city since April and had succeeded in integrating a number of apartment houses and taverns. Lynch and 2 other officials of the National States' Rights Party, Richard Norton, 31, and Joseph Carroll, 19, were sentenced in Baltimore Nov. 21 to 2 years in prison on charges of inciting a riot, disorderly conduct, conspiracy to riot, and violating city park rules.

Street Fighting in Brooklyn

Conflict among Negroes, whites and Puerto Ricans in the East New York area of Brooklyn (N.Y. City) erupted in fighting July 15, 1966. There were renewed clashes July 17 and 18 and riot-like turmoil July 21 and 22. The disorders ended with a city-arranged truce July 23. The fighting at the eastern end of East New York was between blacks and whites, with the whites "defending" a boundary line between their chiefly Italian neighborhood and the black section. 15 blocks to the west the conflict was between blacks and Puerto Ricans, occupying the same area but usually segregated by building.

The initial clashes involved 3 separate fights taking place over 3 hours the night of July 15-16. 11 white youths were arrested; 2 whites and one Negro were hospitalized.

Violence erupted again the evenings of July 17 and 18. A black youth was shot in the back and 2 Puerto Ricans were knifed July 17, and a black woman was shot in the hip July 18. The 2d shooting touched off what police described as 2 "overflow" incidents; the first was a fist-fight between Italians and Negroes, the 2d a fight involving Italians, blacks and Puerto Ricans. 6 persons were injured and 6 arrested.

350 policemen were assigned to the area July 19 (the normal contingent was 40) as 40 black tenants moved out of 2 apartment houses on Alabama Ave., the site of the July 18 shooting. Puerto Rican residents of a 3d apartment house on the same block had moved out the previous week; it was reported by July 20 that more than 200 persons had evacuated the 3 buildings and that the buildings were under 'round-the-clock police guard.

In a series of incidents the night of July 21, one person was killed, one was critically injured by gunfire, 10 policemen and 4 civilians were injured by flying objects and 8 persons were arrested. A black child, Russell Givens, 3, was critically injured by a shot in the stomach from a sniper's rifle early in the evening.

A clash erupted between groups of black and white youths later July 21. The Negroes had been walking toward a restaurant to intercept Mayor John V. Lindsay, who was meeting there with community leaders. The whites had been picketing at a traffic island that demarcated the white and black neighborhoods. The pickets, members of a group known as SPONGE (Society for the Prevention of Negroes Getting Everything), ran through police barricades toward the approaching blacks, who fled, firing at the whites as they went. Eric Dean, 11, a Negro who had gone out with relatives to catch a glimpse of the mayor, was killed in the crossfire; a patrolman calmed angry bystanders by telling them the boy had fainted. Police reinforcements, including about 100 members of the elite Tactical Patrol Force, were rushed to the area as gathering crowds learned of the death and began throwing bricks and firebombs through store windows. The police July 27 arrested Ernest Gallashaw, 17, black, on charges of shooting Dean while firing a caliber .25 pistol at a policeman. (Gallashaw was acquitted Oct. 23.)

The night of July 22-23 was marked by outbreaks of violence as 1,000 extra police patrolled the area. 25 arrests were made. 5 persons, including 3 policemen, were slightly injured, and 2 Puerto Ricans were wounded by blacks firing from a passing car. Crowds of Negroes threw molotov cocktails and shot at police, and police broke up a group of blacks shouting "Get the whites!" Police about to disperse a crowd of about 200 black and Puerto Ricans youths were told, "We've declared a peace," but a fight between blacks and Puerto Ricans broke out later on. Earlier July 22, black and Puerto Rican community leaders had established an Emergency Committee for Peace in East New York and had toured the area calling for an end to violence.

Lindsay and other city officials met at city hall July 23 with 50 East New York residents representing the 3 warring factions. At a news conference following the meeting, Lindsay announced that "it's been agreed by everyone here to make every effort for peace, to cool it off and help calm it." He attributed the unrest to "neglect, mistrust and change, but mainly fear." Police saturation of the area continued, but virtually no incidents occurred July 23 or 24.

Charges that the unrest had been stirred up by "professional demagogues" from outside the city had been aired July 21 by 2

Brooklyn anti-poverty officials, J. Ken Cave and Angel M. Rivera, president and vice president, respectively, of the Brownsville Community Council. Another anti-poverty official, Charles Moore of the Council for a Better East New York, had disagreed; he said there was no evidence for such a conclusion. Police Commissioner Howard Leary described the outbreaks July 21 as "pretty much hoodlumism" on the part of teen-agers, more closely related to "gang warfare" than to the "contempt for the administration" underlying such disorders as the riots in Watts and Chicago. On the issue of outside influence, Leary said July 22 that the police department had "no proof of such activities."

Dayton Turmoil

Rioting and looting by Negroes in Dayton, O. Sept. 1-2, 1966 was touched off by the fatal shooting of Lester Mitchell, 40, black. Nearly 1,000 National Guardsmen were mobilized to restore order. About 30 persons were injured in the outbreak. More than 100 people were arrested. The violence erupted as city officials were preparing for a scheduled visit of Pres. Johnson Sept. 5. (The President appeared as planned at a Labor Day rally at the Montgomery County Fair.) Mitchell had been hit in the head by a shotgun blast early Sept. 1 as he was sweeping his sidewalk; he died that night. The shot reportedly came from a passing car containing 3 white men.

As news of the shooting circulated through the Westside black neighborhood Sept. 1, roving bands of Negroes began throwing rocks at pedestrians and vehicles, breaking windows and looting stores. The violence spread during the day to the downtown area; windows were broken or merchandise looted at about 50 stores. Police reported 2 molotov cocktails thrown at the Gem City Lumber yard, but damage was slight.

Later the evening of Sept. 1 another Negro was reported injured by a shotgun blast as he stood in a crowd in front of a white residence. Police arrested the house's owner, who said he had fired into the crowd to protect his mother after someone had thrown a rock through his window.

Ohio Gov. James A. Rhodes mobilized the National Guard on Mayor Dave Hall's request. The Guardsmen and city police eventually cordoned off the entire Westside neighborhood; 3 bridges leading into the area were closed to keep out sightseers. Authorities imposed a 10:30 p.m. citywide curfew for all juveniles.

Edward A. King, black director of Dayton's Human Relations Council, said Sept. 2 that the black community's major grievance was inadequate housing. But he noted that most Negroes had avoided the rioting and that participants were mainly youths interested in looting. Mayor Hall reported a "return to normal operations" Sept. 2.

Cicero Whites Battle Police

250 civil rights activists marched and demonstrated for 2 hours Sept. 4, 1966 in Cicero, Ill., an all-white suburb southwest of Chicago, in a demand for an end to housing discrimination. Robert Lucas, 41, chairman of the Chicago branch of the Congress of Racial Equality (CORE), led the march. Members of 3 other rights groups—Black Power (a new group), the League of Labor & Education and Brothers for Afro-American Equality—participated.

More than 2,000 National Guardsmen and 500 local, county and state police were on hand to protect the marchers, who drew an estimated 3,000 spectators. 15 persons were injured, including 6 white hecklers bayoneted by Guardsmen, and 39 persons were arrested (most of them from outside of Cicero) on charges of disorderly conduct.

As the demonstrators, about 200 of whom were black, moved down the 30-block march route from the edge of Chicago, onlookers pelted them with rocks, bottles, bricks, eggs and firecrackers. 3 marchers, 4 policemen and 2 bystanders were hit by flying objects. Many members of the crowd shouted derisive epithets and made obscene gestures. Some of the marchers answered the epithets with taunts of their own and displayed signs reading "black power." At one point in the march the demonstrators held a prayer vigil at West 25th St. and South Laramie Ave. for Jerome Huey, 17, a black who had been fatally beaten there by 4 white youths in May while he was looking for summer employment in Cicero. 700 angry whites massed behind police barricades during the vigil.

Later, as the demonstrators were returning to Chicago and were only 50 yards from the city limits, white youths threw a volley of bottles and attempted to rush the marchers. Police pushed back the crowd, clubbing several persons to the ground with night sticks; a Guardsman fired 3 shots from a submachine gun over the heads of the crowd.

The march had resulted in part from a feeling in some rights groups that the Rev. Dr. Martin Luther King Jr. had "sold out" the poor black by signing an open-housing accord with Chicago officials Aug. 26. King, who had called a moratorium on housing demonstrations after reaching the accord, asked Lucas Sept. 3 to call off the march in order to preserve unity in the Chicago Freedom Movement, but CORE ignored the request. Lucas said Sept. 4: The march was being held because Cicero "is the most closed community in the Chicago area, and as long as closed housing goes unchallenged, open housing will remain an impossibility." "We didn't achieve anything concrete enough in the [housing] agreement, and CORE wants to keep the pressure on."

Atlanta Riots Follow Shootings

2 nights of black rioting swept Atlanta Sept. 6-7 and 10-11, 1966. In each case the riot occurred after a Negro had been shot. Sporadic violence continued Sept. 11 and 12. More than 35 persons were injured in the incidents, and about 138 persons were arrested.

The rioting broke out Sept. 6 in the black neighborhood of Summerhill after an Atlanta detective had shot and wounded Louis Prather, 25, black, when Prather resisted arrest for suspected car theft. Prather had been shot at about 1:30 p.m. Shortly thereafter SNCC Chairman Stokely Carmichael, 25, entered the area. He was quoted as telling a crowd of blacks: "We're going to be back at 4 o'clock and tear this place up." Carmichael was seen about 1½ hours later with 2 other SNCC members—William Ware and Bob Vance Walton, 20. The latter 2 then toured the area with a sound truck and, according to black Police Sgt. D. J. Perry, "were bringing different people into the area, and they were saying that ... [Prather] had been shot while handcuffed and that he was murdered by white police." Ware and Walton were arrested and charged with inciting to riot and creating a disturbance.

Shortly afterwards, about 1,000 Negroes, chanting "black power" and "police brutality," began throwing rocks, sticks and bottles at policemen, newsmen and white bystanders. At least 3 cars were overturned, and the windows of many others were smashed. At one point Mayor Ivan Allen Jr., 55, was toppled from the top of a car as he attempted to calm the crowd; he was not injured. Allen had pleaded with the blacks to "go home." Some of the rioters answered him with screams of "white devil," and SNCC members shouted to the crowd: "Don't go—stay here and protest police brutality." About 750 city policemen used tear gas and fired shotguns and pistols in the air to disperse the crowd.

16 persons were injured, 73 persons were arrested, and 20 cars were damaged.

Sporadic violence was reported Sept. 7. A molotov cocktail heavily damaged a building in a black neighborhood, and there were reports of 4 less serious fires. During the afternoon police arrested 10 Negroes in a disturbance allegedly begun by 2 SNCC members. That evening police dispersed a crowd of about 400 blacks who had gathered in the black neighborhood of Vine City.

Mayor Allen warned Sept. 7 that "if Stokely Carmichael is looking for a battleground, he created one last night, and he'll be met in whatever situation he cares to create." "Hundreds of normally good citizens were inflamed out of their normal good senses," Allen said. "They were victims of those who sought to incite violence." Atlanta Police Chief Herbert Jenkins announced the same day that the police force was strengthening its riot control organization in order to deal with what he called the "Nonstudent Violent Committee."

SNCC leaders reportedly had been meeting in Atlanta prior to the outbreak. An Atlanta police source said Sept. 7 that committee members from New York, Philadelphia and Watts were believed to have attended the meeting and to have been in the vicinity of the rioting. Besides Carmichael, other SNCC officials seen during the rioting included Mrs. Ruby Doris Smith Robinson, 23, executive secretary, and Ivanhoe Donaldson, head of the N.Y. City office. But SNCC officials denied that the committee had been responsible for the rioting. Carmichael said Sept. 7 that SNCC "cannot start a rebellion just like that. . . . It is started by conditions of oppression."

Carmichael was arrested Sept. 8 and charged with inciting to riot and disorderly conduct. Carmichael announced through SNCC's Atlanta headquarters Sept. 9 that he would refuse to post the $10,000 bail and would remain in jail "indefinitely." The grand jury Sept. 13 indicted Carmichael and 14 others on the riot charges. Carmichael's bond was reduced to $1,000, and he paid it Sept. 15.

Representatives of 15 Atlanta-based organizations, including the Southern Christian Leadership Conference, the NAACP, the American Civil Liberties Union, the American Jewish Committee and the National Council of Churches, condemned the violence in a letter to Mayor Allen Sept. 9. They warned, however, that "it would be tragic, indeed, if community consensus were to become arrayed against certain individuals and organizations, becoming a substitute for a more constructive response to the conditions which brought it [the riot] about. . . . Whenever there are deprivations and injustices, those who would incite violence will find a ready response to their appeals."

(About 20 blacks, some of them SNCC members, had demonstrated at the 12th Army Corps headquarters in Atlanta Aug. 17 and 18 in protest against the Vietnam war. They had entered the center with recruits Aug. 17, then had begun shouting anti-war slogans. Soldiers quickly ejected them from the building. The following day the Negroes, shouting "black power," fought with police after attempting to enter the center. Several policemen were injured in the incident. SNCC field secretary Larry Fox, 22, and 11 other SNCC members were arrested. They were sentenced Aug. 19 by Atlanta City Court Judge T. C. Little, who tried the cases without a jury. Johnny C. Wilson, about 19, received 120 days in jail for disorderly conduct and failure to obey an officer; the 11 others received jail sentences ranging from 30 to 90 days.)

(About 400 blacks, many yelling "black power," threw stones at police in a black neighborhood of Atlanta Aug. 25. The incident occurred after an officer attempted to make a routine arrest. Police reinforcements dispersed the crowd and made 5 arrests.)

The 2d night of rioting began Sept. 10 after a white man fatally shot Hubert M. (Dukie) Vorner Jr., 16, black, and wounded another Negro, Roy Milton Wright, 16. Police Sept. 13 arrested William Haywood James, 42, and charged him with the murder. The incident touched off rioting on Boulevard, a 4-lane thoroughfare bisecting a predominantly black neighborhood near the center of Atlanta. As policemen arrived to investigate the shooting, a crowd of about 400 Negroes gathered and began throwing bottles and bricks in a wild outbreak that lasted 5-10 minutes. Scattered violence continued until after 2 a.m. Sept. 11 as blacks broke store windows and attacked whites with bricks, bottles and fists. More than 20 persons were injured, including a policeman wounded by gunfire and a TV reporter who suffered a fractured skull. 58 persons were arrested, including Cleveland Sellers, SNCC program secretary.

Outbreaks of violence on Boulevard continued the evening of Sept. 11 as a crowd of about 200 blacks threw bricks, bottles and stones and set several fires. At least one person was injured, and SNCC staff member Wilson Brown was arrested for throwing a firebomb. Police eventually cordoned off a 4-block area along the street.

Violence broke out again the evening of Sept. 12. A crowd of 150 to 300 Negroes, yelling "black power," threw bricks and bottles at policemen and newsmen's autos. At least 5 firebombs were thrown into the street, but they burned harmlessly. Police reinforcements quickly dispersed the crowd. 6 persons were arrested. The violence occurred after the blacks had attended a meeting called by moderate rights leaders. Its purpose was to form a "Boulevard Northeast Youth Council" to help restore order in the neighborhood. At one point, however, black militants disrupted the meeting. SNCC member Willie Ricks grabbed the microphone and shouted, "We're going to put every cracker in Atlanta on his knees. . . . Mayor Allen is the killer." The Negroes answered with shouts of "black power."

The Atlanta Summit Leadership Conference, a grouping of the city's main civil rights leaders, had said in a statement Sept. 7 that the wounding of a Negro by a white policeman was "unfortunate, but not sufficient grounds for anyone or any organization to go into a community and incite the people." The Rev. Dr. Martin Luther King Jr. said in a statement Sept. 7: "It is still my firm conviction that a riot is socially destructive and self-defeating. On the other hand, while condemning riots, it is just as important to condemn the conditions which bring riots into being."

William Haywood James was convicted Feb. 8, 1967 of the fatal shooting of Hubert M. Vorner Jr. The shooting had touched off Atlantia's 2d night of rioting. James had told the court Feb. 7 that black youths standing in front of an apartment building had shouted "Hey baby" at his wife as he drove through the area. He said that when he stopped for a traffic light they attacked him, and he fired his pistol "a couple of times" in self-defense. The all-white jury of 10 men and 2 women returned a verdict of guilty with a recommendation of mercy. James, who was also serving a 6-year prison sentence for assault with intent to murder in an unrelated case, was sentenced to life in prison.

National Guard Quells San Francisco Riots

Racial violence swept black sections of San Francisco Sept. 27-28, 1966 after a white policeman shot and killed a black youth. The city was sweltering in a heat wave, and the rioting started in 95° heat during the hottest day of the year. 3,600 National Guardsmen were called in, and a curfew was imposed. Minor flare-ups did not end until Sept. 30. Altogether, 349 persons were arrested and at least 80 persons were reported injured.

The violence erupted in the Hunter's Point section of San Francisco Sept. 27 after a white policeman, Alvin Johnson, 51, fatally shot Matthew Johnson, 16, a Negro. The policeman said he had fired warning shots first as the youth fled from a car that later was reported stolen.

During the rioting, hundreds of black youths roved the streets, smashing windows, looting stores, hurling bricks and fire-bombs at police and overturning autos. They lured fire trucks into the area by setting false alarms and then attacked the trucks and firemen. By midnight disorder had spread to the Fillmore district 2 miles away. Mayor John F. Shelley imposed an 8 p.m.-to-6 a.m. curfew and sent augmented police forces into the areas with orders "not to shoot," except in self-defense. He barred the use of dogs and tear gas. "You are not going out there to beat people in a vindictive manner but to get people off the streets," he said. At least 50 persons were arrested during the night.

Shelley held all-night talks with neighborhood groups at the Bayview Community Center, but peace efforts failed. Dr. Carlton B. Goodlett, physician and publisher of the *Sun Reporter*, a black weekly, urged in vain that the police be removed from the area while he addressed the mobs himself.

More extensive rioting broke out late in the afternoon Sept. 28. 2,000 National Guardsmen, armed with bayonets, shotguns and automatic rifles, entered the area by 8 p.m. to clear the streets and quell the rioting. Police and Guardsmen exchanged gunfire with rioters, and 100 Guardsmen rode fire trucks to defend them from mob attacks. In the Fillmore district there was a major fire, and sniping at policemen and whites was reported. Black groups opposing the riots equipped themselves with bullhorns and walkie-talkies and canvassed black areas to spread "the word" that "rioting isn't the way."

Shelley Sept. 28 sent a telegram to Pres. Johnson to appeal for emergency funds to remedy the "critical unemployment situa-tion." He asked Cyril Magnin, president of the Greater San Fran-cisco Chamber of Commerce, to meet with business leaders and ask them "to search their employment records and practices and see what could be done to help Negro youths." He called on labor unions to end restrictions on black membership. He appealed to all citizens to end racial discrimination. Magnin met Sept. 29 with heads of the city's 100 largest companies to begin a job search. He announced that the chamber would establish a new employ-ment committee to be headed by a Negro and would work with personnel departments of major companies to fill 2,000 jobs with black youths. The city's Civil Service Commission Sept. 30 an-nounced a program to recruit workers for 774 vacancies at City

Hall. San Francisco already had a human rights commission, and both Shelley's administration and that of his predecessor, George Christopher, had done considerable work in setting up agencies to improve housing and employment conditions for members of minority groups.

(A near-riot had erupted in San Francisco's Fillmore district the night of July 16-17 after a black off-duty policeman shot a black armed robbery suspect who had refused to turn over his gun. A crowd of about 200 persons, some of whom threatened the policeman, gathered at the scene. 7 black youths, including the robbery suspect, were arrested; 5 other robbery suspects got away. Later a molotov cocktail was thrown into the Afro-American Cultural Center 4 blocks away after an integrated dance had ended; the resulting fire was followed by 6 other fires caused by gasoline bombs. All 7 fires were minor and were quickly put out. One of the policemen who rushed to the scene said that "a few trouble-makers . . . tried unsuccessfully to incite a real riot" with cries of "kill whiteys.")

Minutemen Arrested, Weapons Seized

19 alleged members of the rightwing Minutemen were arrested in N.Y. City and other parts of N.Y. State Oct. 30. Police said the crackdown had prevented planned firebomb attacks on 3 allegedly leftist camps and a Brooklyn office serving as campaign headquarters of Dr. Herbert Aptheker, a Communist running for Congress. The Minutemen, a far-right group, trained its members in guerrilla tactics to thwart an expected Communist attempt to seize the U.S.

The 3 camps named as the targets were Camp Webatuck (formerly Camp Unity) in Wingdale, N.Y.; Camp Midvale near Wanaque Reservoir in Midvale, N.J.; a pacifist camp (of the New England Committee for Nonviolent Action) at Voluntown, Conn. The suspects were seized, police said, after they had donned hunting clothes and had started out on the attacks. "Tons of weapons and ammunition" were confiscated, the police reported. The weapons included mortars, bazookas, machine guns, rifles, pistols, grenades and bombs.

15 of those arrested Oct. 30 were indicted by a Queens (N.Y. City) grand jury Dec. 14 on charges of conspiracy to commit arson, illegal possession of firearms and other illegal activity, but charges against 4 of those arrested were dismissed.

The police said that the Minutemen had tried to infiltrate the Army's 11th Special Forces (the "Green Berets") reserve unit at Miller Field (Staten Island in N.Y. City) and had sought to stir up anti-Negro feelings by distributing racist literature purportedly created by black extremists. The counterfeit literature urged Negroes "to kill white devils ... [and] have the white women for our pleasure."

Robert Bolivar DePugh, 42, of Norborne, Mo., who had founded the Minutemen in 1959 and more recently (July 4, 1966) had organized the Patriotic Party of America, was arrested Aug. 20 and was convicted with 2 followers by a federal jury in Kansas City, Mo. Nov. 14 of violating the Federal Firearms Act. The other 2 were Walter Patrick Peyson, 23, of Norborne and Troy Houghton, 33, of San Diego, Calif.

Violence North & West

A virtual epidemic of violence took place in American cities during 1966 as violent incidents ranging from minor to riotous shook more than 2 dozen other cities from New Jersey to California. Among events reported:

Bakersfield, Calif.—In Bakersfield, 100 miles northwest of Los Angeles, violence erupted May 22 in the black Lakeview district where a crowd of about 200 threw rocks and bottles at police investigating an auto accident. About 2,000 Negroes were holding a picnic meeting in a nearby park to discuss the city council's refusal to implement anti-poverty programs. 20 adults were arrested May 22, and 18 juveniles were held for curfew violations. 2 policemen and a white taxi driver were slightly injured, and a black youth was shot in the leg, allegedly while attacking a policeman. A school bus carrying black children was stoned May 23, causing injuries from flying glass to 2 youths and the driver. During the evening a number of molotov cocktails were thrown.

Benton Harbor, Mich.—Racial violence rocked Benton Harbor, Mich. Aug. 28-31 in apparent reaction to what black leaders called "a lack of recreational facilities and bullying by local policemen." For 4 consecutive nights black youths in crowds varying in size from 50 to 400 persons threw stones and bottles at store windows, cars and policemen. Several persons were injured in the incident. At least 13 Negroes and 3 whites were arrested. The violence culminated Aug. 31 in the death of Cecil Hunt, 18, black, who had been shot the previous night by 2 white men in a car.

Gov. George Romney placed more than 500 National Guardsmen and state policemen on riot alert Aug. 31 after Benton Harbor Mayor Wilbert Smith declared a state of emergency. No incidents were reported Sept. 1, however, as black "peace patrols" moved through the black neighborhood to maintain order.

Detroit—Russian-born Rabbi Morris Adler, 59, of Congregation Shaarey Zedek, Detroit's largest Conservative Jewish congregation, was shot Feb. 12 during a Sabbath service in his synagogue. Adler, one of the U.S.' most prominent Jewish Conservative leaders, died Mar. 11 after being in a coma since the shooting. His assailant was Richard S. Wishnetsky, 23, a graduate philosophy student who had been under psychiatric treatment. Wishnetsky ran to the pulpit with a gun and began to read a prepared speech condemning the congregation. Wishnetsky, a member of the congregation, said its members "made me ashamed to say that I am a Jew." He then shot Adler twice and shot himself. Wishnetsky died Feb. 16.

58 persons were arrested in racial disorders in Detroit Aug. 9-11. The violence apparently was touched off when police attempted to arrest 3 blacks for loitering; a black policeman was knifed during the arrest attempt. A crowd of about 150 Negroes then gathered in a 16-block area on the city's east side and began throwing rocks at passing motorists; windows of at least 14 stores also were broken. One white was injured. About 150 policemen, including riot-control specialists, cleared the area and made 7 arrests. Police Commissioner Ray Girardin Aug. 10 ordered the city's 4,000 policemen on 12-hour shifts and canceled all leaves as the violence intensified. A black pedestrian, Tyrone Powers, 26, was wounded by shots from whites in a passing automobile. At least 2 firebomb attacks were reported. Police arrested 30-40 persons, among them 7 white teenagers who were found carrying molotov cocktails. 3 firebomb attacks were reported the night of Aug. 11, and police arrested 15 persons.

Jersey City—Violence broke out in Jersey City June 19 with fights in 2 taverns in a downtown neighborhood occupied by blacks and Puerto Ricans; the disorders spread and were renewed June 20, with youths on rooftops throwing rocks at passing cars. Police described the outburst as a "factional dispute" between black and Puerto Rican residents.

Lansing, Mich.—11 persons were injured and 31 arrested in disorders that swept a section of Lansing's southwest side the nights of Aug. 7 and 8. Both Negroes and whites, mainly teen-agers, were involved in the incidents. The violence broke out when blacks began throwing rocks, apparently in reaction to insults shouted by gangs of white youths. Police were met by a shower of stones when they attempted to break up the disturbance. More widespread violence occurred the night of Aug. 8 when Negroes threw firebombs and smashed store and car windows. Police used tear gas to disperse a crowd of about 200 black youths. Several policemen and at least 4 civilians were injured in the incidents. Part of the black neighborhood was cordoned off by police the night of Aug. 8 to prevent white gangs from entering the area. City leaders and residents of the black area agreed Aug. 9 to maintain the cordon, and only one arrest and one incident—a firebomb attack on an unfinished apartment building—were reported that night. The cordon was lifted Aug. 12 as police reported a return to normal.

Gov. George Romney Aug. 9 had threatened state action against those who had taken part in the disorders. He linked the outbreak of violence to recent talk of "black power." "The only power," he said, "is that of democracy. There can be no private power based on force—not black power nor white power nor shared power."

Milwaukee—A bomb explosion wrecked the Milwaukee office of the NAACP Aug. 9, but no one was injured. The People Youth Council of the NAACP Aug. 10 posted armed guards at the headquarters to prevent any further bombing. Local police objected to the posting of the guards, but District Atty. Hugh O'Connel said no laws were violated.

Turner H. Cheney, 36, grand dragon of the Illinois Ku Klux Klan, was arrested in Milwaukee Sept. 25 after the arrest Sept. 24 of 2 alleged members of the Wisconsin Klan, Robert C. Schmidt, 41, and Robert W. Long, 25, as suspects in 2 Milwaukee bombings. Cheney and Schmidt were charged with the bombing July 1 of the Allied Linoleum Store, operated by John Gilman, former executive secretary of the Wisconsin Civil Rights Congress. Schmidt and Long were charged with the bombing of the NAACP office.

Civil rights workers picketed the homes of 2 judges and a Congressman in suburban and metropolitan Milwaukee Aug. 19-29 and Aug. 31-Sept. 2 in protest against membership by public officials in organizations that barred Negroes. The demonstrators, members of the predominantly black Youth Council of the Milwaukee NAACP, were led by the Rev. James E. Groppi, a white Roman Catholic priest and assistant pastor of St. Boniface parish in Milwaukee's black ghetto. The group objected to the membership of Circuit Judge Robert C. Cannon, County Judge Christ T. Seraphim and Rep. Clement J. Zablocki (D., Wis.) in the Fraternal Order of Eagles, which restricted membership to Caucasians.

The Youth Council demanded that Cannon, Seraphim and Zablocki resign either from office or from the Eagles. The officials replied that they opposed the membership restriction but preferred working from within the organization to repeal it. 60 to 150 demonstrators picketed Cannon's home in Wauwatosa, a Milwaukee suburb, for 11 consecutive nights Aug. 19-29.

The demonstrations sparked angry response among white residents. Large crowds, including Ku Klux Klan members, jeered pickets and threw rocks and firecrackers. About 400 National Guardsmen, mobilized by Gov. Warren P. Knowles Aug. 26, were rushed into the neighborhood Aug. 28 and 29 to protect pickets from crowds numbering in the thousands.

After state officials threatened to obtain a court order barring the demonstrations, the Youth Council agreed Aug. 31 to voluntary restrictions on the picketing in Wauwatosa. The council then shifted its picketing Aug. 31-Sept. 1 to Seraphim's home in northeast Milwaukee. About 45 Council members picketed Zablocki's home in Milwaukee Sept. 2. The situation eased Sept. 3 after the council suspended picketing in order to discuss the issue with Eagles officials.

Minneapolis—About 50 black youths, apparently angered by insufficient job opportunities, smashed some 25 store windows and looted 3 stores in a predominantly black neighborhood on Minneapolis' Northside early Aug. 3. Later Aug. 3 Negroes threatened to burn and loot a Northside shopping center but agreed at a meeting with city and state officials that evening to call a 24-hour halt to the vandalism. Gov. Karl F. Rolvaag and Mayor Arthur Naftalin attended the meeting and promised the blacks 60 jobs with about a dozen local businesses. Minor vandalism in the Northside area was reported Aug. 4.

Muskegon, Mich.—Police clashed with about 1,500 persons, most of them black, the night of Aug. 12 in a downtown section of Muskegon. The incident began when a crowd gathered outside a hotel, apparently after a rumored assault on 2 white men by Negroes, and surrounded a police car that had arrived to investigate the disorder. 70 reinforcements had to be called in before the crowd could be dispersed. 27 persons were arrested—26 Negroes and one white man—and 5 persons, all black, were injured.

New Rochelle, N.Y.—The Rev. Melvin DeWitt Bullock, 38, a Negro, was found beaten to death Sept. 17 in his home in New Rochelle. Bullock, ex-president of the New Rochelle NAACP chapter, had been active in recent drives to end *de facto* segregation in New Rochelle public schools.

Oakland, Calif.—Sporadic outbreaks of racial violence in Oakland Oct. 18-20, coincided with a 3-day boycott of the city's schools. More than 50 persons were arrested, and 13 were reported injured.

The rioting was touched off Oct. 18 after a black woman's car was involved in a traffic accident. 2 arrests were made at the scene of the accident, and the disorders spread when black teen-age gangs rioted in the downtown business area. 5 whites were beaten, and 47 businesses were reported damaged. 19 persons were arrested on charges of burglary, assault with a deadly weapon, battery, disturbing the peace and resisting arrest.

The Ad Hoc Committee for Quality Education, a black Oakland group, launched a 3-day boycott of predominantly black public schools Oct. 19 in protest against alleged *de facto* segregation. About 250 Negroes, many of them nonstudents, rioted for

2 hours Oct. 19 at Oakland's Castlemont High School. The disturbance forced the predominantly black school to close early. The youths smashed windows and school equipment, threw gasoline bombs and rang false alarms. Cafeteria tables were upset when truants and nonstudents reportedly scaled the school fences and charged into the cafeteria at lunch hour. 5 white teachers and 3 white students were beaten. About 30 persons were arrested.

Later Oct. 19 police broke up a group of about 150 black youths who had looted a nearby food market. A little later the raiders, joined by about 150 others, smashed store windows in a 10-block stretch along a major East Oakland traffic artery. A supermarket was forced to close after it was invaded by 75 black youths. A 10 p.m. curfew was imposed on all persons under 18, and police, armed with shotguns and carbines, patrolled the streets.

Molotov cocktails were thrown at an Oakland home and a convalescent hospital at 1:30 a.m. Oct. 20; both were set afire, but the fires were quickly extinguished. 2 black men and a black woman were arrested. 12 more persons were arrested later in the day in connection with sporadic firebomb throwing, but violence was reported to have ended by Oct. 21.

Ossining, N.Y.—400 blacks rampaged through downtown Ossining, N.Y. Oct. 31. 6 policemen were injured. 5 youths were arrested and charged with assault and disorderly conduct. The rioting began when a group of boys and girls throwing eggs and stones at each other were joined by youths from a nearby recreation center. Before leaving the center, where they had been preparing for a dance, the 2d group tore down decorations and fought with each other. The gangs smashed store windows and attacked Ptl. Mario Palmietto when he tried to disperse them. He was found unconscious and was hospitalized.

The executive board of the Ossining NAACP Nov. 2 protested the arrests and accused the Police Department of discriminatory practices in dealing with black youths. It charged that a Halloween masquerader had started the riot by prodding the black youths with a stick. It charged that white youths had destroyed mail boxes and committed other Halloween vandalism without police interference. The board also protested police laxity during Oct. 7 street disturbances caused by whites.

Perth Amboy, N.J.—Puerto Ricans clashed with police in Perth Amboy for 4 nights July 30-Aug. 2. The incidents apparently developed in reaction to a city anti-loitering ordinance enacted in late July. City authorities agreed Aug. 3 to rewrite the ordinance in consultation with a committee of Puerto Ricans.

The incidents began the night of July 30-31 as about 200 Puerto Rican youths gathered at the corner of Hall Ave. and Charles St. to protest the arrest of a Puerto Rican for loitering. There was some rock-and-bottle throwing. Crowds varying in size from 100 to 600 persons gathered at the same intersection the nights of July 31-Aug. 2 and clashed with about 60 of the city's 95 policemen; a total of 37 persons were injured by stones and bottles, and 41 persons were arrested.

A hastily-formed Puerto Rican Grievance Committee, headed by Santos Torres, 24, conferred with city commissioners and Mayor James J. Flynn Jr. Aug. 3. The officials agreed to rewrite the anti-loitering ordinance and to reduce the number of policemen on Hall Ave. (Some observers had said the disorders were caused in part by the presence of the large number of policemen assigned to the intersection.) The officials also promised to consider a number of reforms sought by Puerto Ricans.

Philadelphia—Police raided 4 civil rights meeting places in a black area of North Philadelphia Aug. 13 in a search for suspected caches of weapons, ammunition and dynamite. Armed with rifles and shotguns, 4 squads of 20 policemen each carried out the simultaneous raids. 1,000 policemen were dispersed in the vicinity to maintain order.

$2\frac{1}{2}$ sticks of dynamite were seized in one apartment house, but only civil rights literature was found at the 3 other places. Police arrested 3 persons who were present when the dynamite was found: Barry Dawson, 19, Eugene Dawkins, 19, and Carol West, 18. George Brown, 28, the apartment's occupant, surrendered to police later Aug. 13. Asst. District Atty. Richard A. Sprague identified Dawson Aug. 13 as an official of the Student Nonviolent Coordinating Committee (SNCC), the 3 others as members of a Philadelphia rights group known as the Young Militant Corps.

Acting Police Commissioner Frank Rizzo said Aug. 13 that Winston Ealy, 23, described as "very friendly" with a number of

SNCC members, had informed him Aug. 3 that arms caches were being built up at the 4 locations. Ealy had turned over $2\frac{1}{2}$ sticks of dynamite with detonating caps Aug. 12 to back up his charge.

On information obtained from Dawson, warrants were issued later Aug. 13 charging Ealy and 3 SNCC officials with illegal possession of explosives and with conspiracy. The accused SNCC officials were Fred Meely, 27, regional director and chairman of the Philadelphia chapter; Morris Ruffin, 25, a project director; George Anderson, 21, a full-time field worker. Ealy surrendered to police Aug. 14. He admitted taking 9 sticks of dynamite from a construction site and helping to transport it to the SNCC headquarters, where it was divided among several persons.

James Forman, national director of SNCC, said Aug. 19 that he had "some very good evidence that police had planted the dynamite" that was confiscated during the raid.

White persons demonstrated Oct. 2-5 in front of the home of the first black family to move into the Kensington section of North Philadelphia. During the disorders, 42 persons were arrested. The demonstrations began when Mr. and Mrs. Leon Wright and their 3 children moved into a rented house Oct. 2. A small crowd gathered. Some members of the crowd jeered and hurled eggs at the house. The following night about 500 persons gathered, and some threw bottles and firecrackers at the home. 7 persons, including 4 policemen, were reported injured. Police estimated that more than 1,000 persons demonstrated Oct. 4 in defiance of a preliminary injunction issued on a motion filed by the NAACP. 15 adults and 5 juveniles were arrested Oct. 4 and 22 Oct. 5. Order was restored late in the evening Oct. 6 after 400 policemen were called in.

St. Louis—Demonstrations were staged in St. Louis Sept. 25-28 in protest against the police slaying Sept. 22 of a black robbery suspect. The demonstrations ended in rioting Sept. 28. 14 persons were injured. At a coroner's inquest Sept. 28 police testified that Detective William Finnegan had shot and killed Russell Hayes, 24, the black suspect, when the youth drew a weapon (which turned out to be a tear-gas pistol) on Finnegan and 2 other officers in the car. Hayes' hands were handcuffed behind him at the time of the shooting. Police had failed to notice the weapon when they arrested and searched Hayes. Finnegan did not testify. The coroner's jury returned a verdict of justifiable homicide.

A militant CORE faction demanding Finnegan's dismissal held a protest rally in front of police headquarters that evening. As the meeting broke up, about 50 youths began smashing store and auto windows. Some Negroes stoned firemen answering false alarms and policemen seeking to control the mob. Others hurled a park bench into the path of a bus. 2 firemen and 10 policemen were hit by rocks or glass.

Troy, N.Y.—An incident involving police conduct July 16 led to angry reaction and scattered violence among blacks in Troy, N.Y. The police incident was the arrest of Mary Berkley, 17, black, on a complaint of a disturbance. Miss Berkley claimed the police had pushed her down 2 flights of steps; the police charged her with 2d-degree assault for allegedly kicking and biting them.

About 60 Negroes staged a protest march to city hall July 18. Francis S. Fitch, local NAACP president, said July 22 that Negro teen-agers "were getting ready to riot" and that the NAACP had helped organize the protest march "to burn off some of this energy."

3 small fires set with molotov cocktails and 2 instances of broken windows were reported the night of July 20-21. Firebombs exploded in a grocery store and a clothing store the night of July 22-23, and 3 Negroes were arrested shortly thereafter; police said molotov cocktails had been found in their car. Those arrested included David C. Venson, 19, a leader of a newly formed group of young blacks known as the United Peace Neighborhood Marching Club.

Waukegan, Ill.—Gangs of black youths rioted in the Southside area of Waukegan Aug. 26-28. 14 persons were injured in the incidents, and about 80 people were arrested. The worst violence occurred the night of Aug. 28, when blacks throw molotov cocktails at passing cars and trapped the occupants in flames. After meeting with clergymen, friends and community leaders, Mayor

Robert Sabonjian announced Aug. 31 that Negro grievances would be studied and solutions sought.

Ypsilanti, Mich.—Rock-throwing broke out early Aug. 13 in Ypsilanti, where black youths broke car windows and stoned cars. Police arrested 11 persons, all black, ranging in age from 12 to 19, who admitted participating in the vandalism.

Black Activist Younge Killed in Alabama

Black civil rights worker Samuel L. Younge Jr., 21, was shot and killed in Tuskegee, Ala. by a white service station attendant. Black students from Tuskegee Institute rioted when an all-white jury acquitted the white man of murder.

Younge's body had been found in a Tuskegee alley early Jan. 4, 1966. He had been shot in the head. Marvin Segrest, 67, a white, was arrested later Jan. 4 as Younge's slayer. Younge had been a student at Tuskegee Institute and head of the Tuskegee Institute Advancement League, a rights group. Segrest was a service-station attendant employed near the spot where Younge's body had been found.

Macon County Sheriff Harvey Sadler said Jan. 5 that a friend of Segrest's had come to the police station just before midnight Jan. 3, at Segrest's request, to report "that Segrest had shot twice at somebody but didn't think he hit him." Sadler added that a Greyhound bus driver from Atlanta had reported seeing a white service-station attendant shoot a young black after 11 p.m. Jan. 3. Sadler reported Jan. 6 that Segrest had admitted the shooting. Sadler added: "This is definitely not a civil rights shooting. The boy apparently kept agitating the old man until this happened." Segrest was released on $20,000 bail Jan. 11.

2,000 Tuskegee Institute students and professors marched through downtown Tuskegee Jan. 4 to protest the slaying. About 150 students marched Jan. 6 and 7. The Jan. 6 march was led by Gwendolyn Patton, 22, president of the Tuskegee Institute student body. She asked Mayor Charles M. Keever to convene a special session of the grand jury (scheduled to meet in April). Unless a speedy trial and conviction of Segrest took place, she warned, "you and the city council are going to have to step down and turn over the government to someone who can get these things done."

About 325 Negroes sat on a Tuskegee highway and blocked traffic Jan. 8 after being confronted by police and told they could march no farther. After an hour, the demonstrators voted to march past police, and the police decided to step aside. The protesters, their ranks swelling to 500, marched downtown and blocked business entrances for an hour by sitting on sidewalks near the Macon County courthouse.

Segrest was acquitted in Opelika Dec. 8 by an all-white Lee County jury of charges of 2d-degree murder in Younge's death, and black students rioted in Tuskegee the following day.

Segrest's trial had been moved to Lee County after he charged that he could not receive a fair trial in predominantly black Macon County. Describing Younge's death, Segrest had testified that Younge had started "cussing and raising hell" after being refused permission to use the women's rest rooms. Segrest said that he had fired 2 shots at Younge "to bluff him" and that Younge then had grabbed what "looked like a gun" from his car. (A golf club was found beside Younge's body.)

The Tuskegee Institute student government president had proposed a 9:30 a.m. demonstration for Dec. 9 in protest against the acquittal. But about 700 students rioted for more than 3 hours before dawn Dec. 9. They gathered at a downtown square in Tuskegee, heard speeches, chanted and sang. Then they set fire to leaves in the square and set false alarms. A Confederate statue was painted black, and "black power" was written on it. Bottles and stones were thrown at white-owned establishments, and stores were looted. Although the city's entire 17-man police force was present during the disturbance, no arrests were made. About 13 stores were reported damaged.

Firebomb Kills Vernon Dahmer

Vernon Dahmer, black civil rights figure, was killed in a firebomb attack Jan. 10, 1966. Ultimately, 3 Ku Klux Klansmen received jail sentences for the crime.

Dahmer, 58, died in Hattiesburg, Miss. late Jan. 10 of burns received when molotov cocktails were thrown into his house and adjoining store early that morning. Dahmer's wife, Ellie, 41, and his daughter, Betty, 10, were hospitalized for burns; 2 sons and an aunt escaped injury. The house, store and family car were destroyed in the explosion and fire that followed. Dahmer, a past president of the local NAACP chapter, had announced over Hattiesburg radio Jan. 9 that he would collect poll taxes from local black voters and deliver the money to the sheriff's office.

Dahmer told newsmen at the hospital before dying, "I've been active in trying to get people to register to vote. . . . What happened to us last night can happen to anybody, white or black." He said he had been awakened by gunshots about 2:30 a.m. and had fired several shotgun blasts at a car driving away from his house.

Local authorities later found a car that had been hit with shotgun pellets. The car had been abandoned 3 miles from Hattiesburg in Jones County, headquarters of the White Knights of the Ku Klux Klan. The car's owner had reported it stolen.

Atty. Gen. Nicholas deB. Katzenbach announced in Washington Mar. 28 that FBI agents earlier that day had arrested 13 members of the White Knights of the Ku Klux Klan in connection with Dahmer's death. A search was under way for a 14th man, Sam Holloway Bowers Jr., 41, the White Knights' imperial wizard. The 14 were charged with violating Dahmer's rights.

12 of the arrests were made at dawn in Jones County, Miss., adjoining Hattiesburg; those arrested were released later Mar. 28 and early Mar. 29 on bond ranging from $10,000 to $15,000. They were: Cecil Victor Sessum, 30, exalted cyclops of the Jones County Klavern; Howard Travis Giles, 37, ex-exalted cyclops of the Ellisville Klavern; Lawrence Byrd, 44; Henry Edward DeBoxtel, 29; James Franklin Lyons, 33; Melvin Sennett Martin, 33; Emanuel B. Moss, 52; Deavours Nix, 42; Charles Richard Noble, 23; Billy Roy Pitts, 22; William Ray Smith, 28, and Clifton Eudell Lowe, 50. Lowe's son, Charles Lamar Lowe, 23, was arrested in Houston, Tex. for removal to Mississippi.

Bowers surrendered to the FBI in Hattiesburg Mar. 31 in the company of his 2 attorneys. He was released on $25,000 bond. The FBI had disclosed having found a "small arsenal" in Bowers' home at Laurel, Miss.

A federal grand jury (17 whites, 6 Negroes) in Biloxi, Miss. June 22 returned indictments against 15 alleged Klan members in connection with Dahmer's death. They were accused of violating provisions of the 1965 Voting Rights Act forbidding intimidation of persons for voting or urging others to vote. 14 of the defendants, those arrested in March, were currently free on bond; the 15th, Mordauant William Hamilton Sr., 58, was arrested in Hattiesburg June 23. (The indictments were not made public until after Hamilton's arrest.)

An all-white jury in Hattiesburg Mar. 15, 1968 convicted Sessum of first degree murder for his part in Dahmer's death. Sessum was sentenced to imprisonment for life. During his trial, the state charged that the attack on Dahmer was a Klan plot conceived because of Dahmer's efforts to encourage blacks to register to vote. Smith, an admitted Klan member also convicted in the case, received a life term July 19. Ex-Klan member Pitts, who pleaded guilty to both murder and arson, was sentenced to life in prison, and Byrd was given a 10-year term Nov. 8.

Mistrials were declared in the murder trials of DeBoxtel Mar. 21, 1968, Charles Clifford Wilson July 28 and Lyons Nov. 14. In each case the jurors could not agree on a verdict. The trial for arson of former Ku Klux Klan leader Bowers had ended in a deadlock May 17 with 11 jurors voting guilty and one voting not guilty. Pitts, a key state witness in the trial, had testified May 15 that Bowers had given the orders to firebomb Dahmer's house and kill him if possible. Bowers was arrested on murder charges Nov. 18.

Bowers' murder trial opened in Hattiesburg Jan. 21, 1969 but ended in mistrial Jan. 25 when the jury failed to reach a verdict. The chief prosecutor, James Finch, had charged that Bowers had "planned, directed, masterminded, instituted and inspired" Dahmer's firebombing murder. Pitts, who had testified against Bowers in the arson case, was the prosecution's chief witness in the murder trial. Pitts testified Jan. 23 that Dahmer's death had been planned at a meeting in which Bowers had insisted that the Klan deal with "that nigger Dahmer." According to Pitts, Bowers did not go along on the raid that ended in Dahmer's death but was to act as "backup man" if the murder attempt failed.

James Meredith Ambushed in Mississippi

James H. Meredith, the black student whose entry into the University of Mississippi in 1962 had resulted in racial violence, became a sniper's target as he attempted to walk from Memphis, Tenn. to Jackson, Miss. in support of black voting rights. Meredith was wounded and his attacker arrested. A civil rights coalition took up the march and reached Jackson under a guard of state highway patrolmen. Meredith's attacker was given a 5-year prison term, with 3 years of the 5 suspended.

Meredith was shot from ambush June 6, 1966 shortly after he began a 220-mile voting-rights pilgrimage from Memphis to Jackson, the Mississippi capital. Meredith, then a student at the Columbia University Law School in New York, was wounded as he walked along U.S. Highway 51, 2 miles south of Hernando, Miss., on the 2d day of his march. He had begun the pilgrimage with a few companions June 5. In announcing his plans May 31, he had described the march as a personal attempt to "encourage the 450,-000 unregistered Negroes in Mississippi to go to the polls and register" and also to "point up and to challenge the all-pervasive and overriding fear that dominates the day-to-day life of the Negro in the United States—especially in the South and particularly in Mississippi."

Meredith was hit by 3 blasts from a 16-gauge shotgun. 15 law officers, including 2 FBI agents, and a number of reporters and photographers were in the vicinity of the shooting. Sherwood Ross, a New York and Washington radio announcer serving as Meredith's press coordinator, said he had seen a white man appear in the brush at the side of the highway and shout "James Meredith" twice before firing. An ambulance arrived almost immediately and took Meredith to Memphis, where emergency surgery was performed. Hospital authorities in Memphis said Meredith had suffered 60-70 superficial wounds in the head, back and legs and was in satisfactory condition following surgery.

Aubrey James Norvell, 40, a white resident of Memphis, was arrested at the scene of the shooting and taken to the Hernando jail; Sheriff Lee Meredith of DeSoto County said later that Norvell had admitted the shooting. Norvell, whose car was found to contain a shotgun and quantity of beer, was arraigned June 7 on a charge of "assault with a deadly weapon with intent to murder."

The attack on Meredith brought an immediate reaction from leaders of civil righths organizations. A continuation of Meredith's march was announced at a Memphis news conference early June 7 by the Rev. Dr. Martin Luther King, president of the Southern Christian Leadership Conference (SCLC), Floyd D. McKissick, national director of the Congress of Racial Equality (CORE), and Stokely Carmichael, chairman of the Student Nonviolent Coordinating Committee (SNCC). The 3 leaders and about 20 supporters began their march immediately, encountering hostility from Mississippi state troopers, who jostled them from the pavement to the side of U.S. Highway 51 near Hernando. The marchers resumed walking on the shoulder of the highway for about 2 hours and then announced they would resume the march June 8 and would continue it to Jackson. Meanwhile, black comedian Dick Gregory and a few companions were marching from the site of Meredith's shooting back to Memphis, 26 miles away. The march through Mississippi begun by James Meredith June 5 had been taken up by a civil rights coalition after Meredith was shot.

The "Meredith March Against Fear," the name given the march after the rights organizations took over from the fallen Meredith, covered 260 miles and ended with a rally June 26 in front of the state capitol in Jackson. The march stimulated the registration of about 4,000 Mississippi blacks and involved at least 10,000 Negroes as temporary participants. Voter canvassing teams left the other marchers periodically to concentrate on individual towns.

The marchers had encountered violence June 21 as they held a memorial service at the Neshoba County courthouse in Philadelphia to commemorate the 1964 slaying of 3 civil rights workers near Philadelphia. As the marchers, including about 250 local Negroes, began walking back toward the black community, they were attacked by a crowd of about 300 whites using fists, stones, clubs, bottles and firecrackers. Local police made no move to intervene until a few blacks began fighting back with fists. An outbreak of shooting took place in Philadelphia's black section that evening; Stanley Stuart, a white man, fired a shot into Freedom House, a civil rights headquarters, and suffered a minor neck wound from a shot fired in return. Sporadic shooting followed.

The June 26 rally in Jackson that climaxed the march was attended by a crowd composed largely of Mississippi Negroes and estimated by Justice Department officials at 15,000. More than 1,000 law enforcement officers, including National Guardsmen and state highway patrolmen, were used to separate the demonstrators from 1,500 white Mississippians. There were no major incidents. Speakers at the rally included Meredith, who had rejoined the march June 24, the Rev. Dr. Martin Luther King Jr. and Stokely Carmichael of the Student Nonviolent Coordinating Committee, who called on blacks to "build a power base . . . so strong that we will bring them [whites] to their knees every time they mess with us."

Norvell pleaded guilty in Hernando, Miss. Nov. 21 to the shooting of Meredith. He was given a 5-year prison sentence, but 3 years of the term were suspended. Norvell had changed his plea from not guilty after his attorneys failed to have the indictments dismissed on the grounds that Norvell had been denied his constitutional rights by the alleged systematic exclusion of women and systematic inclusion of Negroes on the county juries.

Disorders in Grenada, Miss.

Shooting incidents and clashes between jeering whites and black demonstrators accompanied a 1966 civil rights campaign in Grenada.

43 black demonstrators were arrested in Grenada July 7 after they sat down in the street and refused to disperse. They were among some 100 whose attempted march on the county courthouse had been halted by police. Those arrested were charged with obstructing traffic. In a statement released July 8 through the Atlanta office of the Southern Christian Leadership Conference (SCLC), the Rev. Dr. Martin Luther King Jr. accused Grenada officials of having "gone back on every promise made" when the "Meredith march" had passed through the town. King also charged that Grenada police had been "harassing, beating and jailing our staff, as well as the local Negroes."

About 300 blacks staged a "sympathy march" July 10 to the jail in which those arrested July 7 were being held. After the demonstrators ignored an order to disperse, 25 highway patrolmen scattered them with billy clubs and gun butts while deputy sheriffs dispersed a crowd of 100 jeering whites.

Earlier July 10 2 white men had been arrested on charges of shooting the previous evening at 3 white men entering a black church. Those shot at (none was hit) were James L. Draper of the federal Community Relations Service, Henry Aaronson, an NAACP attorney, and Oliver Rosengart, an NYU law student. The 2 arrested men were arraigned July 11 on charges of assault and battery with intent to kill and were released on bail; they were identified as Bobby Todd of Grenada and B.C. Bennett of nearby Montgomery County. Bennett and Todd were acquitted Aug. 2 of charges of pointing and aiming a deadly weapon.

City and county officials July 11 issued a statement in reply to 51 demands presented by the SCLC. The statement said: "There will be no concessions of any type or degree made to anyone whatsoever, likewise there will be no acceding to any such demands."

35 Negroes were arrested on charges of obstructing traffic July 13 as they marched through the downtown section urging a black boycott of white merchants.

Negroes clashed with police and whites in Grenada Aug. 8-9. The disorders began when local and state police used tear gas to disperse a black-voter registration rally the evening of Aug. 8. The Negroes, variously estimated at from several hundred to 1,200 persons, had gathered in front of a recently-opened federal voter-registration office for a rally addressed by Hosea Williams, Southern field director of the SCLC. Police routed the demonstrators with tear gas after they had refused to clear the street. Negroes charged that the police had used night-sticks and gunfire as well. Williams said that 2 persons had been injured seriously.

Violence erupted the evening of Aug. 9 when about 300 Negroes marched to protest the Aug. 8 use of tear gas. 150 to 175 whites threw bricks, rocks, bottles, steel pipes and firecrackers at the blacks while local and state police reportedly stood by laughing. One rights worker, Mildred Smith, 19, was knocked unconscious by a thrown piece of pipe that gashed her face. At least a dozen other Negroes were reported injured, none seriously. About 150 Negroes protested the Aug. 9 attacks by marching to the town square Aug. 10. 155 armed state troopers and 75 fish and game wardens protected the marchers and dispersed a crowd of about 500 angry whites. At least 2 whites were arrested for refusing to move.

Demonstrations continued the evening of Aug. 13 when about 150 blacks marched to the courthouse square. 100 policemen carrying shotguns protected the marchers from cursing whites. Police Aug. 14 arrested 19 Negroes, including Leon Hall, director of the civil rights drive in Grenada, when they attempted to enter the all-white First Baptist Church during morning services.

Further violence erupted in Grenada, Sept. 12-13 when a mob of whites attacked black children integrating the city's 2 all-white schools. At least 30 black children and parents were reported beaten. 13 persons were arrested.

The initial clash took place the morning of Sept. 12 when whites (variously reported at from 200 to 400) armed with ax handles, chains and pipes barred about 40 of 160 black students from entering John Rundle High School. At the Lizzie Horn elementary school, black children entered peacefully in the morning but were attacked by a mob on leaving in the afternoon. Receiving little or no protection from local police—who frequently watched without interfering as whites beat black children—black parents and children retreated to the school building until state troopers were summoned to escort them home. 2 boys were hospitalized with severe head injuries and bruises. A 3d was treated for a broken leg. The crowd beat 2 *Memphis Scimitar Press* photographers and a UPI reporter; a constable prevented the UPI man from taking safety on the school grounds.

Violence continued Sept. 13 when whites harrassed Negroes and newsmen. Only 35 or 40 black children were able to reach school. Henry Aaronson, NAACP Legal Defense & Educational Fund attorney, was beaten by 8 white men while nearby police ignored his cries for help. He was released only when his assailants discovered that an NBC camera crew was filming their behavior. The mob then chased the TV personnel. A rock shattered the window of a car to which NBC correspondents and photographers had retreated and struck one on the head.

The mobs Sept. 13 assaulted 2 car-loads of black children. 35 other black children, who were marching to school in a group from the Bell Flowers Baptist Church, were turned back by the mob. Black parents, who charged police with failing to protect the children, started a march to the school the afternoon of Sept. 13 but were stopped a block from the school by state highway patrolmen, who assured them the children would be escorted home safely.

The Justice Department filed suit in Oxford, Miss. Sept. 13 against the city of Grenada, the City Council, Mayor J. D. Quinn, Police Chief Pat Ray, Grenada County Sheriff Suggs Ingram and City Manager John E. McEachin, who were charged with "willful failure and refusal" to protect the black children. The suit asked the U.S. district court in Oxford to grant temporary and permanent injunctions ordering Grenada officials "to provide protection to the children in the future and to arrest and prosecute those who assault or threaten them." A temporary injunction was immediately issued by U.S. District Judge Claude F. Clayton.

About 90 black children attended class Sept. 14 escorted by 150 state troopers and FBI agents; only a few white spectators stood nearby. Local police, under federal court order, arrested 6 white men on charges of assault, disturbing the peace and carrying concealed weapons.

Judge Clayton ordered schools closed Sept. 15 while officials attended the first day of hearings in Oxford, Miss. After hearing 2 days of testimony that police, city and county officials had failed to act against the mob, Clayton Sept. 16 issued a permanent restraining order requiring city and county police to protect Negro children.

These 5 white men were indicted Oct. 4 by a federal grand jury in Greenville, Miss. in connection with the violence: James Richard Ayers, 48, Grenada County Justice of the Peace; Archie Larry Campbell, 19; Doyle Cleveland Vance, 46; Donald Wayne Bain, 18, and Roy L. House. They were charged with conspiracy to intimidate Negro citizens and with willfully obstructing school attendance by Negroes.

Other Southern Violence

Fire Department officials in Natchez, Miss. reported Jan. 1, 1966 that a New Year's Eve fire at the Giant Discount Center, owned by Natchez Mayor John W. Nosser, showed definite indications of arson. The concrete-and-metal structure had been totally destroyed by the time firemen were able to extinguish the blaze. (Nosser's home had been bombed in Sept. 1964, and he had blamed the incident on white segregationists angered by his efforts to reduce racial tension in Natchez.)

The Notchaway Church, a black church near Newton, Ga., was burned Jan. 2. Sheriff Warren Johnson said he had received a phone call Jan. 2 threatening his life if he investigated the fire.

Crosses were burned in at least 9 Mississippi counties the night of Jan. 3, and 7 arrests were made. FBI authorities said that 2 FBI agents had been shot at while observing cross-burnings.

2 white rights workers in Kosciusko, Miss. were hit by shotgun blasts late Feb. 2 when night riders fired into a home housing 9 rights workers. The 2, who suffered only slight injuries, were Donald Salisbury and Richard Klausner, 19-year-old Oberlin College students. Police Feb. 3 halted a march by 100 black schoolchildren demonstrating in protest against the shooting.

A bomb exploded late Feb. 6 in the home of Arthur Lewis, a Negro, in Zachary, La. (near Baton Rouge). Ray Herd, head of the state police laboratory, said Feb. 7 that the bomb damage was similar to that caused by 3 other explosions occurring in the Baton Rouge area since the summer of 1965.

5 Negroes were wounded in Birmingham Feb. 21 when a white motorist fired 8 pistol shots into a crowd of 150 blacks picketing the Liberty Supermarket. The demonstrators had been demanding that the supermarket hire more Negroes and had been protesting the alleged beating of a picket by the supermarket's security guard. Emory Warren McGowan, 23, surrendered to the police later Feb. 21 and admitted the shooting; he was charged with 5 counts of assault with intent to murder and was freed Feb. 22 on $1,500 bail. McGowan contended that he had fired in self-defense after a crowd of demonstrators had surrounded his car as it left the supermarket parking lot and had tried to pull him from it. Witnesses charged that McGowan had driven up to a line of marchers, raced his engine and fired when a crowd began milling around the car. A boycott of Birmingham's white merchants was announced Feb. 24 by the Rev. Calvin Woods. Woods said the tactic had been

decided on at a meeting of a 25-member ministerial committee with representatives of the NAACP and SCLC.

Jefferson County (Ala.) Sheriff Mel Bailey announced in Birmingham Feb. 23 that an unidentified "citizen" had discovered a "bomb factory" in a wooded area near Birmingham Feb. 19. The cache contained several cases of dynamite, blasting caps and timing mechanisms. One timing device was said to be identical to clocks found in Apr. 1965 in unexploded bombs discovered in several Birmingham buildings, including the home of Mayor Albert Boutwell.

Part of a high school in Elba, Ala. was severely damaged Feb. 24 by 2 explosions, apparently of dynamite. The formerly all-white school had admitted 2 black students in Sept. 1965. The explosions occurred shortly after the departure of 200 people who had attended a banquet at the school.

Mississippi state troopers used tear gas Apr. 4 to clear a dormitory of students throwing bricks and bottles at the Lorman, Miss. campus of the black, state-supported Alcorn A & M (Agricultural & Mechanical) College. Later Apr. 4 the troopers turned back an attempted march on the campus by 300 non-student Negroes. A Chancery Court judge Apr. 4 had issued an injunction, sought by the State College Board, forbidding marchers to enter the campus. Gov. Paul B. Johnson Jr. Apr. 4 ordered 250 National Guardsmen to augment the highway patrolmen. The demonstrations were led by Charles Evers, Mississippi field secretary of the NAACP. Evers said Apr. 5 that Alcorn Pres. John D. Boyd, a Negro, was "on'y concerned with pleasing the white folks." He charged Apr. 6 that 8 Alcorn students had been suspended and the chief of the campus police discharged because of civil rights activity. Boyd denied the charges. 2 attempted marches on campus by about 1,000 adults and high school students were turned back by state troopers Apr. 5, and Alcorn students were prevented by troopers from leaving the campus. In a 15-minute melee troopers used fire hoses and tear gas to fend off bottle-throwing demonstrators on campus. Demonstrations were suspended Apr. 6, and the National Guardsmen were withdrawn.

The body of Ben Chester White, 65, a Negro, was found June 12 in a creek near Natchez. He had been shot 16 times with a rifle, and his head had been partly blown away by a shotgun blast. Sheriff Odell Anders, in announcing June 14 the arrest of 3 white men in connection with the slaying, said White had been killed June 10. Those arrested June 14, all identified as KKK members, were James Lloyd Jones, 56, Claude Fuller, 46, and Ernest Avants, 35.

Jones turned state's witness and testified at a preliminary hearing June 17 that he had watched Fuller and Avants shoot White and dump his body in the creek.

About 600 Negroes in Pompano Beach, Fla. rioted the evening of June 21 after a 10-year-old black boy complained that he had been slapped by Arthur Marks, 42, white owner of the Russ Supermarket. As angry Negroes gathered at his store, police arrested Marks on an assault and battery charge. (He was later freed on $500 bond.) 2 blacks were arrested shortly thereafter on loitering charges, and members of the crowd began throwing bottles at cars and policemen and breaking windows, including all those in Marks' store. 2 policemen were treated for cuts, and 25 Negroes were arrested on disorderly conduct and unlawful assembly charges. (All but 4 of those arrested were released on bond June 22.) 150 police using billy clubs and the threat of tear gas restored order shortly after midnight. Police reported no looting or significant property damage. A compromise agreement between police and black leaders was reported June 22; the neighborhood leaders pledged to clear the streets if police strength were cut. Taylor Williams, local NAACP president, said June 22 that calm would have been more quickly restored "if the mayor hadn't called in the outside police." Florida highway patrolmen and police from neighboring Hollywood and Fort Lauderdale had been brought in to augment Pompano Beach's 40-man police force.

An exchange of gunfire between whites and Negroes took place the night of June 28-29 at a black-operated service station in Cordele, Ga. 10 white men, of a group of 25-30 that had gathered at the service station, began shooting after a black youth threw a bottle and smashed a window of a white-driven car. 5-6 Negroes hidden in the vicinity returned the fire. The exchange lasted about 90 minutes and was halted with the arrival of about 25 state troopers from neighboring towns. Nobody was wounded, 5 whites were taken into custody. The incident was reportedly related to a June 26 confrontation between whites and Negroes at a swimming pool at nearby Veterans State Park, which had been desegregated in 1965. Since the swimming pool incident bands of black youths had roamed the town, throwing bricks at cars and stores and setting small fires.

About 200 blacks marched on city hall in Jacksonville, Fla. July 18. When the march headed from city hall toward the business district, clashes broke out between marchers and jeering whites. Negroes then began throwing bricks and firebombs. One store was set afire, 2 white youths were beaten and a white woman was injured by a flying rock. Police arrested Warren H. Folks, 46, a white man, as he attempted to serve a "Klan warrant" on Rutledge Pearson, state NAACP president, who had led the protest march.

Firebombing and other vandalism broke out again in a black Jacksonville neighborhood the following 2 nights. A grocery store was dynamited the night of July 20, and at least 5 black youths were arrested in scattered rock-throwing incidents. Mayor Louis H. Ritter had met earlier July 20 with NAACP Pres. Pearson to discuss demands by black leaders (the demands included the desegregation of the police department and the re-opening of city swimming pools).

Marshall R. Kornegay, grand dragon of the Virginia Ku Klux Klan, offered Oct. 9 to rebuild a black church in Richmond, Va. The church had been damaged by an explosion Oct. 5. Speaking at a Klan rally near Orange, Va., Kornegay said the Klan would rebuild the 2d Bethel Baptist Church with "our own workmanship and our materials." He called the explosion a "dastardly crime" and offered a $200 reward for the apprehension of those responsible.

The House Un-American Activities Committee, reporting Oct. 21 on the KKK, said: "Klans engage in threats, cross-burnings, the firing of churches and schools, bombings, beatings, maimings, murders, and other acts of violence to further their goal of white supremacy as well as other objectives. These acts, however, are not always racially motivated and sometimes are directed against citizens who are not racially oriented but who are conducting themselves to the dislike of the Klans, which take the law into their hands as vigilantes. . . . Klansmen frequently carry pistols, rifles, shotguns, and bombs on their persons and in their autos. . . . Some Klan members have been issued federal licenses as gun dealers and have sold guns to members in wholesale lots. Secret Klan schools instruct in the fabrication of booby traps, bombs, and molotov cocktails and teach the use of bombs, firearms, judo, and karate."

Hundreds of black youths rioted for nearly 6 hours Oct. 31 in Clearwater, Fla. They smashed streetlights and store windows, threw paint on buildings, fired rifles in the air and set trash fires in the streets. 40 Clearwater policemen and 30 Pinellas County deputies including a riot squad armed with bayonets were called in to restore order. 3 persons were arrested. Police Chief Willis Booth said there was "nothing racial" about the outburst, "it was just rowdyism, vandalism and plain hell-raising."

SNCC Chairman Stokely Carmichael was arrested with 2
Negroes in Selma, Ala. Nov. 5 on charges of inciting a riot at the
City Hall. Carmichael and William S. House, 20, were convicted
of the charge Nov. 29. The 3d defendant, Lorenzo Taylor of
Philadelphia, had been convicted previously on a lesser charge.
Carmichael was fined $100 and sentenced to 60 days in jail at hard
labor. House was fined $100 and sentenced to 30 days at hard
labor. Selma Mayor Joseph T. Smitherman had charged that the
3 men had arrived in town in a sound truck with loudspeakers
blaring and had blocked traffic in a black section. He said that
when the defendants ignored police orders to move the truck, one
policeman with a shotgun opened the door and arrested the
driver. Then, Smitherman said, Carmichael "got on the loudspeak-
er and tried to draw a crowd. About 1,000 spectators gathered,
but only 30 to 40 joined" in the demonstration. Smitherman
said he had ordered Carmichael's arrest after Carmichael "lunged"
at an officer. The defendants denied the charges. Carmichael said
he had come to Selma to encourage Negroes to vote for independent candidates in the Nov. 8 elections.

2 Killers Run Amok

8 student nurses of Chicago's Community Hospital were
found slain July 14, 1966 in their 2-story townhouse, on Chicago's
Far South Side, which served as a dormitory. 5 of the students
died by strangulation, 3 by stabbing. (Autopsies showed no signs
of sexual molestation.) The slayer, Richard Speck, was arrested
July 17 after an extensive manhunt.

The victims were: Gloria Jean Davy, 22, of Dyer, Ind.,
Suzanne Bridget Farris, 21, of Chicago, Merlita Gargullo, 23, of
Manila, the Philippines, Mary Ann Jordan, 20, of Chicago, Patricia
Ann Matusek, 20, of Chicago, Valentina Pasion, 23, of Manila,
Nina Jo Schmale, 23, of Wheaton, Ill., Pamela Lee Wilkening,
20, of Chicago Heights. A 9th girl, Corazon Amurao, 23, of the
Philippines, escaped death by hiding under a bed. Miss Amurao
gave this account of the murders:

At approximately 11 p.m. July 13 she was aroused from bed
by a knock at the door. A man entered holding a knife and
revolver. He herded Miss Amurao and her 2 roomates into a 2d
bedroom where 3 of the other students slept. Shortly after the
remaining 3 girls entered the building the man tore up bed sheets
and bound all 9 girls' hands behind their backs. He told them
that he needed money to get to New Orleans. After they gave

him all the cash on hand he led each girl separately out of the room and slew her. During one of his absences Miss Amurao rolled under the bed and hid there until early morning. Shortly after 6 a.m. Miss Amurao went to a 2d-floor window ledge and screamed "They are all dead! . . ." Her screams brought police to the scene.

Richard Benjamin Speck (alias Richard Franklin Lindberg and Richard Franklin Speck), 24, of Monmouth, Ill., an unemployed seaman and laborer, was arrested July 17. He had been identified by a photo shown to Miss Amurao and by fingerprints found in the victims' apartment. Speck, an ex-convict, who had served a 3-year prison sentence in Dallas for burglary and forgery and a subsequent term for assaulting a woman, had been turned over to police by Dr. LeRoy A. Smith, 26, an emergency ward surgeon who had treated Speck in Cook County Hospital early July 17 for self-inflicted arm and wrist wounds. Identification had been aided by tattoos on Speck's arms. Speck had been brought to the hospital by police after he had attempted suicide in his skid-row hotel room. (The police had not recognized the suspect.)

Speck was convicted in Peoria, Ill. Apr. 15, 1967. The jury of 7 men and 5 women asked that Speck be given the death penalty for each of the 8 slayings. (Under Illinois law only the jury can fix the death sentence.) The trial had been transferred from Chicago to Peoria Dec. 19, 1966 because Gerald W. Getty, the public defender, claimed that adverse publicity made it impossible for Speck to receive a fair trial in Chicago.

Charles Joseph Whitman, 25, of Lake Worth, Fla., an architectural engineering honor student at the University of Texas, climbed to the top of the university's 27-story tower in Austin Aug. 1, 1966 and shot 44 persons. 14 persons (including an unborn child) were killed, and 30 were wounded. The 90-minute shooting rampage was ended when Romero Martinez, an off-duty policeman, climbed the tower and shot Whitman, who died immediately. Authorities later found the bodies of Whitman's mother, Mrs. Charles A. Whitman, and his wife, Kathleen Leissner Whitman, 24, at their homes. His mother had been shot in the back of the head and his wife had been stabbed twice.

2 notes found in Whitman's apartment told of his love for both women and expressed concern that they had to die to "save them the embarassment of what [he] was going to do." A longer note included a statement that he hated his father "with a mortal passion." Whitman had apparently killed the 2 women during the night, then had assembled an arsenal (which included 3 rifles,

2 pistols, a shotgun and a knife) and packed a foot locker with food, water and other provisions. After loading everything into the trunk, he carried it to the tower.

An autopsy performed Aug. 2 at Austin State Hospital revealed that Whitman had a pecan-sized non-malignant brain tumor. Medical experts expressed doubt that the tumor had influenced the sniper's psychic behavior. Whitman had indicated in a note that he wished an autopsy performed after his death in order to determine whether he had a mental disorder.

A Texas University psychiatrist, Dr. Maurice D. Heatly, revealed Aug. 2 that Whitman had consulted him earlier in 1966. In his report Heatly had stated that the "massive, muscular youth seemed to be oozing with hostility. . . ." Heatly said that Whitman had expressed an urge to go "up on the tower with a deer rifle and start shooting people" but that the statement had not particularly alarmed him.

Whitman was described by his father, Charles A. Whitman Jr., 47, of Lake Worth, Fla., as a "crack shot" who had been raised in a house with a gun in every room. Whitman had been a Boy Scout leader and a Marine who had won honors in marksmanship. The Pentagon reported Aug. 2 that Whitman had been courtmartialed in 1963 for illegal possession of a pistol in his barracks and aboard ship.

INTENSIFIED URBAN RIOTING (1967)

Growth of Violence in the Cities

75 urban riots were reported in the U.S. in the period Jan.-Nov. 1967. 83 persons died in urban disorders, 16,389 persons were arrested, and the cost of civil strife was estimated at $664½ million. In the previous year there had been 21 riots, 11 deaths, 2,298 arrests and a cost of $10.2 million.

The worst riot since the 1965 Watts outbreak took place in Newark, N.J. July 12-17, 1967. 6 days of rioting brought death to 26 persons. More than 300 fires were started by arsonists, and turmoil covered a 10-square-mile area of the city. At the height of the rioting, police, National Guardsmen and black snipers exchanged gunfire amid burning buildings.

Only days later an explosion of disorder in Detroit July 20-30 surpassed Watts and Newark in violence and intensity. Rioting, burning and looting left 43 people dead, 5,000 homeless and property damage estimated at $250 to $500 million. For the first time in 24 years Regular Army troops were dispatched to help city police and National Guardsmen quell a civil outbreak.

Turmoil began in the spring when black students rioted Apr. 8-10, 1967 in Nashville, Tenn. Disorders flared in Cleveland later in April and in Houston in May.

Armed Spanish-Americans briefly seized a village in New Mexico June 5. In June, racial rioting also exploded in Boston, Cincinnati, Tampa, Atlanta and Buffalo, N.Y.

In addition to the major July conflagrations in Newark and Detroit, rioting flared a 2d time in Cincinnati July 3-4, 1967. National Guard units were called out after a mob beat a policeman to death in Plainfield, N.J., and National Guardsmen were called out to control turmoil in Minneapolis. Rioting in New York City's Spanish Harlem brought death to 2 victims. Black violence swept Cambridge, Md. Philadelphia officials declared a state of emergency after roving black gangs stoned passing cars. 4 persons were killed in Milwaukee disorders. As the wave of racial disorders rolled across the country in July, outbreaks of arson, looting, window-smashing and gunfire were reported in 45 other cities from coast to coast.

Vandalism, looting and arson also broke out in the nation's capital Aug. 1, 1967. Before the month was over, riots had been reported in cities in New York, Illinois, Michigan, Connecticut and Wisconsin. September brought disorders in East St. Louis, Ill., Chicago, Hartford, Conn. and Dayton, O. In November, there was rioting in Winston-Salem, N.C. and renewed violence in Philadelphia and Chicago.

Students and demonstrators protesting the draft and U.S. policy in Vietnam clashed with police in violent incidents in Oakland, Calif., Madison, Wis. and Brooklyn, N.Y. Thousands of marchers participated in a massive Washington, D. C. antiwar protest.

There were fewer reports of racial violence in the South during 1967. Bombings occurred in Mississippi and Alabama, states in which 3 black churches were burned. An open-housing demonstration in Louisville, Ky. was accompanied by clashes between Negroes, whites and police and brief rioting. National Guard troops were mobilized and martial law was imposed in turmoil during which a Negro was killed in Jackson, Miss. Black snipers and police exchanged rifle fire in Prattville, Ala. before National Guardsmen quelled the disturbance. James Meredith completed his "March Against Fear" after recovering from gunshot wounds suffered when he began the march in 1966. Gunfire and attacks by whites punctuated a civil-rights march from Bogalusa, La. to the state capitol in Baton Rouge.

The Rev. Dr. Martin Luther King Jr. had warned at an impromptu news conference in New York Apr. 16, 1967 that at least 10 cities could "explode in racial violence this summer." He described the cities as "powder kegs" and said that "the intolerable conditions which brought about racial violence last summer still exist." The cities he named were Cleveland, Chicago, Los Angeles, Oakland, Calif., Washington, Newark and New York. He said that the other cities, which he did not name, were in the South.

The Senate Permanent Investigations Subcommittee Nov. 1 made public these statistics on riots since 1965:

	1965	1966	1967
Number of riots	5	21	75
Persons killed	36	11	83
Persons injured	1,206	520	1,897
Number arrested	10,245	2,298	16,389
Number convicted	2,074	1,203	2,157
Estimated cost	*$40.1	*$10.2	*$664.5

*In millions

Race Riot in Newark Takes 26 Lives

The country's worst outbreak of racial violence in 2 years erupted in Newark, N.J. July 12-17, 1967. In 6 days of rioting, 26 persons—24 Negroes and 2 whites—were killed; more than 1,500 persons were reported injured; 1,397 persons were arrested. More than 300 fires, 12 of major proportions, were reported. Property damage was estimated at $15 to $30 million. At its height, the rioting spread to 10 of the city's 23 square miles.

For some time observers had held that the city was ripe for such an outburst. Newark's black community had grown from 17% of the city's population in 1950 to 34% of the total in 1960, the year of the last census prior to the riot. According to 1967 reports, Negroes made up 52% to 60% of Newark's estimated population of 405,000. The city's unemployment rate, 7.2% was reported to be nearly double the statewide New Jersey rate. The *N.Y. Times* reported July 15 that average annual household income for Newark proper was $6,890, for the suburbs $11,394. The city's public schools were reportedly to be 80% black. Newark had received $25 million in federal anti-poverty funds in the past 3 years.

The rioting began July 12 in Newark's black ghetto, the Central Ward, when police arrested a black taxi driver, John William Smith, on a driving violation. A brief scuffle between Smith and police outside the 4th Precinct station house was witnessed by a score of residents of a nearby housing project. About 25 taxi drivers loaded black bystanders into their cars and converged on the police station after hearing a false report that Smith had been beaten to death.

As the rumor of Smith's death spread through the community, the mob swelled to 200 to 250 persons, who began throwing rocks and bottles at the station house, smashing its windows. Gangs of black youths then spread through the district and into Newark's downtown area. They set false alarms, smashed windows, looted stores and threw merchandise on the sidewalks. Several carloads of Negroes drove to City Hall to protest police brutality. Order was restored by 3:00 a.m.

Newark Mayor Hugh J. Addonizio met with about 20 of the city's black leaders early the next day and promised to appoint a 10-member committee to investigate charges of police brutality.

Although black leaders contended that police brutality had been the immediate cause of the rioting, they said that a series of other incidents had added to tension in the black community. One of these was Addonizio's recent appointment of white City Councilman James T. Callaghan to the $25,000-a-year post of secretary to the local school board. Black leaders had sponsored Newark Budget Director Wilbur Parker, a Negro, whose academic and professional training, they held, better qualified him for the job. The 2d issue centered on the city's selection of a 50-acre Central Ward site for the construction of a planned New Jersey College of Medicine and Dentistry. Negroes had opposed the plan on the ground it would displace at least 1,800 low-income persons; they wanted the site used for housing.

Violence erupted again at 7:35 p.m. July 13 in front of the 4th Precinct station house when about 200 blacks gathered to protest Smith's alleged beating. Although the marchers reportedly started out in good spirits, the mood changed when one youth tossed a bottle over the crowd and hit the station house. About 150 teenagers then joined in tossing rocks and bottles at the building. After waiting for 45 minutes Police Director Dominick A. Spina dispatched about 60 police, who pushed the mobs to the housing project near the station house.

The disturbance spread to surrounding streets and began moving toward the downtown section of Newark and in the opposite direction as well. 90 more policemen were called in. By 12:30 a.m. snipers had opened fire on police, shooting from cars and rooftops in the West, East and Central Wards. An estimated 3,000 blacks roamed a 20-block area on Springfield Ave., smashing windows and looting stores. Debris from liquor stores, appliance and toy stores was scattered on the sidewalks. A toy store was set on fire with a molotov cocktail, and the flames spread to 2 adjoining stores.

At 1:00 a.m. July 14, Mayor Addonizio and Police Director Spina abandoned their policy of limiting police to containing riot-torn areas and ordered police to "return fire if necessary." 30 minutes later, as the violence spread, Addonizio ordered the city's 1,400-man police force on full alert. Police armed with shotguns were sent to guard firemen fighting a blaze sweeping several stores near Broad and Market Streets. Hundreds of persons were taken into custody by police although only about 75 were formally arrested. At least 4 of the 300 persons listed as injured were treated at Newark City Hospital for gunshot wounds. 3 persons, all black, were killed during the night.

At 2:20 a.m. Addonizio telephoned New Jersey Gov. Richard J. Hughes and asked him to send National Guardsmen and state troopers to the city. Within 10 minutes Hughes summoned the state police and placed New Jersey units of the National Guard on "state alert" (they were not federalized nor was Newark placed under martial law). Guardsmen and troopers began arriving in Newark by 5:00 a.m. July 14. As they went through white sections of the city to the Central Ward they were met by small groups of whites who shouted "Kill the bastards" and "Shoot the niggers."

Gov. Hughes arrived in Newark at about 5:00 a.m. July 14. He telephoned Pres. Johnson later that morning to say that federal aid was not necessary. At a news conference later July 14 Hughes said that "the destruction is unbelievable." He said he was "shocked and horrified" at the "holiday atmosphere [in riot-torn areas of the city]. ... It's like laughing at a funeral." He charged that the rioting was a "criminal insurrection" which had "nothing to do with civil rights." "People who burn and loot and kill are not concerned with civil rights." "I think Negroes in the main are just as ashamed of this as I am. This is the work of the criminal element," he declared.

By the afternoon of July 14, 3,000 Guardsmen, 375 state troopers and nearly all of the city's 1,400 police officers had formed a perimeter around the riot area, a 10-square-mile section bounded by Bergen, Washington and Orange Streets and Chancellor Avenue (about 1/3 of the city). Barbed-wire barricades were put up to seal off the city from the suburbs. Guardsmen and state troopers armed with pistols, rifles and shotguns patrolled the streets in cars, jeeps and trucks. There were reports of sporadic gunfire between snipers and police throughout the day. Looting continued, with rioters forming human chains to move stolen merchandise.

Mayor Addonizio July 14 imposed a 10:00-p.m.-to-6:00-a.m. curfew on vehicular traffic (except food trucks) and an 11:00-p.m.-to-6:00-a.m. curfew on pedestrians. The mayor, appearing at an early evening news conference with Gov. Hughes, declared: "Up to early this afternoon, I thought it was unorganized and the work of just the criminal element. But I have just met with about 35 clergymen, and they indicated to me that it might be controlled possibly by people from outside." Hughes said the situation was "deteriorating."

Guardsmen, police and black rioters exchanged gunfire at a Central Ward housing project early in the evening of July 14 while fires raged in adjacent buildings. Frederick W. Toto, 34, a Newark police detective, was killed in the battle. Police and Guardsmen sprayed the upper stories of the building with bullets as blacks hurled bottles and stones from the roof. The fighting ended when 24 Guardsmen rolled up to the entrance of the building in an

11-ton armored personnel carrier with a mounted machinegun. By
the time they took control of the building, however, the snipers
had disappeared.

Sporadic fighting continued through the night. One policeman
was wounded in a battle at 7th and Wood Streets. Police engaged
black gunmen in a running fire fight at 18th St. and Springfield
Ave. Before dawn July 15, firemen answering a fire alarm on
Springfield Ave. were attacked by sniper fire. One sniper fired 6
shots into the crowded emergency room at City Hospital.

By early morning July 15 the death toll had risen to 15. All
but one, the detective, were black. The injured totaled nearly
1,000, including 5 policemen treated for gunshot wounds. By
afternoon, Gov. Hughes said that 1,012 persons (including 121
women and 176 children under 16) had been arrested, among them
black playwright LeRoi Jones, charged with the possession of 2
loaded .32-caliber pistols. Hughes declared: "It was plain and
simple crime and not a civil rights protest." "Most of them," he
said, had prior criminal records. Hughes said at a news conference
that the city "looks like an atom bomb fell on our streets,"
but he added that the situation was "in control except for
snipers."

Hughes met later July 15 with Mayor Addonizio and black
and white citizens who had formed a Committee of 5 to work out
ways to restore order and open communication between the city's
white and black communities. The committee said it would recruit
volunteers to walk through the streets and urge people "to cool
it." (But the committee said July 16 that its efforts to calm the
rioting had failed because of harassment by the National Guard
and state police.)

It was disclosed later July 15 that Hughes had met secretly
with black leaders for 4 hours the previous night at the home of
Oliver Lofton, administrative director of the Newark Legal Services
Project. Lofton said the discussion had centered on the underlying
problems of the Newark's black community. He said Hughes had
agreed to urge Mayor Addonizio to immediately appoint a Negro
as acting police captain in the 4th Precinct and to urge merchants
in the area to reopen their stores to provide food and other essen-
tials for the community. Lofton said that county prosecutor
Brendan Byrne had agreed to open a grand jury investigation into
charges of police brutality.

Vice Pres. Hubert Humphrey phoned Gov. Hughes July 15
to renew an offer of federal help in coping with the Newark unrest. Hughes declined the offer, declaring that he was satisfied

with police and the National Guard actions to deal with what he again called a "criminal insurrection."

Heavy sniper fire continued through the night of July 15 and into the daylight hours of July 16. By afternoon July 16, 9 more persons had been killed. 2 policemen were overcome by tear gas as they tried to force a sniper from a building. Police also began firing at each other. At 10:30 p.m. July 16 the police radio network warned police to "Hold your fire. You're shooting at your own men." Snipers continued firing at City Hospital for the 3d night, forcing a black-out of the building at 9:30 p.m.

Emergency distribution of food was begun in central Newark July 16. At the peak of the rioting, food deliveries had been curtailed by suppliers, and stocks of black- and white-owned stores had been depleted by looters or had been sold out. Many ghetto residents had not been able to buy food for 5 days. Thousands of Negroes, guarded by armed militia, lined up to receive food rations provided from Agriculture Department surplus stocks. 8 distribution centers were in operation in housing projects and community centers. 5 supermarkets, closed at the outbreak of violence, had reopened, as did some others in response to Hughes' pleas. Hughes asked other businesses to remain closed, but he voiced hope for an early resumption of critical services such as garbage collection.

Members of an *ad hoc* committee organized by Dr. Reynold E. Burch, a black obstetrician, met with Hughes the afternoon of July 16 to protest "excesses" allegedly committed by National Guardsmen and state troopers. The 40-member group produced photos and statements by witnesses to document its charges. Included in the testimony taken by the committee was a statement by Mrs. Nancy Ferguson, a black storeowner, who described how state troopers allegedly shot out the windows of her store and of stores owned by 17 other black merchants in the neighboring 5 or 6 blocks. Only stores bearing the sign "Soul Brother," designating black ownership, were affected. The group sent a telegram to Pres. Johnson, requesting "fully integrated federal troops" to replace police and National Guardsmen who, it said, had committed "wanton destruction of property" and "murders." Many Negroes, the telegram said, had been killed or wounded by "indiscriminate firing." It assailed Hughes and Addonizio for what it said were "inflammatory statements" that had stirred up the formation of white vigilante groups on the edges of the black ghetto.

Hughes contended July 16 that the charges of police brutality were based on "hearsay" and "mostly 2d-hand information." He said he was assessing the situation and promised that "justice will be done" as soon as the facts were clear. He said Guardsmen and state troopers would remain on duty, however, until order was restored and all snipers, whom he called "unregenerate criminals," were arrested. At a news conference early July 16, Hughes had offered executive clemency to any of the 1,650 riot prisoners who volunteered information leading to the conviction of snipers. He estimated that at least 25 snipers were still battling with police in the ghetto area. He said he had been informed that some of the snipers came from outside the city. He asserted that although he had no evidence of a conspiracy, "the rather expert sniping, the jumping from place to place, the cruel and despicable efficiency with which this sniping occurred, indicate some organization and some coordination between those criminals participating in it."

Atty. Gen. Ramsey Clark, interviewed on the ABC-TV program "Issues and Answers" July 16, said there was "very, very little evidence of intercity activity to deliberately activate" the Newark rioting. He added that there was "very little the federal government can do" to implement law enforcement in riot-stricken cities.

In the afternoon of July 16, 40 white businessmen and 10 Negroes attended a meeting called by the Newark Legal Services Project to express "concern in the black community of indiscriminate suppressing of disorders." The group adopted resolutions, calling on Hughes for (1) a reduction of militia in the city; (2) a change in bail policy to permit those charged with minor crimes to be released on personal recognizance; (3) a more severe policy toward white vigilantes; (4) an independent investigation of the rioting by an outside group.

Hughes said July 17 that "the rioting and looting are over." He said: "The restoration of order is accomplished. While sniping incidents continue, it is grinding to a halt." Hughes announced the withdrawal from the city of all but a few of the 3,000 Guardsmen and 375 state troopers. A small force was to remain to assure order and assist in the distribution of food. Hughes curtailed most emergency restrictions by 3:00 p.m. July 17 and lifted the city's curfew.

The city's 26th riot victim, Raymond Gilmer, 20, a Negro, was killed July 17 while allegedly looting a store. (25 cases of looting were reported during the night of July 17.) City Hospital's medical director, Dr. C. Richard Weinberg, said July 18 that some 700 persons had been treated during the rioting; 58 persons, mostly black, had been admitted to the hospital. 75% of them had suffered gunshot wounds.

At a news conference July 18, Mayor Addonizio ascribed the violence to "years of discrimination and bigotry of generations" which were "fueled by the rash of wild and extremist statements and behavior of the past 10 or 12 weeks in our city." "Some outsiders were arrested who have participated in the riot," he said. "We're convinced also that this was a planned situation."

An interracial group of 60 community and civil rights leaders July 18 formed a Committee of Concern to study problems stemming from the riots.

The committee issued a statement calling for an independent commission to investigate charges of "violence and terror visited upon the vast majority of the Negro citizens who were in no way involved in the rioting and were shot, beaten and brutalized by military and police forces without regard to wrong-doing." The statement continued: "A large segment of the Negro people is convinced that the single continuously lawless element operating in the community is the police force itself in its callous disregard to human rights."

Gov. Hughes July 19 and 21 appointed 8 men to a "blue ribbon" committee to investigate charges of police brutality and to determine the causes of the rioting. The committee was also directed to consider Newark's housing, unemployment and education problems. Robert Lilley, president of the New Jersey Bell Telephone Co., was named chairman of the committee. The other members were ex-N.J. Govs. Alfred E. Driscoll and Robert B. Meyner; Catholic Bishop John J. Dougherty, president of Seton Hall University; Bishop Prince Taylor, black presiding bishop of the Methodist Church in New Jersey; Ray Brown, a black lawyer and member of the State Board of Control; ex-State Supreme Court Justice William A. Wachenfeld, and Joseph J. Gibbons, president of the N.J. Bar Association.

In a copyrighted interview in the July 31 issue of *U.S. News & World Report* (reported July 23), Hughes conceded he had no evidence that outside agitators had played any role in the Newark rioting. "Many things are said by people throughout the country which are inflammatory in nature, but so far as a conspiracy from outside moving into Newark—I couldn't say that happened," he admitted. He asserted that while less than 2% of the city's population had participated in the rioting, the nation could "not permit criminal elements who are burning and maiming and killing and looting to hide behind the shield of 'civil rights.'"

The U.S. Marshal's Office in Newark reported Aug. 8 that 90% of those arrested during the riot lived in Newark and that nearly 50% of them were over 25 years old. About 75% of the indictments were for breaking and entering, larceny, or possession and receipt of stolen goods. The Newark Office of Economic Development Aug. 15 reported $10,251,200 in business damages in the rioting—$8,284,060 in stock losses and $1,967,140 in property damages. Liquor stores suffered the most: 151 had $141,745 in property damages and $1.8 million in stock loss; 80 clothing stores suffered $322,550 in building damages and $1,412,375 in stock losses; 72 furniture stores had building damages of $232,000 and stock losses of $1,173,659. The report said: "Of the 889 businesses whose stores were damaged, 2.8%, or 25 stores, were completely demolished while another 15.4%, or 136 stores, were heavily damaged. The remaining 728 stores were either lightly or moderately damaged."

Race Riot in Detroit Causes 43 Deaths

Violence, looting, arson and gun battles swept Detroit, the nation's 5th largest city, July 23-30, 1967 as black rioting swamped police and National Guard control efforts. 43 persons—36 black and 7 white—were killed in the racial violence. The rioting reached a scale previously unknown in a U.S. city in the 20th century.

A plea for help from Michigan Gov. George W. Romney to Pres. Johnson brought the dispatch of federal troops to aid local and state forces in suppressing the disorders. It was the first time in 24 years that the U.S. Army had been used to quell civil strife; the last such use of federal force against urban disorders also had been in Detroit, during the 1943 racial rioting, in which 34 persons died.

The violence resulted in injury to more than 2,000 persons. 5,000 people were homeless as a result of fires that gutted large parts of the city's ghetto areas. 1,442 separate fires were reported to have been set during the rioting, and they caused damage estimated to total $250 to $500 million. 7,202 persons were arrested before the disorders were halted. Firemen attempting to put out fires were attacked by mobs. Rampaging arsonists threw firebombs in downtown Detroit and ranged 6 to 7 miles toward the edge of the city. At the height of the rioting National Guardsmen fired machineguns from Sherman tanks and armored personnel carriers in an attempt to control snipers and rioting.

After the rioting 2 white Detroit policemen were charged with the beating and murder of 2 black youths at the Algiers motel. Other charges of police brutality were investigated, and a controversy developed when Gov. Romney accused Pres. Johnson of "playing politics" in the dispatch of federal troops to Michigan.

Some observers were not surprised that Detroit was the scene of such a serious racial disorder, but other were amazed. According to the 1960 census, blacks comprised 29% (487,000) of the city's 1.67 million population. However, the Michigan Civil Rights Commission reported July 24 that the city's population had dropped 10% to 1.5 million while the black population had increased to 537,000—33% of the total. The black unemployment rate in Detroit was 6% to 8%—approximately double the national average. While the city had only one black councilman, it was the only city in the country that had 2 black Congressmen: Rep. John J. Conyers Jr. (D.) and Rep. Charles C. Diggs (D.). The Aug. 4 issue of *Time* magazine reported that 40% of Detroit's black population owned their own homes. Before the disorders, Detroit had been considered one of the most progressive U.S. cities in its efforts to deal with poverty and racial tensions.

The violence erupted shortly before 4:00 a.m. July 23 when police raided a "blind pig" (after-hours drinking club) on 12th Street on Detroit's West Side and arrested 73 blacks and the bartender. A crowd gathered outside the building. Rumors spread that the police had beaten a man and kicked a woman, and the bystanders began throwing stones at the police. Following the departure of the police and prisoners, a Negro threw a stone through the window of a clothing store, and 50 persons had begun looting the shop before the police drove by again. When the police failed to stop or return, the looting spread. Within an hour, dozens of stores in a 16-block area had been plundered and set on fire.

The looting and arson spread swiftly. Police estimated that at least 5,000 people, black and white, were soon roaming through the West Side and moving into the East Side neighborhoods of the city. The violence ran swiftly along 3-mile and 4-mile sections of Grand River and Woodward Avenues and 12th Street in the downtown section of Detroit and ranged as much as 6-7 miles toward the edge of the city.

An initial force of 600 to 700 National Guardsmen, 200 state troopers and 600 Detroit police sealed off large areas of the city but was unable to disperse the crowds or contain the violence. Gov. Romney placed 7,000 National Guardsmen on standby alert, and city police were ordered to 24-hour duty.

Snipers opened fire on police in the West Side, but the police were ordered to hold their fire in hopes of reducing antagonism and avoiding a major conflagration. Firemen who tried to contain fires, by then consuming a 15-block area, were attacked by mobs with rocks and bricks; at times they were forced to lay down their hoses and retreat.

On several occasions, whites and blacks, armed with shotguns and rifles, were reported to have stood guard for firemen attempting to control the fires. At nightfall a mob of 3,000 rampaged through Detroit's East Side, looting and throwing firebombs, and ignoring a 9:00-p.m.-to-5:30-a.m. curfew imposed by Detroit Mayor Jerome P. Cavanagh. Firebombing and looting spread to almost every section of the city and into the suburbs of River Rouge and Highland Park and the enclave of Hamtramck.

By the evening of July 23, Romney conceded that the situation was "out of control" and declared a state of public emergency. Romney said: "It's a case of lawlessness and hoodlumism and apparently not organized. Disobedience to the law cannot and will not be tolerated in Michigan. I will supply whatever manpower the city needs to handle the situation." Liquor stores and taverns were closed; gatherings of 5 or more persons were prohibited. 7,000 to 8,000 National Guardsmen on standby in Grand Rapids since early in the day were called to the city. Police helicopters equipped with flood lights and submachine guns combed the city in search of rooftop snipers.

In the first day of rioting, 20 persons were injured. 15 of them policemen. At least 650 persons were arrested. With at least 150 fires reported, the city lay under a heavy cloud of smoke.

Before dawn July 24, Atty. Gen. Ramsey Clark informed the White House that Romney was preparing to ask for federal troops for Detroit. At 10:56 a.m. Pres. Johnson received Romney's telegram requesting "the immediate deployment of federal troops into Michigan to assist state and local authorities in reestablishing law and order in Detroit." "There is reasonable doubt," the telegram said, "that we can suppress the existing looting, arson and sniping without the assistance of federal troops. Time could be of the essence."

Within 6 minutes, on order of Pres. Johnson, Defense Secy. Robert S. McNamara ordered 4,700 airborne troops flown to Selfridge Air Force Base, about 30 miles outside of Detroit. The paratroopers, the 3d Brigade, 82d Airborne Division at Ft. Bragg, N.C. and the 2d Brigade, 101st Airborne Division at Ft. Campbell, Ky., were under the command of Lt. Gen. John L.

Throckmorton, 54, former deputy commander in Vietnam. The President sent a personal representative, ex-Defense Secy. Cyrus R. Vance to Detroit to assess the situation. Vance was accompanied by Deputy Atty. Gen. Warren Christopher, John Doar, assistant attorney general in charge of civil rights, and Roger Wilkins, chief of the Community Relations Service in the Justice Department.

While the troops were being moved to Selfridge Air Force Base, the rioting grew worse. Businesses closed; baseball games were canceled, and airlines canceled flights over the city because of the danger of sniper fire. By the evening of July 24, the death toll had reached 15. More than 1,800 persons had been arrested and at least 800 had been injured. 100 new fires were reported.

With nightfall, sniper fire increased. Police were then given orders to shoot. Military barricades were erected to limit entry to the city. The border to the neighboring Canadian city of Windsor was sealed off. At 10:00 p.m. Vance ordered 1,800 troops to the Michigan State Fairgrounds, within the city limits. He declared that the soldiers "will be promptly available to provide assistance and support . . . if they are needed," but he did not order them into active service. Mayor Cavanagh disagreed with Vance's assessment of the situation. He said: "I would certainly like to see the troops in the community at this point." Noting the gravity of the use of federal troops, he added that he "understood the traditional federal desire not to get involved in this type of dispute."

At 10:31 p.m., on the recommendation of Vance, Pres. Johnson signed a proclamation calling on "all persons engaged in such acts of violence to cease and desist . . . and to disperse. . . ." At 11:25 p.m. July 24 Johnson issued an executive order instructing McNamara to "take all appropriate steps to disperse all persons engaged in acts of violence" and to "restore law and order." He also authorized McNamara to call "any or all units" of the Michigan National Guard into federal service. Johnson announced his action in an unusual TV address to the nation near midnight July 24. His executive order authorizing the use of federal troops and a Presidential proclamation commanding all citizens to desist from acts of violence were issued before he spoke to the nation.

The President's address described the events that had led him to order troops to the area and, finally, to be deployed to the riot torn city. Johnson said: Gov. Romney had informed U.S. Atty. Gen. Clark in the early morning of July 24 "of the extreme disorder" existing in Detroit; a telegram from Romney requesting federal troops was sent at 10:46 a.m. and received by the President at 10:56 a.m.; the President issued orders at 11:02 a.m. for the troop movement, and about 5,000 troops were on their way to Detroit by plane within hours. Vance, acting as a special assistant to the defense secretary, was sent to the city for on-the-spot observation and talks with Romney and local officials. Lt. Gen. John L. Throckmorton, in charge of the federal troops involved, reported in the afternoon "that the situation might be controlled" without the use of the federal troops assembling at Selfridge Air Base, northeast of Detroit, but at "approximately 10:30" p.m. Vance and Throckmorton reported that "it was the then unanimous opinion" of state and federal officials in Detroit that the use of federal troops was "imperative" and that "the situation was totally beyond the control of the local authority." The President then had "forthwith issued" the orders necessary to use the federal force in Detroit.

Johnson told the nation that he had taken the step "with the greatest regret, and only because of the clear, the unmistakable and the undisputed evidence that Gov. Romney . . . and the local officials . . . have been unable to bring the situation under control. Law enforcement is a local matter. It is the responsibility of local officials and the governors of the respective states. The federal government should not intervene, except in the most extraordinary circumstances. The fact of the matter, however, is that law and order have broken down in Detroit. . . . And the federal government in the circumstances . . . had no alternative but to respond, since it was called upon by the governor of the state, and since it was presented with proof of his inability to restore order in Michigan. . . ."

Shortly after 2:00 a.m. July 25 the paratroopers had completed a reconnaissance of the area and moved into the East Side of the city, armed with rifles, machineguns and tear gas. They set up barbed wire barricades across the streets as snipers continued firing. National Guardsmen were ordered to the West Side.

2 police stations came under massive sniper attack early in the morning July 25, and 100 National Guardsmen were trapped for awhile.

The violence subsided temporarily later in the day. Romney announced that he was sending National Guardsmen to quell outbreaks of rioting in other Michigan cities: Flint, Pontiac and Grand Rapids.

Mayor Cavanagh announced in the afternoon of July 25 that in view of food shortages, he would provide guards for delivery trucks to replenish supplies. He said that garbage collection would be resumed. A ban on gasoline sales was temporarily lifted for several hours during the afternoon, and businesses were allowed to reopen. 700 refugee centers were opened during the day to care for families that had fled from the rioting or had been left homeless by fires. Cavanagh met with 15 black leaders later in the day to discuss the causes of the violence and to find ways "to pick up the pieces again." He rejected demands made by the Malcolm X Society, a black nationalist organization, which had claimed it could restore order if troops were immediately withdrawn and prisoners were released.

By evening the death toll had reached 26 (21 black and 5 white), 900 persons had been injured and 2,700 were under arrest. More than 950 buildings had been destroyed or seriously damaged by fire and more than 1,500 others looted. Fire Chief Charles J. Quinlan said that 10 new fires were being reported every hour.

After 10:00 p.m. snipers and National Guardsmen fought a gun battle on the West Side. The Guardsmen fired machineguns at the snipers from Sherman tanks and armored personnel carriers.

Cavanagh and Police Chief Ray Girardin came under sharp attack July 25 for not quelling looting and disorders with firmer police policy at the onset of the violence. A banner headline in the city's black newspaper, *The Michigan Chronicle,* read: "It Could Have Been Stopped." The newspaper said that "if the police had stopped looting when it centered on one 12th Street block early Sunday [July 23], when the mood was allowed to become a Roman holiday, the riot could have been prevented." At news conferences early July 23, Girardin and Cavanagh had said they had ordered police to use "restraint" in order to avoid indiscriminate shooting that might have led to "guerrilla warfare." At a news conference July 27, Girardin defended his policy of using the police as a "containment force." "I still believe in putting human lives above property," he declared.

Gun battles between snipers and National Guardsmen continued through the night of July 25 and into the daylight hours of July 26. Snipers shot at firemen fighting new blazes and attacked a police command post at Herman Keifer Hospital. Armed helicopters continued flying low over buildings in efforts to flush out the snipers. Guardsmen in tanks sprayed rooftops and buildings with machinegun fire. There were reports of bullets hitting innocent persons sitting out the violence in their darkened apartments.

The death toll climbed to 36—29 black and 7 white—during the afternoon of July 26, exceeding the 34 deaths recorded in the 1965 rioting in the Watts section of Los Angeles. The number arrested had reached 2,665; 1,163 fires had been reported; more than 1,000 persons had been injured.

Police said that the pattern of shooting indicated that snipers might be organized in bands of 5 to 6 persons. But earlier in the day Vance had said the riot "is not highly organized." He estimated that there were about 100 snipers in the city. He said the rioting had followed a "cyclical" pattern and that the first phase—looting and burning—had ended and had been followed by the sniping phase, which would probably continue for another 24 hours. Vance asserted that the East Side, patrolled by federal troops, was "under control." The West Side, where National Guard patrols operated, remained the source of most of the continued violence.

Gov. Romney and Mayor Cavanagh telegraphed Pres. Johnson July 27 to ask that Detroit be declared a disaster area and be given emergency federal aid. Describing the devastation as a "disaster by any reasonable definition of that term," they declared: "It simply does not make sense not to commit federal assistance to the city of Detroit in view of what has happened there in recent days." Johnson did not immediately accede to their demands, but he ordered a regional officer of the Office of Emergency Planning to meet with Romney. He said he was making surplus food available and was asking hospitals to release emergency drug supplies for use in the city.

Romney lifted the curfew the morning of July 27 but reimposed it later in the day to curtail an influx of sightseers into riot areas. City cleaning crews with bulldozers and cranes began removing debris and knocking down the walls of gutted buildings. Soldiers were ordered to sheathe their bayonets. By July 27 the number of arrests had reached more than 3,400; more than 1,500 persons had been injured; 1,700 stores had been looted. Sporadic reports of sniper fire continued, and 2 more persons were killed during the day, bringing the total slain to 38.

Cavanagh and Romney met with 150 white and black community leaders July 27. Cavanagh called on them to unite in "building the city from the ashes of the present tragedy. . . ." Romney told the group that what had happened in Detroit was "national in scope." He declared that the rioting, however, was different from the racial riot in Newark. Walter P. Reuther, president of the United Auto Workers, told the group: "We can take very little comfort, and it does us no credit, to be the very first city in America to achieve integrated looting." He said: "What we suffered, any city in America can suffer any day of the week. . . . We have left some Americans behind. They are the 'have nots' of America. Ugly economic facts feed their frustrations and their sense of hopelessness, which makes them strike out. If you expect them to act as part of our society, you are kidding yourselves." He told the group that 600,000 union members had pledged their own time to help clean up the city. He asked industry to volunteer the necessary bulldozers and trucks for the removal of debris.

300 state police officers and 600 to 800 National Guardsmen were withdrawn from the city July 28, but 13,000 to 14,000 troops, Guardsmen and police remained on duty. Romney said that police and military officers assured him that "the city is now secure." It was reported July 28 that an estimated $100,000 in loot had been recovered. Police said they were accepting the return of stolen goods without questioning those who returned them.

Cyrus Vance returned to Washington July 29 to report to the President. After their meeting, Vance told reporters that law and order had been restored in Detroit. By noon July 29 1,500 of the more than 7,000 persons arrested during the rioting had been released from jail.

Vance announced July 30 that the 4,700 federal paratroopers would be removed from the city and moved to quarters at the fairgrounds, ready to resume duty if violence should recur. 7,000 National Guardsmen, 200 state troopers and 4,200 city policemen remained on duty.

Gov. Romney ended the curfew Aug. 1 and lifted the state of emergency from the Greater Detroit area at noon Aug. 6. He said: "Recent days and nights have indicated a return of normalcy in the metropolitan area." The last of the National Guardsmen were removed from the city Aug. 6.

The death toll rose to 43 Aug. 5. Detroit police Aug. 7, however, reduced the count to 41, holding that 2 of the deaths had not been connected to the rioting. A 42d death was reported Aug. 9 and a 43d Aug. 14.

2 white Detroit policemen were charged Aug. 7 with the July 26 murder of 2 black youths at the Algiers Motel during the riot. The bodies of 3 black youths had been found at the motel, a mile from the scene of the most serious rioting. Police said the Negroes had died in an exchange of gunfire between policemen and snipers. But motel residents said the youths had been deliberately killed by police who were raiding the motel for snipers. Ptl. Ronald W. August, 28, was charged with the murder of Aubrey Pollard, 19, and Ptl. Robert Paille, 32, was charged with the murder of Fred

Temple, 18. No one was charged in the death of the 3d black youth, Carl Cooper, 17. The officers pleaded not guilty. In a formal statement made by August July 31 and read to the court Aug. 17, the policeman said he had shot Pollard in self defense after Pollard grabbed his shotgun. Recorder's Court Judge Robert De-Mascio Aug. 17 dismissed the charge of murder against Paille. Paille, Ptl. David Senec, 23, a prosecution witness at the examination hearing, and Melvin Dismukes, 24, a black private guard, were charged Aug. 23 with conspiracy to "beat, abuse and intimidate a number of people" in the Algiers Motel. August was named as co-conspirator but not as a defendant since he already faced trial on a murder charge. Dismukes had also been charged with felonious assault in the beating of 2 blacks at the motel.

August was found innocent June 10, 1969 of first-degree murder in Pollard's death. An all-white jury in Mason, Mich. aquitted August after deliberating for 2½ hours. The trial, which opened May 12, had been moved from Detroit at the expense of the defense because of pretrial publicity. (A best-selling book, *The Algiers Motel Incident*, by John Hersey, had been published about the case in 1968.) Charges against Paille for the murder of Temple had been dropped for lack of evidence. Dismukes had been acquitted of felonious assault in connection with the case in May 1968.

The *Detroit News* and *Detroit Free Press* July 31, 1967 had published reports from eyewitnesses in the motel. According to the witnesses, about 16 Guardsmen and state and local police had invaded the motel and had cursed and beaten and threatened Negroes and 2 white teen-age girls. The *Free Press* said that a pathologist it had hired had said that the shots were "fired at close range, from no more than 15 feet away, probably less. 2 of them were probably shot while lying down or kneeling."

2 black youths, Danny Royster, 20, and Charles Latimer, 19, were charged Aug. 7 with the murder of Ptl. Jerome Olshove, 32. They were reported to have been caught by Olshove while looting a grocery store during the rioting. In an ensuing struggle with them Olshove's gun accidentally fired and killed him.

Michael Lewis, 22, a black factory worker, was bound over for trial Aug. 24 on charges of playing a major role in starting the Detroit riot. Lewis had been arrested Aug. 13 on 3 counts of rioting and inciting to riot.

The *Detroit Free Press* charged Sept. 3 that most of the deaths could have been prevented. A copyrighted article by Gene Goltz, 37, William Serrin, 28, and Barbara Stanton said that after interviewing more than 300 persons and reading hundreds of documents, the reporters had reached the "inescapable" conclusion that "a majority of the riot victims need not have died." They said:

18 of the 43 riot victims were shot and killed by Detroit police, and of that number, 14 have been confirmed as looters. . . . The other 4 are a sniper, a possible but un armed arsonist and 2 of the 3 men shot and killed in the Algiers Motel. At least 6 of the victims were killed by the National Guard, 5 of them innocent, the victims of what now seem to be tragic accidents. In 5 more cases, both police and National Guardsmen were involved. . . . 4 of these victims were innocent of any wrongdoing. 2 more persons, both looters, were shot and killed by storeowners. 3 more were killed by private citizens. . . . And 2 looters died when fire swept the store from which they were stealing. 2 victims, one a fireman, the other a civilian, were killed by electric power lines. 5 deaths remain. They are a 19-year-old boy killed accidentally by an Army paratrooper; a 23-year-old white woman shot by an unknown gunman; a Detroit fireman killed by either a hidden sniper or a stray National Guard bullet; a policeman shot as a fellow officer struggled with a prisoner, and the 3d victim of the Algiers Motel slayings, whose assailant is not known. . . . Both the number of snipers active in the riot area and the danger that snipers presented were vastly overstated. . . .

Presidential Commission to Probe Riots

A Special Advisory Commission on Civil Disorders was appointed by Pres. Johnson July 27, 1967 to "investigate the origins of the recent disorders in our cities." The panel was to make recommendations to him, Congress, the state governors and mayors for ways "to prevent or contain such disasters in the future." The President announced appointment of the commission during a televised address to the nation on the riots.

In his address, the 2d in 3 days on the problem of racial violence, Johnson appealed for "an attack—mounted at every level—upon the conditions that breed despair and . . . violence." He proclaimed Sunday, July 30, a National Day of Prayer for Peace & Reconciliation and announced that he was ordering new training standards for riot-control procedures for National Guard units across the country.

The President said that the nation had "endured a week such as no nation should live through; a time of violence and tragedy." He declared that "the looting and arson and plunder and pillage which have occurred are not part of a civil rights protest." "There is no American right," he said, to loot or burn or "fire rifles from the rooftops." "That is crime," he declared. "And crime must be dealt with forcefully and swiftly and, certainly, under law." "The criminals who committed these acts of violence against the people deserve to be punished—and they must be punished," he said.

Those in public responsibility, Johnson said, had "an immediate" job "to end disorder" by using "every means at our command—through local, through police and state officials, and, in extraordinary circumstances, where local authorities have stated that they cannot maintain order with their own resources—then, through federal authority that we have limited authority to use." He said public officials must help "bring about a peaceful change in America," and he warned officials that "if your response to these tragic events is only business-as-usual, you invite not only disaster but dishonor."

Declaring that "the violence must be stopped—quickly, finally and permanently" and pledging that "we will stop it," Johnson said "it would compound the tragedy, however, if we should settle for order that's imposed by the muzzle of a gun." "We seek peace ... based on one man's respect for another man, and upon mutual respect for law," he said. He called for "steady progress in meeting the needs of all of our people." "The only genuine, long-range solution" to the problem of racial violence was in a multi-level attack on the conditions that bred the violence—"ignorance, discrimination, slums, poverty, disease, not enough jobs." It was a time, he said, not for "angry reaction" but for "action, starting with legislative action to improve the life in our cities. The strength and the promise of the law are the surest remedies for tragedy in the streets."

The President warned that "there is a danger that the worst toll of this tragedy will be counted in the hearts of Americans—in hatred, in insecurity, in fear, in heated words which will not end the conflict, but will rather prolong it." He said "most Americans—Negro and white"—were "leading decent, responsible and productive lives" and seeking "safety in their neighborhoods and harmony with their neighbors." "Let us condemn the violent few," he declared, and "remember that it is law-abiding Negro families who have really suffered most at the hands of the rioters." Those "who are tempted by violence," he said, should "think again." "Who is really the loser when violence comes?" he asked. "... There are no victors in the aftermath of violence," he declared.

The commission was headed by Illinois Gov. Otto Kerner (D.). New York City Mayor John V. Lindsay (R.) was vice chairman. Other members (all appointments effective July 27): Sen. Fred R. Harris (D., Okla.); Sen. Edward W. Brooke (R., Mass.); Rep. James C. Corman (D., Calif.); Rep. William M. McCulloch (R., O.); Pres. I.W. Abel of the AFL-CIO United Steelworkers; Charles B. Thornton, president and board chairman of Litton Industries;

Roy Wilkins, executive director of the NAACP; Katherine Graham Pedan, commissioner of commerce of Kentucky; Herbert Jenkins, Atlanta chief of police. Washington attorney David Ginsburg, 55, was named by the President July 31 to serve as executive director of the new commission.

Pres. Johnson called the commission into session at the White House July 29. He asked the panel's members to search for answers to 3 basic questions about the riots: "What happened?" "Why did it happen?" and "What can be done to prevent it from happening again and again?" The President urged the commission to examine why riots had occurred in some cities and not in others; why some persons had broken the law and others had not; whether any of the disorders had been planned, and why some had been impossible to contain; what effect ghetto conditions, federal programs, police-community relationships and mass media had on the riots.

Mississippi Rights Worker Killed by Blast

Wharlest Jackson, 36, a black civil rights activist, had been killed in Natchez, Miss. Feb. 27, 1967, when a bomb exploded in his truck as he was driving home from work at the Armstrong Tire & Rubber Co. plant. This was the 2d bombing aimed at a black employee of the Natchez plant. (Pres. George Metcalfe of the Natchez NAACP had been injured Aug. 27, 1965 by a bomb in his car.) The explosion, shortly after 8:00 p.m., destroyed the truck. Jackson, the father of 6 children, a Korean War veteran and treasurer of the Natchez chapter of the NAACP, had been employed at the plant since Jan. 1955. Recently he had been promoted to mixer, a job held previously only by whites.

A protest rally was held the afternoon of Feb. 28, and Mississippi NAACP field director Charles Evers threatened a national boycott of Armstrong's automobile tires. He charged that the company had "harbored" members of the Ku Klux Klan "for a long time." He said that since his brother Medgar had been murdered in 1963, 41 Negroes had been killed in Mississippi. Nearly 2,000 blacks demonstrated without incident outside the plant gates the evening of Feb. 28. Demonstrators marched from a nearby church to a paved parking lot outside the gates Mar. 1 during a shift change. About 25 Natchez policemen formed a line between the workers who filed in and out of the plant and the demonstrators. Evers and local ministers led about 1,600 Negroes in a silent protest march through Natchez the evening of Mar. 1.

Evers led about 1,000 Negroes in a 2d silent march through town Mar. 4, and NAACP executive director Roy Wilkins Mar. 5 led a motorcade of 25 cars 125 miles from Jackson, Miss. to Natchez to attend Jackson's funeral. At a news conference later Mar. 5, Wilkins said moderation was becoming "noticable" in rural Mississippi: "These killings are the tail end, we believe."

Arsonists & Bombers Strike in South

Fire had destroyed a black church in Collins, Miss. Jan. 21, 1967. The church had been used in the federal Head Start Program.

The Vincent Chapel A.M.E. Church, a black church in Grenada, Miss., was damaged by fire Mar. 4. It had served as headquarters for the Southern Christian Leadership Conference. Grenada Police Commissioner Paul McKelroy said the fire was "definitely not" arson.

Fire destroyed a former Episcopal church in Hayneville, Miss. Mar. 12. The building had served as headquarters for the Lowndes County Christian Movement for Human Rights, Inc., an anti-poverty organization.

The Head Start office in Liberty, Miss., serving 3 counties in Southwest Mississippi, was severely damaged by a bomb explosion Mar. 13.

The Macedonia Baptist Church, a black church in Fort Deposit, Ala., was destroyed by fire Mar. 13.

A bomb exploded in Montgomery, Ala. Apr. 25 outside the home of Mrs. Frank M. Johnson Sr., mother of U.S. District Court Judge Frank M. Johnson Jr. Judge Johnson was a member of a 3-judge panel that had ordered the statewide desegregation of Alabama schools. Mrs. Johnson, an elderly widow, was not injured. The blast loosened the foundations of a car post and knocked out windows.

Spring & Summer Disorders Hit Many Cities

Easter weekend riots had taken place in Ft. Lauderdale, Fla. Mar. 24-26 after about 30,000 out-of-town college students and other young people converged on the city for the annual spring vacation. About 500 persons were arrested in the outbreaks. Similar riots took place in Ocean Drive Beach, S.C. Mar. 25 and in Hollywood, Calif. Mar. 26. 150 young people were arrested in Ocean Drive Beach.

Negroes rioted in Nashville, Tenn. Apr. 8-10. More than 80 persons were reported arrested and 17 injured, 2 of them by gunfire. The rioting began near the predominantly black Fisk University in the early evening Apr. 8 after police ejected a Negro from the University Dinner Club at the request of the management. Within minutes black students began to picket the club, and rioting broke out. The disorder quickly spread to the predominantly black Tennessee A & I State University campus and continued until dawn. Bands of roving youths—students and non-students—threw rocks and bottles at policemen and littered the 2 campuses.

The Nashville rioting started less than an hour after the departure of SNCC Chairman Stokely Carmichael. Earlier that afternoon Carmichael had attended a symposium at predominantly white Vanderbilt University with the Rev. Dr. Martin Luther King Jr. and Sen. Strom Thurmond (D., S.C.). Carmichael, 26, had told a predominantly white audience of about 4,000 persons that for the Negro, "black power" was the only real alternative to domination by a white society. He said: "Our Negro communities can become either concentration camps filled with miserable people who have only the power to destroy or they can become organized communities that make a meaningful contribution to our nation. That is the choice." (In an impromptu speech at Fisk Apr. 7, Carmichael had said: "I am nonviolent right now, but if the white man tries to put his arm on me, I am going to break his arm." "If we don't get changes, we are going to tear this country apart.")

Rioting resumed in Nashville at dusk Apr. 9, and nearly 400 policemen were mobilized to quell the rioters. Negroes fired rifles at passing cars. Policemen were pelted with rocks and bottles, and at one point policemen exchanged rifle fire with snipers. A white-owned grocery store and 2 business buildings were set afire with molotov cocktails. Roving bands of youths shouted "black power." 2 of Carmichael's aides—George Washington Ware of Atlanta and Ernest Stephens of Tuskegee—and 7 people who reportedly had no connection with SNCC were arrested on incitement charges. At 4:00 a.m., several blocks away from the rioting, William Reagan, 21, a Negro, was shot and injured in the neck while driving home from a restaurant. Calvin Conners, 19, a student, was shot and injured in the neck during an exchange of gunfire between police and Negro students on the Tennessee A & I campus. Rioting broke out again at 7:00 p.m. Apr. 10 despite patrolling by student anti-riot squads at Fisk and A & I. Police fired tear gas into rock-throwing mobs of 200 to 300 A & I students. Quiet was restored by 11:00 p.m.

The Interdenominational Ministerial Alliance, an organization of black clergymen, called a meeting of police, city officials, ministers, university officials and students Apr. 11 to find ways of averting further violence. They issued a statement asserting that: Carmichael was not "the sole cause" of the rioting. "The real causes . . . were in existence long before Carmichael was born." Dr. James Lawson, acting president of Fisk, charged that most of the rioters were "outside agitators" brought to Nashville by SNCC.

(Carmichael was replaced May 12 by H. Rap Brown, 23, SNCC's Alabama director, as SNCC chairman. Carmichael said he would remain with the organization as a field worker. At a news conference in Atlanta May 12, Brown said there would be no change in SNCC's black-power policy. He said: "We shall seek to build a strong nation-wide black anti-draft program and movement to include high school students, along with college students and other black men of draft age." "We see no reason for black men, who are daily murdered physically and mentally in this country, to go and kill yellow people abroad [in Vietnam], who have done nothing to us and are, in fact, victims of the same oppression that our brothers in Vietnam suffer.")

Racial rioting flared in the Hough section of Cleveland Apr. 16. According to conflicting reports, the disorders started at or near a carnival. The disturbances spread along Superior Ave. from East 75th St. to East 105th St. Store windows were smashed and several stores looted. 2 youths were arrested while carrying furniture out of one store. 2 others were arrested after they tossed an empty soda bottle at a police car and cracked the rear window.

The Rev. Dr. Martin Luther King Jr. said at a news conference in Cleveland Apr. 26 that Cleveland was a racially "divided city" facing the possibility of increasing violence in the summer. He said: "Negroes are restricted to the East Side [the Hough section] and . . . confined in a mass of substandard housing in high density areas"; Cleveland's mayor, Ralph S. Locher, was "insensitive to the problems of the Negro" and was "more concerned with keeping the community divided to enhance himself politically than in helping to solve its citizens' problems." King criticized the police crack-down on Negro "looters and firebomb throwers." "A get-tough policy should mean getting tough against poverty, inferior education and rat-infested slums," he said.

Open-housing demonstrations, accompanied by several clashes, were intensified in Louisville, Ky. Apr. 11-24 after the city's Board of Aldermen rejected an open-housing ordinance. Several hundred persons were arrested and at least 6 persons injured.

The Rev. A.D. Williams King (a Louisville minister, leader of the open-housing drive and brother of Martin Luther King Jr.) and black comedian Dick Gregory led about 350 demonstrators through downtown Louisville Apr. 11. They began at City Hall, where earlier in the day the 12 Republican aldermen had voted 9-3 against a weakened open-housing law. The marchers, accompanied by about 200 Louisville and Jefferson County policemen and about 200 jeering whites, alternately walked on sidewalks and sat in the streets. At one point they blocked the intersection of Broadway and 4th St., downtown Louisville's 2 busiest streets. White youths on the sidewalk chanted "We Want Wallace."

It was reported that white reaction to the weeks of open-housing marches had grown increasingly bitter. 8 whites had been arrested after they hurled eggs and stones and shouted insults at marchers in a white residential area Apr. 10.

White and black marchers were met Apr. 13 by about 75 whites who burned a cross on the lawn of the Southern Junior High School. King and the Rev. Leo Lesser, a black minister, fell to the street under a barrage of rocks and tomatoes from whites. King was later treated for an eye injury.

At the request of the city, Circuit Judge Marvin J. Sternberg Apr. 14 issued a temporary restraining order forbidding night marches, requiring 12 hours' notice in writing for daylight marches, restricting them to non-rush hours and limiting them to 150 persons. Several hundred persons, however, marched that evening through a white residential section. A police cordon separated the marchers from about 1,000 whites, some of whom threw stones, eggs, firecrackers and other objects. 45 persons were reported arrested for disorderly conduct and parading without a permit.

About 100 demonstrators marched through Louisville's South Side in the evening. They were followed by about 500 whites, who jeered and threw stones, bottles and firecrackers. About 140 policemen were present. 19 white hecklers were arrested. Police used tear gas and smoke bombs Apr. 18-20 to disperse whites who tried to disrupt marches. 150 demonstrators were pelted Apr. 18 with garbage, cherry bombs and rocks. 50 marchers, including King, were arrested. 150 open-housing demonstrators, both white and Negro, climbed Apr. 19 from rented trucks that carried them to white neighborhoods and tried to march despite the reinstatement earlier Apr. 19 of the injunction against marches. Riot police moved in after whites, mostly teen-agers, hurled stones through police car windows. 20 hecklers were arrested. 119 demonstrators were arrested on charges of violating the court injunction.

Demonstrators attempted to march again Apr. 20, but about 70 to 80 were arrested as they climbed out of rented trucks that had brought them to all-white neighborhoods. Police used tear gas to disperse nearly 600 whites, some of whom pelted demonstrators and police with rocks and bottles. King and 6 other demonstration leaders were convicted Apr. 21 of civil contempt for defying the injunction against marches. They were sentenced to 30-hour jail terms, but the terms were stayed until Apr. 24 to allow them to meet with city leaders to find a solution to the housing complaints.

125 demonstrators were arrested the evening of Apr. 21 when they tried to march in Louisville's South Side and in the Churchill Downs neighborhoods of Louisville. But about 300 demonstrators marched through downtown Louisville at noon Apr. 22 without incident. Police made several arrests, however, during a night march on City Hall. The marches were extended to Louisville's affluent East Side Apr. 24. About 50 demonstrators in 2 rented trucks arrived at scheduled march sites but remained in their trucks and conducted a motorized protest, followed by police and press cars, for about 31 miles through downtown and suburban areas.

Negroes rioted on the campus of the all-black Jackson State College May 10-11 in Jackson, Miss. The National Guard was called in and martial law was imposed. One Negro was killed and 2 others were wounded before the rioting ended. According to Kenneth Dean, director of the Mississippi Council on Human Relations, the rioting began late May 10 "[when] 2 Negro policemen arrested a speeder on the campus and students began pouring from their dorms." He said: "The students seemed to have all of the traditional grievances of Mississippi Negroes, but were not rioting over any specific grievance." Police said that 1,500 students including some from nearby Tougaloo College joined the rioting. Calm was restored by daybreak.

Minor incidents took place in Jackson throughout May 11, and serious rioting broke out again at about 8:00 p.m. About 100 rioters built a bonfire on Lynch Street, the main street through the campus. Shouting "Hell no ! We ain't going !" they rushed a barricade police had set up to seal off the campus. They retreated, throwing rocks and bottles, and hit a state highway patrol investigator on the head. They charged a 2d time, and as they retreated again, the police fired shots into the crowd. Benjamin Brown, 22, a black delivery man, was shot in the back of the head and the lower part of the back. He fell on the sidewalk within 60 yards of the policemen. About 50 Jackson policemen stood by without aiding Brown for more than 10 minutes. Finally Brown was carried away from the scene by Negroes. He was taken by ambulance to the University Hospital, where he died at 5:00 a.m. 2 other Negroes were wounded but not seriously. Calm was restored with the arrival of 1,200 to 1,400 National Guardsmen.

19 students from Millsaps College marched May 12 from their campus to the City Hall with signs that said "White Students Protest the Murder of Benjamin Brown." More than 300 Negroes marched from a Methodist Church to City Hall in the evening May 12 to protest the shooting. Black ministers and civil rights leaders said the march had been organized to substitute "nonviolent protest" for the rioting of the past 2 days. Earlier, at a rally at the church, SNCC leaders had urged students to boycott the march and answer violence with violence. At City Hall, however, Charles Evers, Mississippi NAACP director, told the marchers they didn't need SNCC in Jackson and would not gain anything by violence.

Jackson State College Pres. John Peoples said May 12 that 90% of the rioters were "unscrupulous outsiders," not students. Student leaders also attributed the rioting to "intruders—people who have come in and distorted the movement." The National Guard was removed May 13.

One policeman was killed and 2 policemen and a student were wounded in Houston May 16-17 when police and students exchanged rifle fire at Texas Southern University, a predominantly black school. 488 students were arrested; 5 of them were indicted June 2 for the slaying. (Sporadic incidents of violence had preceded the rioting. Students had disrupted classes Mar. 28 by barring doors to buildings to protest the administration's refusal to recognize Friends of SNCC as an on-campus organization and to protest the firing of the group's faculty sponsor.)

Texas Southern students had been demonstrating for various causes, and about 120 students held an evening rally May 16 on the university campus. During the rally a watermelon was hurled at the car of 4 policemen standing nearby. The policemen arrested a student, Douglas Waller, 21, who, they said, was carrying a pistol. As the 4 officers drove from the campus, they became the target of stones and bottles. They stopped and were met with gunshots reportedly fired from Lanier Hall, a freshman dormitory. Ptl. Robert G. Blaylock was wounded in the leg and Ptl. Allen D. Dugger in the cheek. Within an hour more than 600 policemen were in the area, and the campus was sealed off.

Members of the crowd hurled bottles of gasoline and set fire to barrels of tar in a street going through the campus. They tried to erect a barricade across the avenue with pieces of metal from a construction site. At this point Police Chief Herman Short conferred with Houston Mayor Louie Welch, who ordered him to clean up "this damned mess." Police then began shooting into Lanier Hall. The shooting lasted about 40 minutes, and at about 3:00 a.m. 100 police rushed the dormitory. Ptl. Louis R. Kuba was shot in the forehead and died 7 hours later. Morris English, 22, a student, was wounded in the back.

Police began arresting students and searching the dormitory for arms. They were reported to have totally wrecked the building's interior and furnishings. Mrs. Mattie M. Harbert, Lanier Hall house mother, charged May 17 that police had stepped on her and smashed her personal belongings. The police found one shotgun, a rifle and a pistol.

Felony charges were filed May 17 against 5 students for Kuba's death.

Black snipers exchanged gunfire with police after Stokely Carmichael was arrested June 11 outside a black church in Prattville, Ala. Carmichael, who had been arguing with white police officers, was charged with disorderly conduct for allegedly threatening to "take care of" the police and to "tear this town up." Police said they had gone to the church, where Carmichael was addressing a rally of 60 black youths, to investigate reports that a Negro had pointed a shotgun at white passers-by. Negroes said that as whites drove by the rally, they raced their car engines. One witness said the trouble began when Carmichael shouted "black power" at a police cruiser the 2d time it drove by. The police stopped and an argument between Carmichael and Asst. Police Chief Kenneth Hill reportedly broke out. Carmichael was jailed without bond.

Snipers and police exchanged rifle fire in Prattville that evening. About 30 Negroes had gone to the home of Dan Houser Jr., a Negro, in the "Happy Hollow" section of Prattville and, according to police, had started shooting from inside the house. The blacks reportedly charged that police had fired into the house first.

Within a few hours Gov. Lurleen B. Wallace (D.) sent 150 National Guardsmen to Prattville with orders to "shoot to kill if this be necessary. ..." The shooting ended around midnight when 25 Negroes filed out of the house. 10 were arrested. During the reported battle, 3 policemen and a black dog handler were injured. The next day Houser claimed that no shots had been fired from his house, and his wife said the house had not been hit by bullets. Reporters could find no damage to the house from gun fire.

Houser was hospitalized early June 12 for eye and facial injuries apparently suffered in a beating. Prattville Police Chief O. C. Thompson said Houser had been questioned at City Hall early in the morning but that he had been released unharmed. But Houser June 15 filed a $100,000 damage suit against the Autauga County sheriff and 4 Prattville policemen for conspiring to deprive him of his civil rights by beating him.

Violence erupted in the predominantly black West Side of Dayton, O. June 12. Black youths set fires, smashed windows and looted stores. Police sealed off the area. The violence began when Negroes attacked a white man after a speech by SNCC Chairman H. Rap Brown. The rioting continued sporadically June 15 but ebbed after Dayton officials organized a black "youth patrol" to keep peace. The youths, wearing white helmets, began patrolling the ghetto by 8:00 p.m. Although some officials attributed the outbreak to Brown's inflammatory speech, others said the youths were "keyed up" and that any other incident would have served to ignite the rioting.

Violence broke out in black sections of Tampa, Fla. June 11, 1967 shortly after police shot and killed a black robbery suspect. The violence, which continued June 12-13, was quelled after city officials enlisted the aid of 100 black youths from the ghetto neighborhoods. In 3 nights of violence, 65 to 80 arrests were reported.

The outbreak began when Ptl. J. R. Calvert began chasing 3 youths he had discovered robbing the Tampa Photo Supply Co., near Central Avenue, a street of stores and nightclubs bordered by a public housing project. According to Calvert, the youths refused to stop on command. He fired 2 warning shots and then shot at one of them, Martin Chambers, 19, a Negro, and hit him in the back. Chambers was pronounced dead on arrival at the hospital.

Less than 3 hours later crowds had gathered, and violence had broken out on Central Avenue and in the housing project. Police and rioters exchanged rifle fire. The rioters set an entire block afire and looted stores. A white man, Carl DeWitt, was dragged from his car, beaten and taken hostage by rioters. Police, armed with guns, bayonets and dogs, moved into the area to restore order. About 20 persons were arrested, 15 were injured; one policeman died of a heart attack.

Gov. Claude R. Kirk Jr. called 500 National Guardsmen to Tampa June 12. Kirk visited the riot-torn area and asked Negroes to stay in their homes. Rioting, however, spread June 12 to other black sections. Firemen in the old Spanish section of Ybor City were forced to call for assistance from police when rioters hurled fire bombs at fire trucks. Rampaging gangs of youths roamed the streets throwing rocks and setting fires. Many buildings were entirely destroyed. There were reports of sniper fire. The National Guard was shifted from the Central Avenue section to quell new outbreaks of violence in the Ponce de Leon and College Hill housing projects in the western section of the city.

Robert L. Gilder, president of the Tampa branch of the NAACP, June 12 attributed the rioting to Tampa's unemployment situation and to "police brutality." (The unemployment rate for Tampa's Negroes, about 16% of the city's population, had remained steady at about 10% for the last 10 years. The situation had been made worse by job competition from 10,000 Cuban refugees who had come to the city in recent years.) Gilder said the rioters were anxious to meet with Mayor Nick Nuccio, but, he said, he had not been able to persuade the mayor to come to the area of unrest.

Tampa's prosecuting attorney ruled June 14 that the shooting of Chambers was justifiable homicide. Tampa's Commission on Community Relations, at Williams' suggestion, June 14 recruited about 100 black youths aged 15 to 20 to help prevent further violence in the city. The youths, clad in white helmets, patrolled the black residential areas June 14, and no further violence occurred. The National Guard units were sent home June 15. Police battled rock-throwing black youths for 4 hours in black neighborhoods of Lansing June 14-15. 17 persons were arrested June 15, and 2 policemen were injured.

One Negro was killed and 3 others were seriously wounded as unrest swept black residential areas of Atlanta June 19-20. The disturbances erupted one day after ex-SNCC Chairman Stokely Carmichael was arrested when he joined a crowd June 18 in the black Dixie Hill section of west Atlanta. He was charged with failure to move when requested by an officer. 4 others were arrested and jailed with him. All 5 were released on $50 bond the next morning.

Early June 19 Douglas Richmond, 21, a Negro was wounded by a black policeman. According to the police version of the incident, black policemen had been sent to investigate a burglar alarm at a grocery store in the Dixie Hills section. One of the policemen, Robert McKibben, said Richmond started kicking the police alarm box and persisted despite the officer's order to stop. McKibben arrested Richmond for "malicious mischief"; but when he tried to take the youth into custody, the youth's friends interfered. Richmond reportedly struck McKibben with a broomstick, while the others hit him on the back and arms with rocks. McKibben then fired his gun at Richmond and wounded him in the thigh. Richmond was charged with drunkenness, disorderly conduct, cursing, resisting arrest and assault on an officer. According to SNCC, however the policemen had sought Richmond's aid in stopping the alarm.

Violence erupted in the evening of June 19 after Carmichael told a crowd of about 350 Negroes at a church near the Dixie Hills shopping center that "the only way these honkies [whites] and the honky lovers can understand is when they're met by resistance." "They've got everybody marked, ready to shoot," he declared. But "they've got us surrounded tonight, so we'll just walk around and play it cool." 100 policemen were sent to the area after the crowd began throwing rocks. They restored order in an hour. 4 policemen and 2 civilians were reported injured.

Negroes assembled in the shopping center in the evening June 20, and began throwing rocks at policemen. The police ordered the crowd of several hundred persons off the streets and fired shots in the air to speed their dispersal. As the Negroes retreated there was a series of explosions; Timothy Ross, 46, a Negro, who was standing in the doorway of the nearby apartment building, was killed. Catherine Duncan, 51, Marion Ward, 34, and Reginald Rivers, 9, all black were injured. According to Police Superintendent J. F. Brown, neither of the 2 policemen standing a short distance from the doorway had fired in the direction of the Negroes. 2 black witnesses, however, charged that the police had opened fire after a gas bomb exploded near them.

Atlanta Mayor Ivan Allen Jr. immediately went to the Dixie Hills area. He proclaimed a state of emergency and ordered a 9:00-p.m.-to-6:00-a.m. curfew in the section. Later the curfew, denounced by Carmichael and others because of the hot weather, was lifted.

Negroes rioted in the predominantly black East Side section of Buffalo, N.Y. June 27-30, and 85 to 100 persons were reported injured. 205 alleged rioters were arrested. Property damage was estimated at $100,000. The disturbance began June 27 after a black youth reportedly threw a stone at a passing bus and hit a passenger. Bands of young Negroes numbering 300 to 350 gathered, threw rocks and set fires in a 10-block area. 75 policemen were rushed to the scene, and 22 persons were arrested before quiet was restored at about 1 a.m. June 28.

Mayor Frank Albert Sedita, 60, met early June 28 with 40 to 50 Buffalo city officials and black leaders. He reportedly agreed to meet with the city's business leaders in the effort to find jobs for the city's 3,500 unemployed youths and avert further violence.

Rioting started again in Buffalo June 28 shortly after 7:00 p.m. despite patrolling by more than 400 policemen. A white couple driving through the area was dragged from their car and beaten before the police could rescue them. Several cars were overturned and other whites beaten. Gangs of youths totaling more than 1,000 battled with police, who were armed with shotguns and tear-gas guns. The youths were temporarily disabled by tear gas, but they reassembled in a short time, and battling continued through the night. 4 or 5 blacks were wounded, one seriously, by gunshots, at least some of them reported to be from snipers. Late in the evening 2 policemen were also reported shot. By 11:00 p.m. 40 persons, 11 of them juveniles, had been arrested. 35 to 40 persons were injured.

Sporadic incidents of rock throwing, looting, firebombing and gunfire were reported in Buffalo June 29, while store fronts remained barricaded and helmeted police patrolled the city, their car windows taped to prevent shattering. More than 100 persons were taken into custody by the police. At a news conference early June 29, Mayor Sedita charged that "out-of-towners are the cause of the trouble." He said he had been told that a man had offered black youths a dollar for every window they broke. Later in the day, at a meeting called by the Youth Council of the NAACP, Sedita told about 200 black youths that he planned to meet with business and industry leaders to work out a summer job program. His pleas to "give me a week's time . . . a chance to get the message across" were met with angry shouts of "You gotta do more for us," "We want jobs for everybody" and "If we don't get what we want we're gonna turn Buffalo into a living hell."

Rioting was renewed the evening of June 29. About 40 persons were reported wounded, many by shotgun pellets. Small crowds were dispersed by tear-gas bombs. Looting was reported, and 46 persons were arrested. Temporary calm June 30 was broken shortly after 10:00 p.m. Looting, rock-throwing and sniper fire were reported. A police car was stoned. 100 additional policemen were brought into the area.

At a meeting of business and civic leaders June 30, black leaders presented Sedita with a list of demands. These included: (1) "a minimum of 3,000 jobs to be provided youngsters from the Negro area"; (2) "immediate reduction of the number of police in the

Negro community and the removal of such antagonistic and pro-
vocative shows of force as shotguns in hand and out of car
windows and police dogs"; (3) the "immediate halting of the
indiscriminate use of tear gas"; (4) reduction of bail for those
arrested. At the meeting, the Bethlehem Steel Corp. offered 100
summer jobs in its Lackawanna plant for youths 16 to 20 years
old. The mayor announced that the finance committee of the Erie
County Board of Supervisors had agreed to appropriate $294,000
to hire 600 youths for work in county parks. He said the Post
Office and the Board of Education had promised 350 jobs. But
Ambrose Lane, head of the Community Action program, Buffalo's
anti-poverty group, said the jobs were "coming at a late date and
were too few." (The Buffalo Urban League reported July 2 that
750 Negro youths had signed up for jobs during recruiting
July 1-2.)

U.S. urban rioting reached new intensity in July 1967. In
addition to major disorders in Newark, N.J. and Detroit, Mich.,
rioting broke out a 2d time in Cincinnati July 3-4. There were
lesser disturbances in Atlanta, Kansas City, Mo., Tampa and
Waterloo and Des Moines, Ia, and Erie, Pa. Riot reports streamed
in from Hartford, Conn., Fresno, Calif. and Jersey City, Paterson
and Elizabeth, N.J. Plainfield, N.J. was wracked by violence.
Disorders occurred in New Brunswick, N.J., Cairo, Ill., Nyack,
N.Y. and Durham, N.C. Guardsmen quelled rioting in Minneapolis; there were violent outbreaks in Englewood, N.J., Youngstown, O., New Britain, Conn., Birmingham, Ala. 3 days of rioting
occurred in New York City's Spanish Harlem. Racial disturbances
were reported in Mt. Vernon, N.Y.; Toledo, O.; Pontiac, Grand
Rapids and Flint, Mich. Arsonists set a major fire in Cambridge,
Md. Vandalism, firebombing and looting broke out in South Bend,
Ind.; Phoenix, Ariz.; Saginaw, Mich and Chicago. Philadelphia
officials proclaimed a state of limited emergency. Mobs rioted in
San Francisco, Peekskill, N.Y., Passaic and Palmyra, N.J.,
Wilmington, Del., Memphis, Tenn., Long Beach, Calif. and New-
burgh, N.Y. Major rioting occurred in Milwaukee. Firebombings
swept Portland, Ore., San Bernadino, Calif., West Palm Beach,
Fla. Youth gangs clashed with police in Providence, R.I.; white
gunmen were arrested after black rioting in Wichita, Kans.

Illinois Gov. Otto Kerner ordered National Guard units to
Cairo, Ill. July 19 after 3 days of rioting in the city. The racial
violence had begun July 17 after reports of the death of a 19-
year-old black soldier in the city jail. Police claimed the soldier had
hanged himself with his shirt, but most Negroes in the city of

9,000 apparently believed that he was a victim of police brutality. That night arsonists burned down a warehouse and damaged 3 stores and an automobile. Snipers opened fire the night of July 18 on a police car cruising outside the Pyramid Courts public housing project, the home of about 1,000 of Cairo's 3,000 Negroes. During the same night, firebombs started blazes at a lumber yard and a cotton warehouse. About 100 Guardsmen took up stations in Cairo July 19, and an 8 p.m. curfew was declared.

Spokesmen for young Cairo Negroes warned Mayor Lee Stenzel and city officials July 20 that unless their demands for new job opportunities, more recreation facilities, and an end to police brutality were met, there was likely to be a renewal of the firebombing. Following 2 days of meetings, city officials agreed July 23 to hire one black fireman and one more black policeman. They also agreed to help open up jobs in industry to Cairo Negroes.

Police and National Guard units were summoned to put down violence that erupted in the wake of black rights demonstrations in Durham, N.C. July 19-20. 2 persons had been injured July 19 when some 300 Negroes began smashing windows in the downtown area of Durham following a demonstration at City Hall for desegregated public housing. It was reported July 20 that cars used in the protest were registered to Operation Breakthrough, the city's antipoverty organization. 300 Negroes conducted a 2d Durham protest march the evening of July 20 as police and 120 National Guardsmen called in by Gov. Daniel K. Moore lined the streets. Police arrested one white heckler. There were no serious incidents. Negro leaders had warned the marchers earlier: "If just one person picks up a brick and hits one of those white people there's going to be shooting and somebody's going to be killed."

600 National Guardsmen were moved into Minneapolis July 21 to curb racial violence that had beset the city for 2 days. The disorders began July 19 with an outbreak of street fighting and firebombing. Violence erupted again on the North Side the next night, and the disorders included car burnings and sniper fire. Mayor Arthur Naftalin requested July 21 that 300 Guardsmen be sent to the North Side to aid Minneapolis police. But Gov. Harold LeVander sent 600 troops to the area, where most of the city's 12,000 blacks lived. Despite the burning of a Catholic church that night, there was no major rioting and only 7 arrests were made, compared to 36 during the previous 2 days. Fire Department officials reported 22 confirmed cases of arson during the disturbances. Black leaders blamed police brutality for the rioting, but

Naftalin said that a major factor was the shortage of jobs for teenagers. The National Guard was withdrawn from the ghetto July 25. Except for the firebombing of one tavern, all was reported to be quiet in the riot area.

Englewood, N.J., a New York suburb just 2 miles from the New Jersey side of the George Washington Bridge, was torn by 3 nights of racial violence July 21-23. The disorders began early in the evening of July 21 in the 4th Ward, where nearly all of the city's 12,000 blacks (40% of the population) lived. Rock-and-bottle-throwing mobs raced through the streets and smashed store windows. Although little looting was reported, 8 policemen suffered minor injuries. The riot was brought under control by local police reinforced by policemen from nearby communities. 5 Negroes were arrested and several were reported injured. Violence flared again the next evening when several stores were looted and small fires were set. Shotgun-carrying policemen, sealing off the riot district, fired on one sniper but reported no serious injuries. 8 blacks were arrested. After meeting with ghetto residents July 22 and 23, Mayor Austin N. Volk characterized their grievances as "not momentous." A white-owned grocery store was set afire by a molotov cocktail July 23, but otherwise the town remained quiet. (Federal housing officials revealed July 25 that the government had turned down plans for 2 urban-renewal projects in Englewood after the city had refused to take steps to integrate the projects. Black leaders had cited dilapidated housing as a major grievance in the ghetto.)

2 buildings were dynamited and 3 others were burned in Youngstown, O. July 22. The destruction was accompanied by disorders in which 3 men were beaten. 2 black and 5 white persons were arrested. Leaders of the black community July 27 presented to the City Council a list of demands that included the addition of 25 Negroes to the city's police and fire departments, the creation of a civilian police review board and improvement in city services in the "ghetto neighborhoods."

More than 200 black youths smashed windows and looted stores in Birmingham, Ala. July 22 after a white policeman had wounded a black burglary suspect. 400 National Guardsmen were called in to quell the rioting. 11 persons were reported injured and more than 70 arrested.

Racial disturbances involving firebombing and looting were reported in Rochester, N.Y. July 23-25. Rioting broke out at 10 p.m. July 23 when 200 youths began throwing stones at a Public Works Department sprinkler truck that was watering down a street to prevent drag races. The disorders spread, and by early July 24, 400 members of the 562-man police force were called to duty. The police sealed off a 20-block area. At least 50 persons were arrested July 23-24. In another part of the city 2 Negroes were wounded early July 24 when they were fired at by a group of whites in a passing car. They were not seriously injured. But Thomas Lee Wright, 21, black, was fatally shot when he tried to run a police barricade in the 3d Ward. Rochester City Manager Seymour Scher, responding to demands for legal action against the policeman who killed Wright, said July 25 that the shooting was "an unavoidable by-product of lawlessness."

Rioting broke out in the black section of Mt. Vernon, N.Y. July 24-28. (Negroes comprised about 30% of the city's 72,000 inhabitants.) Mayor Joseph P. Vaccarella July 26 declared a state of emergency and imposed a 10-p.m.-to-6-a.m. curfew on the 5-to-6-block area. Police reinforcements were called from the neighboring cities of White Plains, Yonkers and New Rochelle. Under terms of an agreement between community black and white leaders, police were withdrawn from the black neighborhood July 28. The curfew was lifted, and black leaders consented to patrol the area and persuade youths to "cool it." The police also granted permission for an outdoor grievance meeting attended by 100 Negroes later July 28.

Neil McArthur, deputy assistant U.S. manpower administrator, told county antipoverty officials, local aldermen, civil rights leaders, businessmen and residents July 29 that he would call on the Federal Employment Service to find jobs for residents. Mayor Vaccarella agreed to a proposal by Negroes that $250,000 be allocated for 200 new jobs for unemployed persons. But City Controller Nicholas Yannantuono rejected the proposal July 31, declaring the funds were not available for the program. Later July 31, Rep. Ogden R. Reid (R., N.Y.) announced that the Labor Department had agreed to appropriate $215,000 to underwrite 409 new training jobs in Westchester County; 200 of the jobs were for Mt. Vernon.

2 Negroes were killed in racial disorders in Pontiac, Mich. July 24-25. One of the dead was Alfred Taylor, 17, who was slain by a shotgun blast fired by Michigan State Rep. Arthur J. Law. Law said he had fired the gun at a half-dozen black youths when they threw a trash basket through the window of his food market. A policeman was wounded by a sniper, and 87 persons were arrested.

A firebombing spree in the Detroit suburb of Flint, Mich. July 24 resulted in the arrests of more than 100 young blacks.

Charges—ranging from arson and inciting riot to vandalism and disorderly conduct—were dropped the next day after the youths agreed to spread through the streets urging others to "cool it." The mayor of Flint, Floyd McCree, a Negro, July 25 began to speed action on a proposed open-occupancy housing ordinance.

3 Negroes were wounded in racial violence in Grand Rapids, Michigan's 2d largest city, July 24-25. The wounded men were members of a task force attempting to cool off tempers. They reportedly were shot by a sniper. Officials reported that about 40 fires were set, that more than 40 persons were injured and that more than 200 people were arrested during the disorders. Gov. George Romney proclaimed a state of emergency in the city of 200,000 July 25. Sporadic looting occurred July 26, but the city remained relatively calm. 250 National Guardsmen had arrived July 25, and a curfew had been imposed.

Racial disorders broke out in the black section of the near South Side of Toledo, O. July 24-26. There were reports of scattered firebombings and vandalism but no serious injuries or deaths. A 300-man police force was put on duty to quell the disturbances, and 48 persons were arrested the first night. About 20 fires were set. Gov. James A. Rhodes July 25 ordered 500 National Guardsmen to standby alert in an armory at the edge of Toledo. Mayor John Potter imposed a 9:00-p.m.-to-6:00-a.m. curfew on all persons under 21 later that day. 7 firebombings were reported late July 25. About 37 persons were arrested. Firebombings and looting continued July 26.

Philadelphia Mayor James H. J. Tate issued a proclamation of limited emergency July 27, on the 2d night of scattered disorders in predominantly-black South Philadelphia. Roving black gangs were reported to have stoned police cars and smashed windows. Several hundred police were reported to have been sent to quell the rioting. The proclamation, issued on the advice of Police Commissioner Frank Rizzo and made effective until Aug. 14, prohibited groups of 10 or more persons from gathering at public or private places for purposes other than organized recreation. Tate said he had issued the orders because the city "is now faced with the threat of an eruption similar to the violence that has flared in other cities throughout the country."

A biracial group of 150 Philadelphia civic leaders and gang representatives, called the Appeal for Reason Committee, issued a statement July 28 scoring the proclamation as "premature and an incitement to riot." 30 demonstrators protesting the limited state of emergency were arrested July 30. Police reported July 31 that 40 rifles and an unknown number of pellet guns and bows and arrows had been stolen over the weekend from a wholesale distributing company in the city.

250 Philadelphia businessmen attended a luncheon with Mayor Tate Aug. 3 and agreed to hire at least 1,500 unemployed persons. Tate told the group: "It would be very foolish indeed for us to pretend that the same tragedy could not strike Philadelphia again . . . unless we, who have the most to lose, do something about it." "One of the major causes," he said, "is the frustration of a large number of our citizens—frustration arising from discrimination, lack of opportunity, boredom, crowded and unwholesome living conditions. One of the things that could go a long way toward alleviating this pent-up pressure is a job."

Gangs of Negroes rampaged through the West Side district of Wilmington, Del. July 28-29, setting fires, looting stores and firing guns. The violence was reported to have lasted about 4 hours and was restricted to 6 square blocks in the black section. At 2:00 a.m. July 29 Mayor John E. Babiarz imposed a 2:30-a.m.-to-6:30-a.m. curfew on the city. 80 to 100 persons, most of them aged 18 to 25, were arrested on charges of looting, disorderly conduct and possession of firearms. 7 injuries from gunshots were reported.

19 persons were arrested in Wichita, Kan. July 31 during a night of rock throwing and firebombing by bands of black youths. City Commissioner A. Price Woodward, a Negro, acting as mayor in the absence of Mayor Clarence Vollmer, imposed an emergency curfew at 1:00 a.m. Aug. 1. Order was restored by dawn, and the curfew was lifted during the day. Violence flared again in northeast Wichita Aug. 3-5. 20 blacks and whites were wounded by shotgun blasts from ambush early Aug. 4. 4 white youths were arrested Aug. 5 and charged with felonious assault for the shooting after 100 Negroes had threatened to "burn this town down" unless the whites were apprehended. Despite the arrests, 300 blacks rampaged through the neighborhood at about 3:00 a.m. Aug. 5. Several policemen suffered cuts when mobs threw rocks and bottles at them, and 2 stores were reported to have been firebombed. After a special City Council meeting Aug. 5, Mayor Vollmer imposed a 10-p.m.-to-5-a.m. curfew. A sniper wounded a pedestrian Aug. 7, and minor fires were reported throughout the day.

Black and white gangs clashed in predominantly black South Providence, R.I. July 31-Aug. 2. 350 police were called in to restore order July 31 after gangs of black youths threw stones at a white man who used a gun to defend his lemonade stand against mob attack. The stand was destroyed by the youths. 2 Negroes were shot in the mêlée, neither seriously. Sporadic sniper activity was reported Aug. 1. Gangs of white youths shouting "White Power" tried to attack black gangs in the evening. 20 persons were injured as snipers and heavily armed police traded gunfire; 13 persons were arrested. Looting was reported during the day. 72 persons, most of them whites, were arrested in the early morning of Aug. 2. A special session of the City Council Aug. 2 gave Providence Mayor Joseph A. Doorley emergency powers to handle the disturbances. Doorley imposed a 9:00-p.m.-to-6:00-a.m. curfew on the 100-block area where most of Providence's 15,000 Negroes lived. 50 antipoverty workers, most of them black, wearing white helmets, aided police Aug. 2 in patrolling the streets, but several fires were reported in the evening. In a special TV appearance Aug. 3, Doorley thanked police, residents and "soul patrol" members for their cooperation in restoring order in the city.

Arson, vandalism and looting were reported in the black ghetto of northwest Washington Aug. 1. About 50 store windows were smashed and 11 minor fires reported. The disorders began at 12:30 a.m. Aug. 1 when firemen fighting a 2-alarm blaze were pelted with rocks and bottles by a crowd of about 400 onlookers. Gangs of youths then began roaming nearby streets, mainly in the Shaw Urban Renewal Area, a mile-square area 8 blocks north of the federal buildings on Constitution Ave. A white soldier was beaten and robbed. The Police Department's Tactical Squad was called in and order was restored by 5:00 a.m. 34 persons were arrested and charged with disorderly conduct or failing to obey police orders to move on. The Washington Urban League provided $25 bail each for the release of most of those arrested. Julian Dugas, director of the city's Neighborhood Legal Services project, said that the arrests were "inflammatory" because most of those taken were bystanders and were not involved in the disturbances.

Washington's governing body, the 3-man Board of Commissioners of the District of Columbia, issued a statement Aug. 1 congratulating "the vast majority of our citizens" for their restraint during the "relatively minor disturbance." The commissioners appointed a task force to study citizens' grievances. The commissioners met later the same day with Rufus Mayfield, 20, and 40 other black youths to hear their grievances and demands for the release of those arrested. The Labor Department Aug. 3 awarded a $300,000 grant to a black youth employment group called Pride, Inc., organized by Mayfield. Mayfield said that Pride, Inc. would hire some 900 youths at $56 a week for a month-long slum clean-up and rat control program in the 10 areas of the city covered by the antipoverty Neighborhood Development Program. The city's Department of Sanitation said Aug. 3 that it would provide 434 jobs for youths under a $100,000 federal grant to the Neighborhood Youth Corps.

Black demonstrators marching from Bogalusa, La. to the state capitol in Baton Rouge was attacked by whites despite police and National Guard escorts. The march, started Aug. 10 as a protest against the lack of job opportunities for Negroes, ended after 106 miles with a rally at the capitol Aug. 20. The marchers, whose numbers varied between 15 and 92, were escorted by 175 state policemen. The police were joined Aug. 18 by 650 National Guardsmen who had been activated by Gov. John J. McKeithen.

15 white men broke through the police escort and attacked 20 black marchers in Holden, La. Aug. 15. Several Negroes and a deputy sheriff were knocked down in the brief scuffle, and 2 white men were arrested. In Satsuma, La. Aug. 16, about 75 white men charged through the police guard and attacked 25 marchers. Police used billy clubs and carbine butts to disperse the attackers. 4 persons, including a policeman, were treated for head wounds. 8 men were arrested on charges of battery and disturbing the peace. The marchers were met by crowds of white hecklers as they moved through Denham Springs, La. Aug. 18. 2 Negroes were struck by bottles, others were pelted with eggs. March leader A. Z. Young praised the authorities for their protection. He said that without it, "there would have been slaughter out here— slaughter."

Sporadic violence flared in New Haven, Conn. Aug. 19-23. Nearly 450 persons were arrested during 5 days of looting, arson and vandalism. According to Police Chief Francis McManus, the disturbances began late Aug. 19 after Edward Thomas, 31, a white restaurant owner, shot and wounded Julio Diaz, 35; Diaz allegedly had threatened Thomas with a knife. Within a short time bands of black youths were roaming the Hill and Dixwell sections of the city. Looting broke out in a 4-block area. Police together with leaders of the Hill Parents Association, a community group, and Yale students, members of Students for a Democratic Society, urged the milling crowds to disperse. Police finally brought out riot sticks, shotguns and tear gas; but only one tear gas canister was fired. By midnight order was restored.

The New Haven disorders were resumed Aug. 20. That evening Mayor Richard C. Lee declared a state of emergency and imposed an 8 p.m. curfew. 200 state troopers were called in to augment the 400-man city police force. A 12-block area in a black and

Puerto Rican neighborhood was sealed off and placed under heavy patrol, and a 250-man National Guard unit was put on standby alert. 3 cars were set afire, 2 stores burned and dozens of stores looted. Sporadic violence was reported Aug. 21. The number of arrests rose to 263 by evening. Mayor Lee conferred with black leaders and city officials throughout the day Aug. 21. Negroes gathered outside the circuit court, where black prisoners were being arraigned, and signed affidavits charging police brutality. Black youths circulated a petition demanding "an immediate commitment by the city to a massive program of jobs, housing and educational programs to close the economic gap between blacks and whites." 40 black leaders met at the Zion Evangelical Church in the evening of Aug. 21. They issued a 2-page manifesto calling for the immediate lifting of the curfew, a million dollar loan for rehabilitation of the area and an apology from police for alleged brutality.

Gangs of black youths roved New Haven late Aug. 21, in defiance of the curfew. Looting, arson and vandalism continued. More than 100 arrests, mostly on charges of failure to observe the curfew, were reported during the night Aug. 21 and early Aug. 22. Police arrested several carloads of white youths who, they said, were driving around with firearms "looking for trouble." 150 state police replacements arrived in the city the evening of Aug. 22. Mayor Lee said Aug. 22: The disorders were "disorganized, sporadic, but there has been a good deal of it," although "not one single shot" had been fired in New Haven since the disturbances began. About 130 persons were arrested Aug. 23, but Lee expressed hope "that the worst of our problems are behind us."

Boston Clash Over Welfare Grievances

A sit-in by a group called Mothers for Adequate Welfare (MAW) in Boston's predominantly black Roxbury district turned in to rioting June 2-5, 1967 after demonstrators charged that they had been assaulted by poilce. The outbreak was Boston's first large-scale racial rioting in recent years. 60 to 75 persons were injured, and 75 to 100 were arrested.

The rioting followed a demonstration at a city Welfare Department building in the Grove Hall section of Roxbury. About 30 MAW members had staged a sit-in to protest what they alleged was the department's termination of welfare payments without notice or investigation, the hostility of social workers and the rudeness of police on duty at the welfare center. At 5:00 p.m. the women padlocked the building's doors and locked themselves, 20 social workers and about 10 policemen in the center.

As police reinforcements arrived with ladders and attempted to enter the building through a window, black youths gathered and began throwing stones and bottles. Police inside the building formed a flying wedge and charged out of the center. They were bombarded with bottles, stones and rocks by the crowd outside. (The demonstrators in the building charged they had been assaulted by the police locked in with them.)

Black leaders arrived and tried to restore order, but the violence was only temporarily quelled. By 11:00 p.m. mobs raged through the district, setting fires, looting stores and throwing rocks and bottles from rooftops and side streets at policemen and firemen. Snipers fired shots from the rooftops. 1,700 policemen, some armed with bayonets and submachine guns, were mobilized to put down the estimated 1,000 rioters. A command post was established at the nearby Franklin Park football stadium.

At least 25 stores were reported looted; 2 multiple alarm fires were attributed to the rioting. Scores were injured, including about 30 policemen, firemen and newspaper reporters. A 15-year-old white girl, riding through the area in a car, was struck in the head and suffered a skull fracture. More than 40 persons were arrested, including 3 prominent black leaders. They were arraigned in special court sessions June 3 on charges ranging from assault and battery to trespassing.

Shortly after midnight June 3, after a degree of order was restored, black community and civil rights leaders met with Police Commissioner Edmund L. McNamara. The meeting was not reported to have produced tangible results. Mayor John F. Collins called an emergency meeting with black leaders June 3, but only the district's 3 state legislators showed up. The mayor issued a statement denouncing the rioting as "the worst manifestation of disrespect for the rights of others this city has ever seen." A black leader, the Rev. Virgil Wood, said, however, that "war was declared on the black people by the police force last night, and in all likelihood this will happen again until the whole attitude of the administration changes." The Rev. James P. Breeden, a black member of the Commission on Race & Religion of the Massachusetts Council of Churches, declared: "The people of Roxbury did not riot, the police did. The policemen inside the building roughed up the mothers, and those who arrived on the scene . . . panicked and began laying into bystanders."

Police cars patrolled the riot-torn section during the day. But rioting and looting resumed in the evening. Rioters littered the area with debris as they tossed bottles and stones, set fires and smashed windows. A fireman was shot in the wrist by a sniper when his crew responded to one of several false alarms. About 1,900 policemen were sent to the district to stem the rioting. They sealed off a 15-block area, and by midnight order was restored. 68 persons were arrested.

Roving bands of black youths, however, continued to set fires, smash windows and loot stores June 4.

The Roxbury Tuesday Luncheon Group, an inter-organizational committee composed of members of civil rights, self-help and human relations organizations, June 6 organized a mass meeting for Roxbury teenagers (believed by many to have kept the rioting alive) at the district's St. Hugh's Church. Youths were urged to come and "speak your piece" on the causes of the riots. The white press was barred. 200 teenagers attended the meeting, which lasted beyond 10:30 p.m. There was no rioting that night. A 2d meeting was held June 7 and again there was no rioting. The youths reportedly organized "safety patrols" and special committees to plan recreational facilities and jobs.

'Rebels' Seize N.M. Courthouse in Land Claim

About 40 armed Spanish-American "rebels" raided the Rio Arriba County, N.M. courthouse in Tierre Amarilla June 5, 1967 and freed 11 rebels arrested in connection with the group's plan to take control of lands illegally granted to their forbears by the Spanish crown. After exchanging shots with local police, wounding 2 of them and holding the town briefly, the rebels took 2 hostages and fled into the mountains. They later traded gunfire with state troopers and National Guardsmen called into the area. One hostage escaped, the other was released unharmed.

The leader of the group, Reies Lopez Tijerina, 41, was captured June 10 at a roadblock near Bernalillo, north of Albuquerque. 17 members of his group were captured later. They were arraigned in Santa Fe June 22 on charges of kidnapping and assault with intent to commit murder.

The group, known as the Political Confederation of Free City States, was asserting their claim to about 2,500 square miles of northern New Mexico. The 11 rebels freed by the raid had been under arrest for unlawful assembly as part of a reported attempt to seize part of the Carson National Forest and surrounding area in Oct. 1966.

About 40 members of families of the insurrectionists had been taken into custody by Guardsmen June 6 and held as hostages. New Mexico Gov. David F. Cargo told a House Agriculture subcommittee June 14 that a major cause of the rebellion was the "unbelievable" poverty of the area's Spanish-Americans. An employee of a state antipoverty group, Uvaldo Valasquez, had been arrested with Tijerina at the roadblock, and the state's antipoverty office had offered to obtain legal aid for some of the rebels. But the director of the antipoverty group, HELP, told the House subcommittee June 12 that there was no connection between his agency and the rebellion and that no antipoverty funds had been given to the Tijerina movement.

Cincinnati Riots

Rioting, looting and fire swept through black sections of Cincinnati, O. June 12-15, 1967, and more than 300 persons were arrested before order was restored.

The rioting began June 12 following a demonstration by about 300 persons at the Samuel Ach Junior High School in Avondale, 2 miles northeast of downtown Cincinnati. They were protesting a death sentence given Posteal Laskey, 29, a Negro charged with the murder of a white secretary. Peter Allen Frakes, a Negro, carrying a sign reading "Freedom for Laskey," was arrested and charged with interfering with pedestrian and vehicular traffic.

After the protest marauding gangs of black youths formed in the area and battled with police for nearly 2 hours. 3 persons were slightly injured, and 7 were arrested.

Rioting erupted at about 7:00 p.m. June 13 in Avondale and spread to the Evanston and Walnut Hills sections, both integrated residential neighborhoods, and to Norwood and the Old West End—encompassing 5 to 6 square miles of the city. There also were reports of violence in Lockland, 18 miles northeast of the city. Police Chief Jacob Schott estimated that "thousands" of teenagers and adults were roaming through the city. By 9:00 p.m. more than 900 policemen were in the area.

Shortly after 9:00 p.m. June 13, at the request of Cincinnati Mayor Walton S. Bachrach, Gov. James A. Rhodes sent in about 800 National Guardsmen armed with rifles and gas masks. Some arrived in jeeps with mounted machine guns. At least 13 persons were reported injured in clashes, and 47 arrests were reported.

Earlier June 13 the City Council had held a special session with black leaders and clergymen. The Negroes charged police with behavior that "served only to inflame an already tense situation." They also called for (1) the repeal of the city's no-loitering law; (2) the release of persons arrested; (3) employment opportunities for the city's youths. (The unemployment rate of Cincinnati's Negroes [about 150,000 of the city's 500,000 population] was reported as 13% to 15% compared with 3%-4% for whites; the black teenage unemployment rate was said to be more than 20%.) Negroes walked out of talks with the mayor and City Council June 14. They charged the National Guard had dispersed some of their group while they were waiting outside for their turn to testify. Black leaders insisted that the trouble could be traced to the failure of city officials to act on demands for new jobs, swimming pools and other recreational facilities. The Rev. Otis Moss Jr., a Negro, asserted that the violence was being spearheaded by "an active and militant minority" that was difficult to control.

Violence raged unabated in parts of the city and suburbs June 14, James Shirk, 15, a white youth, was shot and wounded by Negroes riding in a car.

Violence spread to the Cincinnati Workhouse June 15 on the arrival there of 12 Negroes who had been convicted of participation in the rioting and sentenced to a year in prison and $500 fines. The 409 black and white workhouse inmates fought with prison guards, police and National Guardsmen for more than 3 hours. Police fired tear gas shells into the cell blocks to force the prisoners outdoors, but once outside they began ripping up bricks from a walk and attacking the guards. About 50 National Guardsmen were sent into the prison to quell the rioting.

Sporadic cases of gunfire and window smashing were reported in Cincinnati June 15 despite National Guard patrols. Firemen answered more than 45 fire alarms and extinguished more than 20 fires. About 100 of the more than 300 persons arrested during the 3 nights of violence were tried June 15.

The National Guard was removed from Cincinnati streets June 17 and withdrawn from the city June 18.

Violence erupted again in Avondale July 3-4. Gangs of black youths began roaming Avondale streets shortly after 9:00 p.m. July 3, smashing windows, looting stores, stoning cars and setting fires. 12 to 15 persons were reported injured; 6 suffered minor injuries. 26 fires occurred during the night, causing an estimated $1 million in damage. Order was restored by 5:00 a.m. July 4, but further outbreaks of firebombing and vandalism the night of July 4 resulted in 11 arrests.

Cincinnati Safety Director Henry Sandman swore in the city's firemen as special policemen July 6 and instructed them to carry shotguns in every truck for protection against snipers.

Violence broke out again in Avondale July 26, when black youths stoned firemen fighting a blaze in a housing project. The youths set fires and looted stores. Walter Evans, 46, a bystander, was accidentally wounded in the hip when police fired over the heads of the youths.

Black Activists Charged with Plot to Murder Moderates

15 Negroes (11 men and 4 women), allegedly members of the pro-Peking Revolutionary Action Movement (RAM), were arrested in N.Y. City early June 21, 1967 on charges of plotting to murder moderate civil rights leaders. The 15 were specifically charged with plotting to assassinate NAACP Executive Director Roy Wilkins, Urban League Executive Director Whitney Young Jr. and at least 3 other moderate rights leaders and of conspiring to advocate criminal anarchy. A 16th black defendant Maxwell Stanford, 33, alleged leader of RAM, was arrested the same day in Philadelphia.

The arrests followed indictments handed down June 20 against 17 Negroes by a Queens (N.Y. City) grand jury. Although a warrant was issued for the arrest of the 17th accused, John Anderson (also known as John Shabazz), he was not immediately arrested. Also seized in the pre-dawn raids by 150 policemen in Queens, Brooklyn and Manhattan were 30 weapons, including rifles, shotguns, carbines, 1,000 rounds of ammunition, 150 to 275 packets of heroin, walkie-talkies, subversive literature and radio receivers and transmitters.

Mob Kills Policeman in Plainfield, N.J.

A white policeman was shot and beaten to death by a mob of black youths in Plainfield, N.J. July 16, 1967. National Guard units were sent to the city after violence had swept through its black neighborhoods, but order was restored only after 4 days of looting and vandalism. More than 100 persons were arrested, and 10 were reported to have been injured during the disorders.

The unrest broke out July 14 when a gang of 40 black youths threw rocks at police cars and store windows. They dispersed when additional police arrived. Looting and firebombing began in Plainfield's West End section at 10:00 p.m. July 15 and continued until 3:00 a.m. July 16. Molotov cocktails were tossed at several stores, and a fire truck was hit and destroyed by a fire-bomb. One fireman suffered minor burns. 38 persons, including 10 white motorcyclists and 3 white men carrying baseball bats, were arrested during the disorders.

Rioters began stoning cars driving through the black section July 16. A few police patrol cars and the fire chief's car were damaged. By the evening of July 16, more than 300 black youths were rampaging through a 14-block area of the neighborhood, smashing store windows, looting and throwing molotov cocktails and stones. Snipers shot at a fire station.

A mob converged on the corner of Front St. and Plainfield Ave., where Ptl. John V. Gleason Jr., 36, was on traffic duty. It swept through the area and began to pursue some young whites who had tried to stop a looter. When Gleason attempted to stop the looter, he was attacked by a crowd of about 30 Negroes. According to witnesses, Gleason drew his gun and fired into the mob, wounding a black youth, Bobby Williams, 7. The crowd then wrested the gun from Gleason and shot him with it. One of the witnesses, David Hardy, a reporter for *The Plainfield Courier-News*, said: "It was really brutal. They got shopping carts and threw them on him. They beat him and stomped him. He was raising his hand and they just kept kicking him." When other witnesses tried to intervene the mob attacked them with rocks and bottles. Gleason was dead by the time help arrived.

Shortly after the slaying, at 11:15 p.m. July 16, Leo F. Kaplowitz, Union County prosecutor, announced that 100 National Guardsmen had been sent to Plainfield at the request of Mayor George S. Hetfield. 60 police reservists were added to the city's 75-man force to deal with the rioters, many of whom carried rifles and automatic weapons. The Guardsmen formed a perimeter around the riot area. A 10:00-p.m.-to-6:00-a.m. curfew was imposed. It was reported late July 16 that 46 semiautomatic rifles and ammunition had been stolen from the Plainfield Machine Co. in Middlesex, N.J.

Looting and sporadic sniper fire continued July 17, though with lessened intensity. State troopers moved into the city and were joined by another 30-man unit of National Guardsmen the next day.

In the evening of July 17, black leaders and youths held a closed meeting with Mayor Hetfield, State Atty. Gen. Arthur J. Sills, N.J. Community Affairs Commissioner Paul N. Ylvisaker and Col. David Kelly, superintendent of the State Police. Sills announced early July 18 that white and black leaders had agreed on a peace plan, under which National Guardsmen, state troopers and police would withdraw from the West End riot area and black leaders would assume responsibility for maintaining order in the district.

300 heavily-armed National Guardsmen and state troopers conducted a house-to-house search for the stolen Middlesex weapons in the 128-unit West End Gardens public housing project and 14 other "selected spots" in Plainfield July 19. They acted without search warrants under Gov. Richard J. Hughes' proclamation of "a state of disaster and emergency" in Plainfield. The proclamation had been signed July 17 but had been withheld while city officials negotiated. (Earlier in the day, 12 black youths had been released on their own recognizance on condition they asked other Negroes to return the stolen rifles.) Due to what was termed a misunderstanding, 4 armored personnel carriers started moving into the riot area before the search. They were stopped by Paul Ylvisaker, who sprinted to the middle of an intersection shouting: "Stop, Stop." "This is a peaceful community. This will be an orderly search." The heavy equipment was withdrawn and 20 jeeps and 12 trucks brought in the searchers.

Crowds gathered to protest the search procedure. Doors and windows reportedly were broken, beds were torn apart and clothes and linens were said to have been strewn on floors. The search, conducted like a military operation, continued for more than 2 hours. Many Negroes whose homes were searched complained of serious damage to their property. The Plainfield Human Relations Commission and the New Jersey branch of the American Civil Liberties Union July 19 denounced the search. The ACLU group said the search was "an unconscionable violation of the constitutional rights of the Negro community" and "a deliberate attempt to provoke rioting." State Police Col. Kelly conceded there had been a "misunderstanding" about the search techniques to be used and said that when this became known the search was ended. 3 guns were found during the search; one had been found earlier. The Union County prosecutor said July 19 that the search had not been expected to produce the stolen weapons. "The search," he said, "is a symbol of law and order, and it is vitally important for this community to see that symbol."

Plainfield remained calm July 20. Several hundred policemen from 50 northern New Jersey communities attended funeral services for Ptl. Gleason. While police were absent from the riot area, "talk squads" of young Negroes patrolled in an effort to prove that order could be maintained without the presence of white police.

All National Guard units were withdrawn from Plainfield July 21. All but administrative personnel and one operational unit of the state troopers were removed, and the curfew was lifted.

Gail Madden, 22, and George Merritt Jr., 24, both Negro, were convicted in Elizabeth, N.J. Dec. 23, 1968 of first degree murder in the killing of Ptl. Gleason. 2 other defendants were acquitted; 6 others had been acquitted previously. During the trial, witnesses testified that Merritt had attacked Gleason with a butcher knife and that Miss Madden, who weighed more than 250 pounds, had jumped up and down on him. The jury recommended life imprisonment rather than the death penalty.

New York City Turmoil

Rioting and anti-police disorders broke out in the East Harlem ghetto of New York City known to its Puerto Rican residents as *El Barrio* (The Neighborhood) July 23-25, 1967. The 3 days of rioting spread through 125 blocks of the community—famed as the first stop for Puerto Ricans arriving in the U.S. Before the riots subsided, 2 persons were killed, stores were looted, cars were overturned and set afire, 36 persons were injured, and 13 persons were arrested.

The violence began at 12:30 a.m. July 23 when an off-duty patrolman shot and killed Renaldo Rodriquez, 25. Rodriquez, wielding a knife, allegedly had lunged at another off-duty policeman when the officer attempted to arrest him after finding him standing in the street over another Puerto Rican, knife in hand.

News of the killing of Rodriquez spread quickly, and crowds began to converge on the area. Bottles and bricks were soon being rained on passing squad cars. Although a few stores were looted and trash cans set afire, most of the crowd's hostility was directed at the police. At about 4 a.m., the city's white-helmeted Tactical Patrol Force—a special elite police unit often used for riot suppression—was given orders to clear the area. According to Puerto Ricans in the crowd and some newsmen who witnessed the melee, the police waded into the crowd swinging their nightsticks. Their first charge was turned back by a barrage of bricks and bottles, but their 2d succeeded in clearing the streets.

Mayor John V. Lindsay arrived in the neighborhood from his summer home shortly after 4 a.m. July 23. He wandered through a crowd of about 75 Puerto Ricans, listening to their complaints. He was cheered with *"Vivas"* and was clapped on the back by ghetto residents. A meeting between Lindsay and 10 ghetto residents took place later that morning at the mayor's residence. Lindsay then said at a news conference that he would investigate charges of police brutality and would discuss with Police Commissioner Howard R. Leary the possibility of keeping the Tactical Patrol Force out of the Spanish Harlem area. A delegate confirmed to newsmen later that their basic grievance was over the special force. "However bad the precinct police might be," he said, "they know us." Puerto Rican community leaders met with Leary and other city officials later July 23. A Lindsay assistant said the Puerto Ricans had been promised that there was "no intention of bringing in the Tactical Patrol Force at this time."

But the special force entered the district again late July 23 to break up a crowd throwing bottles at police cars. Minor cases of arson and looting were reported during the night.

The worst night of rioting began shortly after dark July 24, when bands of youths stoned police cars and looted stores. Police in the district opened fire on roof tops after reporting sniper fire. Flaming brands from a bonfire lit in the middle of 3d Ave., a main thoroughfare, were used in a futile attempt to set a gas station afire. Crowds swarmed through the streets, overturning trash cans, smashing windows and setting small fires. 2 ghetto residents were killed during the July 24 rioting, both by .38-caliber bullets of the type used by the police. Police reported at first that one of the victims, a Puerto Rican boy of 16, had fallen from a rooftop and died of a broken neck and that the other, a 44-year-old woman found dead in her home, had been killed by a .22-caliber bullet. The reports were corrected after autopsies.

More than 100 *El Barrio* residents and anti-poverty workers roamed the district's streets urging knots of angry Puerto Ricans to return to their homes but largely to no avail. Rioting spread from Spanish Harlem to the heavily Puerto Rican slum in the city's south Bronx July 24. The Bronx disturbances were confined largely to looting and the setting of small fires, although some sniper shots were reported.

By the night of July 26, rioting had subsided.

In the aftermath of the disturbances, city and community officials began to seek ways to avert further rioting. The police July 26 were placed on a 6-day week to provide more men during evening hours. The director of the city's Neighborhood Youth Corps program announced July 26 that he was deploying the corps' 1,867 teenaged workers to East Harlem to spread a message to "cool it." The Police Department July 28 ordered precincts in Spanish-speaking neighborhoods to assign a Spanish-speaking patrolman to each squad car.

The leadership of the Puerto Rican Community Conference July 27 blamed Lindsay and his administration for failing to act on recommendations made by the city-sponsored conference in April. The group blamed poor police tactics and use of the Tactical Patrol Force for the outbreak and continuation of the violence. The Puerto Rican Bar Association July 30 praised the police for using minimal force in quelling the riots.

A band of about 200 black teenagers looted stores in New York's exclusive 5th Ave. shopping district July 26. The teenagers, who had attended a rock-'n'-roll concert in Central Park, swept through the theater district, jostling passersby. On reaching 5th Ave., they smashed the windows of 2 men's clothing stores and a shoe store and took an estimated $26,000 worth of merchandise. Among the loot: $56 Alpaca sweaters regarded as a ghetto status symbol. The raiders fled as police arrived, but 22 youths were arrested. 4 later were revealed to be employes of city-sponsored anti-poverty and youth projects.

Minor rioting and looting broke out in the Bedford-Stuyvesant area of Brooklyn July 29, but order was quickly restored. The Police Department moved a large contingent of black patrolmen into the area July 30 and issued a set of instructions to police officers ordering courtesy and restraint.

Rap Brown & Arson in Cambridge, Md.

Fire swept the black business section of Cambridge, Md. in the early hours of July 25, 1967. The fire, apparently set by arsonists in the 50-year-old, all-black Pine St. Elementary School, raged out of control after the city's white volunteer firemen refused to take action against the blaze.

The fire and accompanying violence followed a Cambridge speech in which H. Rap (originally Hubert Geroid) Brown, 23, chairman of the Student Nonviolent Coordinating Committee (SNCC), had exhorted a crowd of 400 young Negroes the previous evening to "burn this town down." (Brown's apparent incitement of the Cambridge disturbances led to his arrest in Washington, D.C. 2 days later.) Brown reportedly told the black Cambridge audience: "You better get yourselves some guns. The only thing honkies [whites] respect is guns." He singled out the Pine St. school as a "firetrap" and told the crowd "you should've burned it down long ago."

After ending his speech a few minutes before 10 p.m. July 24, Brown gathered a group of about 40 men and began a march toward the white business center of Cambridge. The marchers were met by helmeted police who ordered them to halt. When they kept marching, the police fired shotguns loaded with pellets into the crowd. Brown received a minor wound, which was later treated at a local hospital. One other Negro received a superficial wound. The marchers dispersed.

Violence erupted along Pine St. at about 11:15 when blacks attacked a car driven by white youths. The car returned a few minutes later, and its occupants sprayed the street with buckshot. Black residents sought protection in doorways and under porches. About an hour later a city patrolman was wounded by a shotgun blast as he sat in his parked squad car in the black section.

The fire began in the Pine St. school at about 2:15 a.m. July 25. It spread quickly to the unpainted wooden buildings near it. Cambridge Police Chief Bryce Kinnamon kept the volunteer fire department's equipment on fire-preventive duty in the white business district for 2 hours while a black church, stores and other black-owned buildings were consumed by the flames a block away. Kinnamon was quoted as telling a group of 30 Negroes who offered to operate a fire truck: "You shot one of my policemen. Don't give me that stuff." When the fire equipment finally moved into the black section 2 hours after the first alarm, many Negroes helped fight the blaze. Nearly 20 buildings were destroyed.

Gov. Spiro Agnew toured the district later July 25 and told newsmen that Brown was to blame for the disturbances. As Agnew spoke to local officials, 700 National Guardsmen took up stations in town on his orders. It was the 2d time in recent years that the National Guard had been sent to the city of 13,000 (4,000 Negroes) to curb racial violence. Cambridge, located in Maryland's Eastern Shore section, had been the scene of more racial violence than any other city in the state. Agnew said July 28 that Cambridge was a "sick city" in which "segregation is completely obvious."

Cambridge police officials announced July 27 that 2 men had been arrested for shooting the policeman July 24. A 3d suspect, Lemanuel Chester Jr., 21, arrested July 29 and charged with inciting to riot, was the leader of the militant Cambridge Black Action Federation. Newsmen said Chester had made no statement at the July 24 rally.

In the aftermath of the rioting, Cambridge was reported relatively quiet despite the National Guard's use of tear gas to break up an unruly group of Negroes July 26.

Meanwhile, within hours after his Cambridge speech, Brown was being hunted by state police and the FBI as a fugitive from Maryland charges of "inciting to riot" and "counseling to burn." A federal fugitive warrant was obtained July 25, empowering the FBI to seize Brown for fleeing across a state border to avoid arrest. The FBI arrested Brown at the Washington National Airport July 26 as he was about to board a flight to New York. Brown told newsmen at the federal courthouse in Alexandria, Va. that he had been on his way to New York to surrender to the FBI under a deal worked out with the FBI by his lawyer, William M. Kunstler. The FBI denied that it had made any deal for Brown's surrender. The Justice Department, following a procedure often used to allow precedence to usual extradition processes, then dropped the federal fugitive warrant. Alexandria police had obtained a warrant and prepared to arrest Brown. After being ejected from the comparative sanctuary of the federal courthouse, Brown stood on the steps of the building, surrounded by fist-shaking black nationalists, and declared that he would not move. 4 Alexandria policemen, however, dragged him into a waiting squad car. He was released on $10,000 bail at 1 a.m. July 27.

Speaking later July 27, in the heart of Washington's black ghetto, Brown repeated the advice he had offered in Cambridge: "You better get you a gun. The honky got respect for but one thing, a gun." He assailed Pres. Johnson as a "wild, mad dog, an outlaw from Texas" who had sent "honky, cracker federal troops into Negro communities to kill black people." Brown said at a SNCC-sponsored rally that evening: "There should be more shooting and looting." "If Washington, D.C. don't come around, Washington, D.C. should be burned down," he added. Brown predicted that "the rebellions will continue and escalate." "I say violence is necessary," he asserted. "It is as American as cherry pie."

Brown was indicted *in absentia* by a Dorchester County grand jury in Cambridge Aug. 14 on charges of arson, inciting a riot and acting in concert with others in disturbing the public peace. 5 others indicted were: Lemanuel Chester Jr., on charges of inciting a riot and disturbing the public peace; Gladys Fletcher, about 30, and James duPont Fletcher, about 40, on charges of arson; James Lee Lewis, 30, and Leon Lewis, 25, on charges of assault with intent to murder a Cambridge policeman and simple assult.

Brown was arrested in N.Y. City at 2:30 a.m. Aug. 19 on a federal charge of carrying a gun across state lines while under indictment. The complaint, filed in U.S. District Court in New Orleans, alleged that Brown had carried a .30-caliber "Enforcer"

semi-automatic carbine on an Aug. 16 flight from New York to
New Orleans and on a return flight to New York Aug. 18. When
a boarding agent at New Orleans International Airport had asked
Brown Aug. 18 whether he was carrying a gun, Brown said he was
and gave the weapon to the agent for transportation on the flight
to New York. Brown was released at 5:20 p.m. Aug. 22 on $15,000
bail.

After his release Brown addressed a crowd of about 100 Negroes from the top of the courthouse steps. "It was black power
that got that bail reduced [from $25,000 originally set]," he de-
clared. "We're at war! We are caught behind enemy lines, and
you better get yourself some guns." Pointing to whites in the
crowd, he said: "That's your enemy out there. And you better
not forget, because I ain't going to." Brown had said Aug. 6, at
a rally of about 1,500 Negroes in Queens (N.Y. City), that the
1967 summer's racial riots were only "dress rehearsals for revolution." He urged Negroes to arm themselves against a "honky
[white] conspiracy of genocide." Brown said that both the late
Pres. Kennedy and Pres. Johnson, whom he called "lynching Johnson" and the "greatest outlaw in history," had "tricked black
people." He declared that the U.S. was "escalating its war against
black people," but he warned: "If you play Nazis with us, we
ain't gonna play Jews." Brown told a cheering crowd of about
3,000 blacks in riot-stricken Detroit Aug. 27: "You did a good
job here." But he said the riots in Detroit would "look like a
picnic" when Negroes united to "take their due." "The honky is
your enemy," he shouted. "Within 20 years we will be just like
the buffalo. We're going to have to defend ourselves. The white
man is not going to defend us." After the speech Negroes hurled
rocks and bottles at 2 white TV newsmen, but both escaped unharmed.

Rioting in Chicago

Scattered vandalism, firebombings and looting broke out on
Chicago's South and West Sides July 26-Aug. 1, 1967. 2 persons
died of bullet wounds in the racial violence, and at least 120 persons were arrested.

In the Hyde Park area of the South Side, molotov cocktails
were used to set off fires in at least 6 stores July 26. Youths
smashed windows in the Lake Meadows Shopping Center on the
near South Side. A Chicago Transit Authority bus was pelted
with bottles and rocks and 5 persons injured. Near the Comiskey

Park stadium black crowds gathered and chanted "Black Power!" At least 10 fires were reported on the West Side. Firebombs were hurled onto the Eisenhower Expressway. 250 policemen were called in, and they cordoned off portions of the West Side. At least 22 persons were reported arrested July 26 and 35 more July 27.

Herman Hancox, 31, a Negro, was shot to death July 28 by a black policeman who said Hancox had attacked him with a knife.

Police exchanged gunfire with black youths July 29 after the youths had fired on a patrolman. No injuries were reported, and police said they had brought the situation under control with a "minimum of force." During the night police officers sitting in their patrol cars on the South Side were fired on by snipers. No one was injured.

A store on the West Side burned to the ground July 29 after 5 molotov cocktails were thrown through the rear window. 9 black teenagers were arrested.

Julius Woods, 40, a Negro, was shot to death Aug. 1 outside a food and liquor store after an argument with the store's owner, Nicholas James Nicholaou, 34. According to UPI, Woods had gone to the store to get his son's bicycle, allegedly taken by Nicholaou on the ground that the boy had broken a store window. Woods reportedly was shot twice by Nicholaou. Crowds gathered at the store in response to rumors that Woods had been shot by police, and teams of policemen were sent out to spread the news of Nicholaou's arrest on charges of murder. The section was cordoned off. By 2 a.m. police had dispersed the milling crowds. 54 persons were arrested.

The *Chicago Daily News* Aug. 5 corrected rumors about Woods' death. According to the *News* 2 black youths broke the liquor store window July 31 while scuffling on the sidewalk. False rumors began to spread through the neighborhood that Nicholaou had the youths arrested. The *News* reported that the next morning Woods, a transient with a minor police record, drank some beer and then went to the liquor store. Woods, who was not related to either of the boys, demanded to know why Nicholaou had the youths arrested and, according to one witness, told Nicholaou: "I'm going to kill you." Then, the *News* said, Nicholaou fatally shot Woods.

The Rev. Jesse L. Jackson of the Southern Christian Leadership Conference said Aug. 3 that he had asked Illinois Gov. Otto Kerner and Mayor Richard J. Daley to declare the city a disaster area to forestall further rioting. "Chicago is sitting on a powder keg," he declared. "We have more evidence of the possibility of riots here than in other cities."

(Police and Negroes had clashed for more than 2 hours in Chicago May 21 following a memorial service for the late black nationalist leader Malcolm X. Participants said that police had been "harassing" the meeting after several whites had attempted to "invade" the service, attended by 500 blacks. Police contended, however, that the Negroes had marched from the service to a busy intersection, causing traffic congestion and forcing police to disperse them. Stones and bottles were tossed at police as the crowds milled around in the street. Police arrested 30 persons on charges of disorderly conduct, resisting arrest and inciting to riot.)

(Fighting between white and black students broke out in the cafeteria of the Waller High School in Chicago's Near North Side Nov. 21. The clashes spread to 2 other schools. At least 12 persons were injured and 84 arrested. The fighting reportedly followed a false rumor that white youths had pushed a black youth into the path of an elevated train. Fighting spread to the school's corridors and outside to the playground areas. Within an hour school officials closed the school. Some rioters then marched to 2 nearby schools, hurling bricks and stones and setting off fire alarms as they went. Police reinforcements were sent in to stop the more than 2,000 rioting students. Order was not restored until 8 p.m.)

Milwaukee Riot Precedes Open-Housing Campaign

Rioting battered Milwaukee's predominantly black "Inner Core" neighborhood on the near North Side July 30—Aug. 3, 1967. A 24-hour curfew was imposed in the city, the nation's 11th largest, and Wisconsin National Guard units were called in. 4 persons were killed in the disturbances; at least 100 were reported injured, and 705 persons were arrested. Property damage was relatively light.

The violence erupted at 9:30 p.m. July 30, when black gangs began setting fires, smashing windows and looting stores. There were exchanges of gunfire between police and Negroes. By 3:00 a.m., when a rainstorm forced rioters to take cover, 2 persons, a policeman and an elderly white woman, had been killed. 83 persons were injured, including 12 policemen and a fireman; 145 to 180 persons were arrested. 28 fires were reported.

Mayor Henry Maier asked Gov. Warren P. Knowles to alert National Guard units at 12:40 a.m. July 31. Shortly afterwards, Maier notified the White House of the situation. Finally, at 2:27 a.m. July 31, after 2 policemen had been wounded by snipers,

Maier called in the National Guard. He proclaimed a state of emergency and ordered a 24-hour curfew for everyone except doctors, nurses, policemen, firemen and newsmen. The sale of liquor and beer, arms, ammunition and gasoline in containers was prohibited by the mayor.

Gov. Knowles immediately dispatched a force of 1,450 National Guardsmen to the city. The metropolitan area was sealed off, and police barricaded areas of the downtown Inner Core, a $5\frac{1}{2}$-square-mile section inhabited by most of Milwaukee's approximately 80,000 Negroes (about 10% of the city's population). All stores and public and private facilities were closed. Public and private transportation came to a halt. 7:00 p.m. curfews were imposed on all Milwaukee suburbs.

By 10:20 a.m. July 31, 450 National Guardsmen had established patrols in the main riot area in the Inner Core. Within the ghetto, they cordoned off a 105-square-block area. Some 1,000 Guardsmen were on standby in nearby staging areas. At noon, Maj. Gen. Ralph Olson, acting state adjutant general, called in an additional 2,400 Guardsmen to help the 1,900-man city police force. Maier lifted the curfew from 4:00 p.m. to 6:00 p.m. July 31 to permit residents outside the riot area to buy food. Guardsmen carrying loaded guns escorted milkmen into the riot areas to deliver free milk to residents.

The Rev. James E. Groppi, 36, assistant pastor at the St. Boniface Roman Catholic Church, and an adviser to the Youth Council of the Milwaukee branch of the NAACP, and 6 other members of the council were arrested that afternoon and charged with violating the curfew. Groppi, who was released on bail, reportedly had warned the city's Common Council the previous week that a "holocaust" was inevitable unless the city enacted an open-housing ordinance.

During the night of July 31, the police responded to reports of sniper fire by patrolling in 4 rented armored Brinks trucks. Maier Aug. 1 lifted the curfew until 7:00 p.m. and limited National Guard activities to standby duty at the city's armories. In an interview Aug. 1 he told newsmen: "The curfew has been a good . . . cooling-off device." He said that only .005% of the city's Negroes had participated in the violence but that these were a criminal element "beyond the reach of any program now in existence."

Scattered sniper fire erupted again in the evening of Aug. 1 after blacks attacked firemen fighting a blaze in the Inner Core. By Aug. 2 the death toll had risen to 4, and arrests had reached 539.

Groppi and 24 other civil rights leaders Aug. 2 denounced city officials for having failed to do anything to eliminate the causes of the rioting or to alleviate black frustations stemming from bad relations with the police and bias in employment, education and housing.

The withdrawal of the National Guard force—which had grown to 4,800 men—was begun Aug. 2. Maier lifted the curfew at 5:30 a.m. Aug. 3 but announced 2 hours later that it would be reimposed at 9:00 p.m. because of reports of firebombings, vandalism and lootings. Later in the day the mayor asked businessmen to help solve the economic problems of the black ghetto by providing summer jobs for unemployed youths.

Angry whites clashed with police and demonstrators led by the Rev. Groppi and the Milwaukee Youth Council in confrontations that started when Groppi's group began a series of daily open-housing demonstrations in Milwaukee Aug. 28. By Oct. 22 more than 375 persons had been arrested.

From the start the marches provoked bitter and violent reaction from white residents of Milwaukee's predominantly Polish South Side. At least 6 persons were injured Aug. 28 in a clash between whites and marchers; 16 persons were arrested. After the disturbance, Mayor Maier called on South Side residents to observe a "voluntary curfew." (Maier refused an offer from Gov. Warren P. Knowles to call out the Wisconsin National Guard.)

200 open housing demonstrators, guarded by an armed police escort, marched again Aug. 29 and were met by nearly 2,000 whites who lined the 2-mile march route to Kosciuszko Park. Many of the whites carried signs that read "white power" and "Polish power," and some chanted "kill, kill, kill!" Eggs, rocks and bottles were thrown at the marchers. Twice during the march police used tear gas to quell disturbances. At least 6 persons were hospitalized; more than 50 persons were arrested. Late Aug. 29 the marchers were escorted by police to Freedom House, the headquarters of the Youth Concil. Policemen charged that snipers fired on the police escorts. Several firebombs were thrown, and Freedom House was set ablaze by a firebomb. The Youth Council blamed the police for the fire. (Freedom House had suffered $2,000 in fire damages Aug. 12 when it was one of 11 arson targets.)

Early Aug. 30 Mayor Maier issued an emergency proclamation banning "marches, demonstrations and parades" between 4 p.m. and 9 a.m. for the next 30 days. Groppi denounced the ban and said it did not apply to rallies. More than 100 of his followers gathered for a rally at the charred remains of Freedom House at

7 p.m. Aug. 30. More than 100 policemen soon arrived to disperse them, but they refused to move. Finally the police charged them and arrested 15. The crowd reassembled on the private property of Freedom House, and for 45 minutes members of the crowd stood confronting police while singing "We Shall Overcome" and "We Shall Not Be Moved." The police finally moved in and arrested more than 50 persons.

Marches took place Aug. 31 and Sept. 1 despite the ban. 58 persons, including Groppi, were arrested Aug. 31 for defying the "state-of-emergency" order. Joseph P. Fagan, chairman of the Wisconsin Department of Industry, Labor & Human Relations and a spokesman for the governor, accused the mayor Sept. 1 of "suspending the Bill of Rights." Maier Sept. 1 said he would remove the ban the next day. In making the announcement. Maier denounced Fagan and Groppi.

Groppi and Negro comedian Dick Gregory led 1,400 predominantly black demonstrators on a peaceful march from St. Boniface's Church to City Hall Sept. 2. The marchers then continued on to the South Side, where they were met by white hecklers; there were several incidents of fistfighting. Before 1,000 demonstrators marched Sept. 3 from the church to downtown Milwaukee, Groppi told reporters that the marches would continue "until we have a fair-housing bill that says a man can live where he wants."

The Milwaukee Common Council met Sept. 5 and voted 18-1 to ratify the mayor's emergency proclamation banning marches. The dissenting vote was that of Mrs. Vel R. Phillips, the only black member of the council. After the vote Groppi marched out of the meeting accompanied by 200 Negroes and whites. They went to St. Boniface's Church, and Groppi said there would be no "cooling off." He said at a rally of 800 persons: "I saw in the Common Council a worse form of racism than I saw in the South Side last week. ... I heard a man say that I preach hate. I preach brotherhood and justice. One of the best ways to teach brotherhood is to preach black power."

500 demonstrators marched downtown the evening of Sept. 5, but only 50 marchers demonstrated Sept. 6. Dick Gregory said at a rally of 600 that "we've got to escalate this thing." Despite his militant stance, however, Groppi was reported to be unwilling to accept the support of advocates of black rebellion such as H. Rap Brown.

A planned marathon lie-in by rights activists at the mayor's office turned into a spree of destruction Sept. 7 when about 75 black youths, "commandos" of the Youth Council, vandalized the reception room of Maier's office. Under orders from Maier not to interfere, policemen watched for nearly 4 hours as the youths pushed and taunted them, ripped stuffing from chairs, broke windows, took over the interoffice phone switchboard and the receptionist's desk, made paper airplanes from memo pads and stuck "black power" stickers, lipstick and hand lotion on a photo-mural of downtown Milwaukee. A clerk was stranded inside the mayor's conference room. Policemen moved in to rescue him and struggled briefly with the youths. The mayor finally told the police to clear the office. The youths, reduced in number to 35, were given 2 minutes to leave or face arrest for disorderly conduct. They conferred and then marched out of City Hall. (Andrew Tyler, a "commando sergeant" in the Youth Council, told an interviewer Sept. 21 that efforts by outside black groups to inject violence into the open-housing drive had been rejected. About 25 Chicago Negroes had distributed photos and buttons of Stokely Carmichael and Malcolm X Sept. 17 and had urged Milwaukee Negroes to riot.)

Groppi and about 1,000 supporters marched through the South Side again Sept. 9. White hecklers held placards that read "Burn, Groppi, burn," and others shouted "White nigger." The police kept the 2 groups separated. But during the homeward journey, after darkness, several brawls broke out.

Groppi, Dick Gregory and Mrs. Vel Phillips Sept. 10 led more than 2,300 demonstrators, including civil rights workers from 7 Middle Western states, in a 15-mile protest march to the South Side. At a pre-march rally at St. Boniface's Church, the demonstrators unanimously voted to boycott Milwaukee's largest brewery, the Joseph Schlitz Co. Gregory told the marchers: "This is not a brick and bottle throwing march today. If you see anybody throwing a brick or bottle, hold him." During the march police fired 30 rounds of tear gas at white hecklers who threw bottles at marchers. 2 whites and 3 marchers were arrested during an outbreak of fistfighting in the suburb of West Milwaukee, where several marchers threw bottles and smashed windows. A mob of whites waited for marchers to return to West Milwaukee, but Groppi led them back on a different route. Some whites then turned on the police, who fired tear gas at the mob.

During an evening march of more than 700 demonstrators Sept. 11, whites pelted marchers with bricks and bottles, and the demonstrators returned the fire.

At a Sept. 12 press conference Maier denounced white violence and hatred, which he said was reminiscent of Nazi Germany. He said he was "forcedrafting" 9 civic and religious leaders, including the Most Rev. William E. Cousins, archbishop of Milwaukee and Groppi's superior, to seek a solution. Maier urged the group to meet "immediately" because "the city verged on civil war last night and no one knows what lurks ahead." White demonstrators carrying a cardboard coffin lettered "God Is White" and "Father Groppi Rest in Hell" paraded outside the archbishop's residence in the evening, but Cousins Oct. 13 refused to serve on Maier's Special Community Relations Commission; 3 appointees had refused previously.

Black marchers avoided the white South Side Sept. 12-13 and demonstrated instead in the black North Side. South Side whites meanwhile gathered in their home neighborhood the evenings of Sept. 12 and 13 to heckle black marchers who did not appear. The whites, armed with bottles, clashed instead with policemen. Faced with a crowd of 2,000 whites Sept. 13, the police used tear gas to halt the bottle-throwing and disperse the mobs. 3 policemen and 2 civilians were injured.

Archbishop Cousins Sept. 13 announced his support of Groppi in his drive for open-housing legislation. In what was reported to be the first time in the 97-year history of the *Catholic Herald Citizen,* the archdiocesan weekly, the archbishop addressed his 700,000 parishioners in an editorial. The archbishop's editorial said: "Do I agree with everything that Father Groppi has said and done? I certainly do not." But "we are being diverted by emotion and mob psychology into fighting a straw figure while the real enemy goes unscathed." "People are so disturbed by his actions that they lose sight of the cause for which he is fighting, that of freedom and human dignity. As Christians we favor the same just cause."

The priests' Senate of the Milwaukee Archdiocese Sept. 15 voted 21-7 to support Groppi and his open-housing drive. The Senate, a 3-month-old body elected by 729 priests to advise and consult with the archbishop on church problems, met in closed session. "To the extent that Father Groppi's efforts are directed toward a living charity and social justice, the Senate concurs with Archbishop William E. Cousins in retaining Father Groppi in his present assignment," the statement said.

Rights demonstrators picketing City Hall Sept. 15 were joined by a delegation of nuns from Chicago. About 80 clergymen and nuns arrived later from other parts of the country to participate in the open-housing marches. About 650 Negroes and whites, including clergymen, nuns and laymen who had arrived from out of town in response to pleas from Groppi, were greeted with jeers

and curses as they marched from the North Side to the South Side
Sept. 16.

A vigil was held Sept. 29-Oct. 7 at the Lincoln Memorial in
Washington, D.C. in support of the Milwaukee open-housing
demonstrations as an "alternative to violence." Mrs. Vel Phillips,
attending the closing ceremonies, said: This is the last stand for
nonviolence." Mrs. Phillips met Oct. 6 with officials of the Justice
Department and the Office of the Vice President. She said she was
"encouraged that the people here in Washington realize the depth
and urgency of our problem." TV correspondent Jim Burns had
said on the ABC "Issues and Answers" program Sept. 24, however, that Mrs. Phillips had told him Sept. 23 that "Milwaukee
might some day become . . . the 'cradle of the real American revolution in the United States,' meaning by that an armed revolt
against the white people of that city."

The Milwaukee Common Council Dec. 12 finally enacted an
open-housing ordinance by 13-6 vote. Mrs. Phillips voted against
the ordinance, which she denounced as "mere tokenism." Groppi
assailed the ordinance as "an insult to the black community" and
promised that the demonstrations "will continue and intensify."
The only change in the existing state law, which excluded an estimated 60% of Milwaukee housing, involved a transfer of enforcement powers from a state agency to the city attorney's office. The
ordinance exempted owner-occupied homes, duplexes and apartment buildings of 4 units or less.

Riot Remedies Sought, 'Conditions' & 'Agitators' Blamed

Local and national leaders urged a variety of remedies for the
social ills that produced the unprecedented urban violence.

The 441,169-member National Association for the Advancement of Colored People (NAACP), the nation's largest civil rights
organization, held a tense and acrimonious 58th annual convention
in Boston July 10-15, 1967. Convened as U.S. cities were wracked
by another summer of racial violence, nearly 2,000 delegates
weighed problems ranging from the organization's own internal
leadership and its image as a non-militant civil rights group to
the recent racial riots and the Vietnam war. Executive Director
Roy Wilkins, who made the keynote address July 10, defended the
militants who, he said, "have shaken up Negroes and whites, both
of whom badly needed the treatment. Their service outweighs their
disservice." But he warned against racialism that would exclude
whites from the rights movement. Wilkins had been under fire

from militants within the NAACP for his previous criticisms of the ideology of black power. The convention July 15 passed a package of resolutions that included one condemning the Newark riots but adding that "much of the blame for this unfortunate eruption must be placed on the city administration for its failure to take corrective action to meet any of the grave social ills of the Negro community." Wilkins, speaking on CBS-TV's "Meet The Press" program July 16, backed the use of troops to quell riots wherever and whenever necessary. He restated his view that riots could be avoided by ending the conditions that caused them.

The largest and most diverse group of black American leaders ever assembled met in Newark, N.J. July 20-23 for a 4-day National Conference on Black Power. A militant and separatist mood dominated the delegates, representing 197 black organizations in 42 cities throughout the U.S. The delegates included civil rights activists, labor leader, educators, anti-poverty workers, politicians, clergymen, representatives of traditionally moderate Negro groups, and avowed revolutionaries. The conference, planned since Sept. 1966, was organized by Dr. Nathan Wright Jr., executive director of the Department of Urban Work of the Episcopal Diocese of Newark. The idea for the conference originally had been advanced by Rep.-elect Adam Clayton Powell, who did not attend the meeting but was named honorary co-chairman with Rep. Charles C. Diggs (D., Mich.) and Floyd B. McKissick, national director of the Congress of Racial Equality (CORE). When asked July 21 whether black violence was destined to continue in the U.S., McKissick said: "No sane person could say we are not due for more violence. You will have violence as long as you have black people suppressed." He said that white people who "control the government, the money and the ghettos" were responsible for the violence. " ... It is the responsibility of the whites to eliminate the conditions that cause violence. It is the conditions themselves that make for violence, and only white people have the power to change them," he declared.

The black power conference delegates July 22 unanimously passed a resolution demanding "full restitution and reparation to all of our black brothers and sisters and their families [in Newark] and that all of our black brothers and sisters be released from jail without bail immediately." The resolution assailed what it called the "massacre of black people" by police, and charged that in the Newark violence "black men and women were indiscriminately murdered, beaten and arrested," and "the wanton destruction of black people's property in the entire black community was

maliciously undertaken." The resolution said the delegates "vigor-
ously affirm the exercise of our unchallengeable right of self-
defense." The conference July 23 issued a report denouncing the
Newark riots as "the inevitable results of the criminal behavior
of a society which dehumanizes people and drives men to utter
distraction."

The Republican Coordinating Committee charged July 24 that
"widespread rioting and violent civil disorder have grown to a
national crisis since the present [Democratic] Administration took
office." The committee, in a statement on the growth of urban
disorders, warned that "we are rapidly approaching a state of
anarchy, and the President [Lyndon B. Johnson] has totally failed
to recognize the problem. Worse, he has vetoed legislation
and opposed other legislation designed to re-establish peace and
order within the country." The statement said: "When city after
city across the nation is overwhelmed by riots, looting, arson and
murder which mounting evidence indicates may be the result of
organized planning and execution on a national scale, the federal
government must accept its national responsibility" for the situation. "Factories for the manufacture of molotov cocktails have
been uncovered by the police," "simultaneous fires have been started
in widely separated areas upon the . . . outbreak of rioting," and
"public and private meetings of riot organizers from many sections
of the country have been repeatedly reported in the press." The
committee called on the President to back a GOP proposal for
"full-scale investigation of civil disorders" and "Republican
legislation designed to prevent rioting."

Making public the Republican statement, the GOP Congressional leaders, Sen. Everett M. Dirksen (Ill.) and Rep. Gerald R.
Ford (Mich.), told newsmen that the Republican legislation cited
by the document was a Distict of Columbia anti-crime bill vetoed
in 1966 and a bill, making it a federal crime to cross state lines to
incite a riot, passed by the House of Representatives July 19 but
opposed by U.S. Atty. Gen. Ramsey Clark as ineffective. Dirksen
said there were unproved indications that "there is a timetable"
to the rioting. Dirksen said he had information about the existence of a molotov cocktail factory in New York. Ford, asked who
might be responsible for organization of the rioting, named Stokely
Carmichael.

Congressional leaders of both parties called July 25 for an
investigation of the continued urban disorders. The Republican
proposal, introduced in both houses, called for a joint Congressional committee to study (1) the causes of the riots, (2) the ability

of police forces to cope with the riots, and (3) evidence of "any [riot] conspiracy" or involvement in the unrest by "any Communist or other subversive organization." Senate GOP leader Dirksen, sponsor of the proposal, said he wanted the investigation "to see if there is a touch of Red" behind the riots. In the House, GOP leader Ford said: "I can't help but believe that there is in the background some national plan" in the disorders.

Senate Democratic leader Mike Mansfield (Mont.) said July 25 that he did not want a probe to become a "political football" and he preferred that a Presidential commission be formed to look into the unrest. The Senate Permanent Subcommittee on Investigations was directed to investigate the riots. The subcommittee probe was selected Aug. 1 by the Senate Rules Committee from among 5 proposals for investigations submitted to it. Sen. John Sherman Cooper (R., Ky.) urged that the investigation specifically be focused on "economic and social" factors involved in the riots. The Rules Committee rejected Cooper's suggestion by a vote of 6-2, but it did direct the subcommittee, under Sen. John L.Mc-Cellan (D., Ark.), to search for the "immediate and long-standing causes" of the riots.

Rep. William C. Cramer (R., Fla.), author of the House-passed anti-riot bill, said July 19 that it was "aimed at those professional agitators" who traveled from city to city to "inflame the people . . . to violence and then leave the jurisdiction before the riot begins." Many similar speeches were delivered in an emotional 5-hour debate preceding the vote for passage. Rules Committee Chairman William M. Colmer (D., Miss.) called the riots "an organized conspiracy . . . backed by the Communists." Unless it were checked, he said, we "are going to have a nation-wide state of anarchy." The legislation had not been requested by the Administration. It was opposed by Rep. Emanuel Celler (D., N.Y.), chairman of the House Judiciary Committee, who said he considered the bill "a futile gesture, neither preventive nor curative." "The basic disorder," he said, "is the discontent of the Negro," and the bill "will not allay his anger and frustrations" but "arouse" them "more deeply." Rep. Frank Thompson Jr. (D., N.J.) July 19 called the measure "a bill of attainder aimed at one man—Stokely Carmichael."

The Senate Judiciary Committee opened hearings Aug. 2-3 on the House-passed anti-riot bill. Sen. James O. Eastland (D., Miss.) was chairman. The first witnesses heard by the committee were police officials of Cambridge, Md., Cincinnati and Nashville, Tenn., all recently the scenes of racial disorders. All of the witnesses deplored the role of outside agitators in inciting riots in their cities. The Cambridge police chief, Bryce Kinnamon, said Aug. 2 that the "sole reason" for the Cambridge riot July 28 was an inflammatory speech made by H. Rap Brown. Kinnamon produced a tape recording of Brown urging Cambridge Negroes to burn and kill. Brown and Stokely Carmichael were named by Capt. John A. Sarace of the Nashville police force Aug. 2 as organizers of his city's April riots. Cincinnati Police Chief Jacob W. Schott told the committee Aug. 2 that the antiriot bill "would help in curbing these people who move around causing these problems." 2 Plainfield, N.J. police officials Aug. 3 told the committee that riots in Plainfield were directed by an outside source, but they could not name the source. Some members of the Judiciary Committee spoke out against the proposed legislation Aug. 2. Sen. Philip A. Hart (D., Mich.) said that the bill "and 97 more like it would not have stopped [the riot in] Detroit." Sen. Sam J. Ervin Jr. (D., N.C.) said it served as "a manifestation of Congress's outrage" but was impractical because "it defines a crime which can hardly be proved by evidence." Sen. Edward M. Kennedy (D., Mass.) said the bill "may constitute a fraud on the American people" by giving the impression that Congress had taken effective action against the riots.

Rep. Edwin E. Willis (D., La.), chairman of the House Committee on Un-American Activities, had said July 26 that committee investigators had detected the involvement of "subversive influences" in some riots. The Senate Internal Security Subcommittee, headed by Eastland, had heard Detective Sgt. John Ungvary of the Cleveland police force testify May 2 that the 1966 Cleveland riots were planned and ignited by black nationalist groups and that there was evidence of "Communist influence" and "exploitation" of the riots.

An amended Administration bill to defend persons exercising federally protected civil rights was passed by the House Aug. 16 by 326-93 vote. The bill was amended to prohibit interference with policemen or firemen performing their duty during a riot. Proposed by Rep. Jim Wright (D., Tex.), the amendment was accepted by voice vote. Another amendment, suggested by Rep. Fletcher Thompson (R., Ga.), to exempt from criminal prosecution (under the bill) law officers lawfully carrying out their duties or enforcing lawful ordinances and laws, was approved by 74-42 vote. A further change, adopted by voice vote, provided that the "speech and peaceful assembly" rights protected under the bill did not extend to inciting to riot. This amendment was proposed by

Rep. William C. Cramer (R., Fla.) to keep the bill from preventing prosecutions under the anti-riot bill. The measure was finally enacted Apr. 10, 1968 after further modification by the Senate.

Sen. Robert C. Byrd (D., W. Va.) July 25, 1967 advocated "brutal force" to contain urban riots and said adult looters should be "shot on the spot." Rep. James G. O'Hara (D., Mich.) and about 40 other Representatives proposed July 27 that a fund of about $300 million be made available for local police handling of civil disorders. Sen Robert F. Kennedy (D., N.Y.), testifying before the Senate Committee on Banking and Currency July 25 on his proposed slum-housing program, said: "Those who break the law and shatter the peace must know that swift justice will be done and effective punishment meted out for their deeds. No grievance, no sense of injustice, however deep, can excuse the wanton killing of other Americans—whether they are policemen or firemen doing their duty or innocent bystanders in the streets of their city."

Office of Economic Opportunity Director Sargent Shriver told the House Education & Labor Committee July 31 that "all America is responsible for the riots. All of us here in this room. We are all actors in this American tragedy."

4 black rights leaders appealed in a joint statement July 26 for an end to the riots in ghettos. The 4 leaders, all of them political moderates, were the Rev. Dr. Martin Luther King Jr., A. Philip Randolph, president of the A. Philip Randolph Institute, Roy Wilkins, and Whitney M. Young Jr., executive director of the National Urban League. Their statement said: "Riots have proved ineffective, disruptive and highly damaging to the Negro population, to the civil rights cause and to the entire nation." "Killing, arson, looting are criminal acts and should be dealt with as such. Equally guilty are those who incite, provoke and call specifically for such action. There is no justice which justifies the present destruction of the Negro community and its people. We are confident that the overwhelming majority of the Negro community joins us in opposition to violence in the streets." The statement was also critical of the stand taken on the riot problem by whites and Congress. White Americans, it said, were "not blameless" because they generally supported restrictions against Negroes. The 90th Congress, it said, had "exhibited an incredible indifference to the hardships of the ghetto dwellers."

King attacked Congress July 26, saying that it had "created the atmosphere for these riots." King said July 28 that "the long

summer of riots have been caused by the long winters of delay"
on social development legislation.

Adam Clayton Powell Jr. July 26 called the riots "a necessary
phase of the black revolution." He made the statement at a news
conference in Bimini, the Bahamas, his residence since his exclusion
from the House and subsequent re-election.

Stokely Carmichael said Aug. 1 that the Negro was fighting
"guerrilla warfare" to attain his rights and that a "revolutionary
movement" would be initiated to help him. He made the remarks
at a news conference in Havana, Cuba, where he was attending
the conference of the Organization for Latin American Solidarity.
An "honorary delegate" to the conference, Carmichael addressed
it Aug. 2 and said the American Negro was ready to destroy
"Yankee imperialism" with urban warfare. In a broadcast over
Havana radio earlier Aug. 2, Carmichael had addressed a message
to Maj. Ernesto (Che) Guevara, Cuban guerrilla leader said to be
operating in Latin America. He said: "We eagerly await your
writings in order to read them, digest them and plan our tactics
based on them."

A call for an "action program" against "the tragic epidemic
of riots" in U.S. cities was sounded by 8 Republican governors
meeting in New York Aug. 10. Among the state executives' recommendations: (a) establishment of a center to provide information
to states on urban programs; (b) prompt and firm action by police
forces in the early stages of civil disorders; (c) agreements among
local law-enforcement groups for pooling of resources to resist
rioting; (d) new riot control equipment and procedures for the
National Guard; (e) a coordinated public and private attack on
the social causes of civil unrest. The meeting was attended by
Govs. Nelson A. Rockefeller (N.Y.) (sponsor of the meeting),
George W. Romney (Mich.), Raymond P. Shafer (Pa.), John A.
Love (Colo.), Spiro T. Agnew (Md.), John H. Chafee (R.I.), John
A. Volpe (Mass.) and Nils A. Boe (S.D.).

In a speech at the Chautauqua (N.Y.) Institution Aug. 4,
Romney had declared that "those Americans who preach revolu-
tion and preach the use of guns should be charged with treason."
"There is a criminal element in all races," he said, "and we must
enforce the law without fear or favor among the races." He said
Stokely Carmichael was guilty of "treason" for a recent speech
in Havana, Cuba advocating a revolutionary movement in the
U.S.

Romney, a prospective GOP Presidential contender, toured 17
areas in 12 states Sept. 11-30 to get first-hand information on urban

problems. During a tour of Brooklyn (N.Y.) Sept. 15, Romney said "a lot of people are very frustrated and bitter, and it's time to do something because there's tinder in the cities that will make Vietnam look like child's play, and I mean just that." At the end of his tour, Romney Sept. 30 issued a statement in which he said: "Time is running out for those who have responsibilities for the tranquility of our nation." "As I have rubbed elbows with those who live in the ghetto, as I have listened to the voice of revolt, I am more convinced than ever before that unless we reverse our course, build a new America, the old America will be destroyed." "The seeds of revolution have been sown. They cannot be rooted out by force. While we must maintain law and order, we must either achieve orderly progress or change will be inflicted with mortal wounds. Either we shall join hands, hearts and minds and march together on paths of fulfillment for all, or we shall find ourselves torn asunder."

Atty. Gen. Ramsey Clark announced Nov. 1 that the Justice Department would hold training conferences for mayors, police chiefs and other municipal officials throughout the nation on the prevention and control of civil disturbances. Clark said that the purpose of conferences, to be co-sponsored by the International Association of Chiefs of Police (IACP), was "to combine knowledge on effective methods of preventing and controlling disturbances, to develop and refine these methods, and to search for new methods." The National Advisory Commission on Civil Disorders had recommended such conferences to Pres. Johnson, and the President directed Clark to arrange them.

The U.S. Civil Rights Commission Nov. 22 issued a study on the frustrating conditions that led to violence. The report, "A Time to Listen . . . A Time to Act," contained testimony of ghetto residents to "provide insights into what slum residents think and feel about the conditions in which they live." The report held that the summer riots and the growing black militancy should be viewed in the context of the "great frustrations, of laws and programs which promise but do not deliver, of continued deprivation, discrimination and prejudice" in an increasingly prosperous society. The report said: "The problems of our cities and the people who live in them will not be resolved by a search for culprits or conspirators or for solutions which do not cost money or effort. Nor can it justly be argued that remedies for the discrimination suffered by millions of Americans who live in slum ghettos should be deferred on the ground that to do otherwise would be to reward violence."

Racial Violence Continues Into Fall

As the summer of 1967 waned, there appeared to be no diminution in demonstrations escalating into violence.

Violence broke out in East St. Louis, Ill. Sept. 10 shortly after SNCC Chairman H. Rap Brown told a cheering crowd of more than 1,000 blacks that "America has no use for Negroes" and urged them to "stop singing and start swinging." Reports of looting and arson continued Sept. 11-13. At least 5 persons were injured, more than 55 arrested. 40 county deputy sheriffs and 30 state troopers were brought to East St. Louis Sept. 10 to aid 60 city policemen in quelling looting and firebombing. Police barricaded a 3-block area of the city. The night police chief said that the vandalism was centered "in the commercial section of the colored district," where several stores and 2 cars were firebombed.

Roosevelt Young, 18, a black high school dropout, was shot and killed by a policeman in East St. Louis late Sept. 10. Police said that the shooting occurred when the youth, being questioned about a stolen car, tried to grab a gun from a policeman and then fled. They denied that the incident was related to the disorders. But 30 young Negroes shouting "black power" marched on police headquarters and the newsroom of the *Metro East Journal* Sept. 11 to protest the shooting.

During the East St. Louis disorders, firemen in the area answered 58 calls Sept. 11-13, several stores were looted and a drug store was set afire. White motorists were pelted with bottles and bricks, and some of them were dragged from their cars and beaten. But Police Commissioner Russell Beebe asserted that only "1/10 of 1% of the Negro community" was responsible for the disturbances. 2 black youths were hospitalized Sept. 13 for burns and flesh wounds, and at least 6 Negroes were arrested on charges of disorderly conduct and suspected arson.

Boyce Perry, chairman of the executive board of IMPACT House, an East St. Louis gathering place for young Negroes, denied Sept. 14 that his organization taught revolt. But Oliver Smith, IMPACT House's assistant director, asserted that "every black man in town supports the disturbances. Who's to say the violent way is wrong? Let's see what it accomplishes."

Violence flared for more than 5 hours on Chicago's South Side Sept. 14 following a black rally sponsored by the SNCC in protest against alleged police brutality. Speakers at the rally charged that police had kicked Corinne Roby, 18, a Negro, in the

stomach when they arrested her Sept. 12. The police said that
Miss Roby had tossed a bottle at them. The violence began after
black students at the nearby Forrestville High School were let out
for the day. They joined the SNCC rally, and youths began
smashing windows and throwing rocks and bottles. Police headquarters sent in tactical forces, and a 240-block area was cordoned
off. The police, using bullhorns, urged people to go home and
stay off the streets.

Sniper fire began shortly after dark, and Chicago policemen
returned the fire with carbines and submachineguns. 11 persons
were injured, 5 of them policemen. About 50 persons were arrested
on charges of aggravated battery, mob action or disorderly conduct. State Sen. Charles Chew, a Chicago Negro, visited the scene
of the disturbance and said: "Black agitators from Chicago and
outside of Chicago are stirring them up."

66 persons were arrested in Hartford, Conn. Sept. 18-19 after
racial violence erupted during a demonstration calling for stricter
enforcement of the state's open housing laws. Some 150 demonstrators, mostly black and Puerto Rican, had started a scheduled
3-mile march from the city's predominantly black North End late
Sept. 18. They were heading for the South End, an almost entirely
white middle-class neighborhood with many European immigrants.
But the march, led by black restaurant manager John Barber, 30,
broke up about 2 miles from the planned destination when the
marchers reached Hartford's new shopping and business center and
began throwing rocks and bottles. Several policemen were injured,
and about 24 store windows were broken. 25 marchers, half of
them white, were arrested, mostly on charges of breach of the
peace. A crowd of hostile whites awaiting the demonstrators in the
South End then dispersed. Police Chief John J. Kerringan said:
"We had adequate protection for them [the demonstrators]—perhaps 250 men. But they became unruly and started throwing
things, so we moved in and broke it up."

Hartford police used tear gas Sept. 19 to disperse black
youths who were pelting cars passing through the North End.
14 policemen, some guarding fire trucks answering false alarms,
were injured; dozens of cars were damaged.

Incidents of window-smashing and looting broke out in the
predominantly black West End section of Dayton, O. Sept. 19
following a demonstration of 500 to 600 persons protesting the
fatal shooting Sept. 17 by a white off-duty policeman of Robert
Elwood Barbee, 41, of Findlay, O., a black civil rights worker. It
was reported that Barbee was shot when he ran from detective

R.S. Collier and another detective, who said they saw a pipe in his belt and thought it was a gun. 131 persons were arrested, 1/3 of them juveniles, and more than 50 were reported injured.

Racial violence erupted in Winston-Salem, N.C. Nov. 2 after the death of James Eller, 32, a Negro who had been struck by a white policeman. More than 250 persons were arrested Nov. 2-4 for reasons directly and indirectly related to the disturbances. The disorders began after the burial of Eller, who had been blackjacked by Ptl. W. C. Owens. Owens, who had arrested Eller for public drunkenness, said it was necessary to subdue Eller by force when he became disorderly. Owens was charged with murder and suspended.

Gangs of black youths numbering nearly 500, roving Winston-Salem in small bands late Nov. 2, began setting fires, throwing rocks and bottles, overturning autos and looting stores. Policemen fired shots in the air to disperse a crowd of about 100 Negroes who had gathered after dark between white and black sections of the city. Gov. Daniel K. Moore ordered 200 National Guardsmen to the troubled city, and a squad of state troopers were sent to aid police. Nearly 50 persons, including 8 policemen, were injured and more than 100 were arrested.

The Winston-Salem Board of Aldermen Nov. 3 granted Mayor M.C. Benton Jr. emergency powers. At nightfall the mayor imposed an 11 p.m.-to-dawn curfew, and an additional 600 National Guardsmen were sent to the city, increasing the combined force of police and Guardsmen to 1,200 persons. Finally, with order restored, half the National Guardsmen were withdrawn from the city, and the curfew was suspended Nov. 5.

The Ohio National Guard was called in Nov. 13 to quell violence on the predominantly black campus of Central State University in Wilberforce, O. The school was closed Nov. 14. Before classes were resumed Nov. 27, Dr. Harry E. Groves, 46, a Negro, had announced his resignation as president of the university (effective in 6 months at the expiration of his contract). The disturbances began Nov. 13 when Michael Warren, 23, a black senior, returned to the campus. He had been suspended Nov. 9 after allegedly threatening to kill Dr. Rembert Stokes, the black president of predominantly black Wilberforce University nearby. Warren had gone to Wilberforce University Nov. 2 to recruit students for a CSU demonstration and reportedly had told Stokes: "When the revolution comes, I will kill you."

When police attempted to arrest Warren Nov. 13, about 30 to 50 students barricaded the entrance to the building in which the

youth was attending classes. About 100 sheriff's deputies were sent
to the campus but failed to disperse the students. Greene County
Sheriff Russell Bradley was summoned to the campus by Dean
Charles Flowers, and students squirted a fire extinguisher in his
face. Bradly then called for the aid of the National Guard and
the Ohio Highway Patrol. Violence broke out that evening after
a student rally. About 100 to 200 students from the rally began
throwing bricks and rocks at the police, and 9 policemen were
injured. Policemen arrested more than 90 students, many of whom
they reportedly dragged kicking and screaming from the dormitories.
The students were charged with disorderly conduct and released
on bond. Sidney Davis, president of the county chapter of the
NAACP, accused the police Nov. 14 of brutality. He said he saw
police "use clubs on students" but didn't intervene because "we
can't fight police."

More than 3,500 students from 10 predominantly black high
schools clashed with more than 400 policemen in Philadelphia
Nov. 17 during a demonstration outside the Board of Education's
administration building. At least 22 persons were injured, and 57
were arrested. The students had marched on the building in
protest against the "white policy" of the board. Earlier in the
week 12 to 16 students had been reported suspended from a techni-
cal-vocational high school for participating in a demonstration
calling for the inclusion of black history courses in the school
curriculum. A Board of Education spokesmen said Nov. 17 that
they had not been suspended and that the board had promised
to start the courses requested. During the demonstration outside
the administration building Nov. 17, policemen attempted to
arrest a youth who was standing on top of a car. Students surrounded the policemen, and the disorders followed. School Board
Pres. Richard Dilworth blamed police for the outbreak. Originally,
he said, the police had agreed that only plainclothesmen would
be assigned to the demonstration. The trouble began with the
arrival of 2 busloads of uniformed policemen, he said. Then, for
more than an hour, gangs of youths roamed the streets, smashing
car windows, throwing rocks and assaulting passers-by. Newsmen,
clergymen, office workers and others said that policemen used
nightsticks on the youths.

Violence at Anti-War Demonstrations

Demonstrations against the Vietnam war, war contractors and
the draft were held throughout the U.S. Oct. 16-21, 1967, and the
protests frequently led to violence.

About 3,000 anti-war demonstrators showed up at the Oakland, Calif. draft induction center Oct. 17 in an effort to bar entrance to inductees. It was the 2d such attempt in 2 days. A force of 400 police and highway patrolmen routed the demonstrators with clubs and chemical sprays. 20 persons were arrested in the 10-minute mêlée. Many demonstrators had come from an all-night rally held in defiance of a court order on the University of California campus at Berkeley. The Northern California Radio-Television News Directors Association accused Oakland police and California highway patrolmen of unprovoked attacks on newsmen during the demonstration.

About 6,500 persons staged a silent demonstration Oct. 20 in the vicinity of the Oakland draft center. They used cars and traffic signs, benches, trash cans and other property taken from city parks in an attempt to block 16 intersections leading to the building. Buses carrying 40 employes of the center and 250 inductees arrived at the center after a 2-hour delay. About 1,000 police dispersed the crowd and arrested 21 demonstrators. In one incident, police clubbed 20 demonstrators, injuring 10.

About 1,000 University of Wisconsin students had demonstrated Oct. 18 on the Madison campus in protest against the presence of job recruiters of the Dow Chemical Co., which manufactured napalm used in Vietnam. A riot erupted after police were called in to end the demonstration. Some of the school buildings were damaged. 70 persons, mostly students, were injured.

Chicago police clashed Oct. 19 with 100 demonstrators, mostly University of Chicago students, who attempted to break into the city's induction center. 18 persons were arrested on charges of interfering with policemen, resisting arrest and disorderly conduct.

The appearance of 2 Navy recruiters on the campus of Brooklyn (N.Y.) College Oct. 19 precipitated a violent clash between protesting students and N.Y. City police who were called to the campus to keep order. About 1,000 students and 200 police were involved in the fighting at the height of the incident. About 40 students and 2 faculty members were arrested. The fighting started when police were called in to remove students engaged in a sit-down in the lobby of Boylan Hall in protest against the arrival of the 2 Navy officers. The college was virtually shut down Oct. 20 when more than 8,000 of the 10,000 students boycotted classes in protest against "police brutality." College Pres. Francis P. Kilcoyne approved an agreement to: (1) refrain from calling in police in "internal campus matters"; (2) drop charges against students involved in the Oct. 19 demonstration; (3) station armed forces recruiters in a room or an office, rather than in Boylan Hall.

Thousands of Americans participated in a massive demonstration in Washington Oct. 21 in protest against U.S. policy in Vietnam. Demonstrators first attended a rally at Lincoln Memorial, and then many of them marched to the Pentagon in nearby Arlington, Va., where they held another rally and a vigil that continued through the early hours of Oct. 23. Many demonstrators at the Pentagon were arrested after clashing with Army troops and federal marshals who had been called out to prevent the Defense Department's headquarters from being stormed. The demonstrators included a wide variety of participants, among them radicals, costumed black nationalists, hippies and students. The demonstration, organized by the National Mobilization Committee to End the War in Vietnam, was the culmination of nationwide anti-draft protests that had started Oct. 16.

Army and police authorities estimated that 55,000 persons had taken part in the Lincoln Memorial rally. But David Dellinger, 52, editor of *Liberation* magazine and chairman of the National Mobilization Committee, said the true figure was 150,000. The crowd in front of the Pentagon was reported to number 35,000. According to military authorities, 681 persons were arrested, most of them in the Pentagon area, during the 2-day demonstration. 13 U.S. marshals, 10 soldiers and 24 demonstrators were reported injured in the clashes, and the Pentagon steps were spattered with blood. In an address at the Lincoln Memorial rally Oct. 21, Dellinger declared that the demonstration was "a beginning of a new stage in the American peace movement in which the cutting edge becomes active resistance."

Following the Lincoln Memorial rally, 30,000 to 35,000 of the demonstrators crossed the Arlington Memorial Bridge over the Potomac River and marched on the Pentagon. They were restricted by a government permit to a huge parking lot on the north side of the Pentagon and to a 20-acre grass triangle below the mall entrance. Less than 2 hours after their arrival, about 2,000 demonstrators, crossing the lines authorized by the permit, pushed up the steps and clashed with marshals backed by troops. At this point, troops carrying tear-gas grenades emerged from the Pentagon building to reinforce the guard. About an hour later another crowd of 3,000 dashed to another entrance of the building. 30 demonstrators managed to get into the Pentagon but were quickly ejected by troops and club-wielding marshals. Shortly before the demonstrators surged toward the Pentagon, Dellinger had announced that some marchers would commit civil disobedience by crossing into the off-limits area. He and novelist Norman Mailer were the first to do so and were arrested.

Dellinger announced after a meeting of the National Mobilization Committee in Washington Oct. 22 that the group had decided to change its tactics from peaceful parades to "confrontations" with the government by sit-ins and other acts of civil disobedience. Dellinger said: "We have been calling for a step-up to a new phase in the movement. We were gratified and enthused that so many people came in from all over the country ready for this."

INDEX